DESIGN INTEGRATIONS:

RESEARCH AND COLLABORATION

DESIGN INTEGRATIONS:

RESEARCH AND COLLABORATION

Edited by Sharon Poggenpohl
and Keiichi Sato

First published in the UK in 2009 by
Intellect, The Mill, Parnall Road, Fishponds, Bristol, BS16 3JG, UK

First published in the USA in 2009 by
Intellect, The University of Chicago Press,
1427 E. 60th Street, Chicago, IL 60637, USA

A catalogue record for this book is available from the British Library.

Cover Design: Holly Rose
Copy Editor: Jennifer Alluisi
Typesetting: John Teehan

ISBN: 978-1-84150-240-3

Printed in Canada by Friesens.

CONTENTS

CONCLUSION

INTRODUCTION

1

TIME FOR CHANGE: BUILDING A DESIGN DISCIPLINE

Sharon Helmer Poggenpohl

Design is reaching a transitional moment that requires a critical look at its current and future states. The look that will unfold in these pages is not from the standpoint of design as an object, but from the standpoint of design as process or action—a look from the inside of design by international teachers and practitioners who support a change from craft to discipline. Design's craft origins cannot support the evolving context of design action needed now. This is not a new or unique call to action (Krippendorff, 1995; Owen, 1998; Buchanan, 2001); nevertheless, it is timely. Transformations from a status quo do not happen suddenly, and do not evolve because one or a few people believe it is necessary, but because the idea of change resonates with many individuals and institutions worldwide, especially those who practice a new version of design and who teach the next generation of designers to build on the past rather than replicate it. Such transformations also respond to cultural change in the broadest sense. In this case, it also depends on design faculty that understands academic structure from a broader perspective and use institutional supports like research offices, peer-reviewed journals, interdisciplinary opportunities, and conferences to their advantage. What unfolds in this book is a fairly specific argument: that design practice and education are changing, particularly in relation to the two themes this book addresses, research and collaboration. If design is to develop as a discipline, it must necessarily develop further based on these themes.

The first and last chapters of this book frame the focus on design integration; the first chapter argues for a necessary change in design education and practice, while the last chapter looks to the future of design. Between these chapters are two sections, research and collaboration, each of which starts with an examination of its theme and ends by introducing the next chapters in its section. Let's now explore the argument for change.

Craft or Discipline?

Both crafts and disciplines have methods to support their work, but how these methods are learned and applied is different. Crafts often have traditional, stable methods learned by observation and trial and error during an apprenticeship. Disciplines have an array of methods as well as ongoing inquiry into new or improved ones, introduced with theoretical perspectives and used in practical situations on a variety of problems. Craft methods are often not transferable to situations beyond the craft's immediate domain, while disciplinary methods are frequently empty of content or context and are transferable or adaptable to other situations. Another way to look at the difference between craft and discipline is to examine their outcomes. Crafts lead to trade organizations and disciplines lead to professions. Research is intimately tied to disciplinary evolution in its development of grounding knowledge for professional work.

Disciplines do not have to be invented; scaffolding for their growth exists organizationally within the university. Other disciplinary histories and evolutions can inform an immature domain like design. Lee Shulman, former president of The Carnegie Foundation for the Advancement of Teaching, observed in *The Wisdom of Practice* (2004b, 456), "...we recognize that the communities that matter most are strongly identified with the disciplines of our scholarship. 'Discipline' is in fact a powerful pun because it not only denotes a domain but also suggests a process: a community that disciplines is one that exercises quality, control, judgment, evaluation, and paradigmatic definition." Others (Weingart and Stehr, 2000, 51) have suggested that disciplines are like cartels—they organize the marketplace for the employment of their students to the exclusion of those lacking such credentials. Arguably, design in its craft configuration lacks the processes just mentioned as its singularity or idiosyncrasy has limited reach and authority among practitioners and marketplace.

What is Tacit or Explicit?

Among others, Jürgen Habermas (1998, 33) has drawn a useful distinction between "know-how" and "know-that." Know-how is the understanding of a competent practitioner to understand how to produce or accomplish something—a craftsperson or one with habituated skills. Know-that is the explicit knowledge of how one is able to know-how; for example, a teacher who abstracts principles for or from application exhibits know-that. To illustrate the difference even more specifically, compare a design practitioner who can intuitively select, size, and position type for legibility to an educator who knows why the type is better perceptually and how the typographic variables interact with page or screen space, reading ease, and comprehension.

Another way to draw this distinction is to discuss what is tacit and what is explicit. Tacit knowledge, according to Michael Polanyi (1983, 166), is what we know that we cannot tell. He offers the example of how we can identify a particular human face, yet be unable to describe exactly how we recognize it in a crowd. He compares this to the police system that facilitates the selection of facial elements (eyes, noses, mouths, etc.) to form a composite face from an array of possibilities. We can use this method by matching the features to our remembrance, yet we are unable to tell exactly how we do this. Our remembrance and its realization through building a composite face are tacit; the method for building the facial representation is explicit.

Much of the forming activity of design is tacit, developed through interaction with representations or prototypes that we manipulate, observe differences in, react to and change until a desired (imagined, discovered, appropriate) form is achieved. It is difficult to talk about the action of making something a little smaller (how small?) or shifting something to a more remote place (how remote?)—we sense the need and perform the action much before we can articulate the reason why. In a fluid situation of forming something, such moves are left unspoken and unanalyzed; one simply sees the improvement—it is experiential. (Massimo Vignelli is reported to have said much design is about getting the scale right—a little bigger or smaller or moving something a little.) This is the shortcoming that makes design appear elusive, special, inarticulate, and even unknowable. As long as designers consider themselves to be first and foremost aesthetic finishers of ideas that are well advanced in the development process, they will be trapped by the tacit and unable to provide a clear explanation.

Much has been made of the tacit nature of design, yet other disciplines have emerged from tacit understanding—medicine, engineering, and marketing, for example. Tacit approaches to design maintain a sense of mystery, where intuition is the foundation, and learning is based on a master-apprentice model involving close observation and imitation. Craft is absorbed and sensibility is slowly acquired, but the assumptions of the craft are often obscure and not open to question. Some aspects of undergraduate education may never transcend the tacit. Tacit skills developed over time by practicing designers are valuable experiential guides that mark their competence and sensibility; they are not without value.

Complex design projects, those with dense contextual relationships, those requiring an extensive system, or those that are highly customized, require a foundation in explicit theory, principle, or method to provide a grounding for design and its consistent and thoughtful development, especially if developed by an interdisciplinary, collaborative team. This does not rule out tacit moves or aesthetics; it is not an either/or situation, but an intelligent understanding and integration of the two. Design practice can be characterized as a dance that moves between the tacit and explicit.

Two well-known examples can clarify the tacit-explicit dimensions of knowing. Josef Albers, through understanding the relational effects of color and through phenomenal experimentation, developed a theory of color relations, *Interaction of Color* (1963). The initial observations were no doubt tacit, but after some number of them, he probably began to actively investigate and identify principles observed through his color experiments. From these qualitative and rather extensive (but personal) color actions, a pattern emerged from which a theory was developed as an explicit set of understandings that could be shared. Karl Gerstner, in his *Compendium for Literates* (1974), exemplifies 124 dimensions of writing. Writing included for him all forms of visible language—handwriting, typography, color, spatial organization, and methods of reproduction (see figures 1.1–1.3). He began these experiments to discover basic aspects of writing based on his own curiosity:

> The deeper I delved into the subject the more surprised I was that, although there is any amount of literature on "writing"— histories of development, textbooks, collections of examples, studies of function—there was virtually nothing so basic as a system analysis. Was this because writing refuses to fit into a rigid system? And perhaps also because—in spite of the risks involved—a start had to be made... (1974, 4).

Figures 1.1-1.3
Examples of Gerstner's dimensions of writing including figure-ground relationship and typographic manipulation

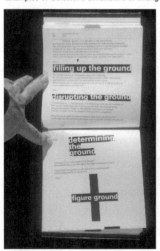

Using Fritz Zwicky's (1969) morphological method, he transformed his writing explorations into a system. What began for both Albers and Gerstner as a kind of tacit experience at a specific level of engagement, through analysis yielded an explicit understanding of the phenomenon of color interaction for Albers, and for Gerstner, a more systematic understanding of the extensive structural dimensions of writing. Both moved from phenomenal particulars that were largely tacit to a higher level of abstraction and analysis, which revealed explicit structural characteristics leading to principles, theories, or systems understanding.

Theory emerges from an analytical perspective that seeks to identify patterns found in an activity or phenomenon. It may be bottom-up, like the afore-mentioned examples, or it can be an adaptive approach, taking a theory from one domain for use in design interface and interaction, such as J.J. Gibson's theory of affordance (1979) in psychology. Theory, in this case, is a shortcut or reminder of the relationship between possible action and the form characteristics that signal and support the action. For example, in literature, the playwright Jean Genet (1962) writes of a man's necktie as a tool with which to strangle the wearer; the tie affords the act of strangling. Seeing the form-action relationship can be ordinary or extraordinary. In this way, theory becomes a new filter through which to see and interpret the world.

While much design education is tacit and directed to developing sensibilities of visual, material, cultural, and historical contexts, what can be made explicit—theory, method, or tool—is often either ignored or looked upon with suspicion. Theory has an undeservedly bad reputation ("Oh, that's just theory!"). Theory is a generalized explanation; yes, it is abstract, but it helps us to remember the salient issues of whatever we are trying to do or think about. Method, contrary to pervasive belief, is not a straightjacket the designer blindly submits to or a guarantee of a superior outcome, but a way of classifying and understanding actions appropriate to a category of problem. Methods are like tools and we are toolmakers and users, in many forms, both digital and physical. We can blindly use the tools in predictable ways, creative ways, or we can develop new ones, but the tools themselves are inescapable. But the identification or generation of theory, the development and testing of method, or the creation of a tool is an explicit activity based on critical analysis and trial and error. These more formal elements emerge from an analytical look at design's actions and challenges—yet they may be initially grounded in the tacit just as Albers' and Gerstner's explorations were. The theory, methods, and tools that result are evolutionary; they are the building blocks from which better editions emerge. Not everything can make the transition from tacit to explicit; some actions and sensibilities may be inherently tacit. But making some now tacit activities explicit, developing formalisms and methods with which to learn and do design, enhances design performance. This is a difficult task, but a task that must be addressed if design is to become a discipline.

Where is Design Located in a Development Process?

Notions of the scope of design action have changed. Some designers have moved from the aesthetic configuration that typically happens near the end of a project to the beginning where what may develop is unknown. Here another kind of process unfolds, one initially divorced from physical making and more deeply engaged with processing information and understanding the context through the generation of frameworks or conceptual diagrams, defining the problem to be addressed, asking questions, accessing research, constructing new research, and entertaining possibilities. We are reminded of Herbert Simon's (1969, 55) definition of design as "changing existing situations into preferred ones." This newer situation wants disciplinary resources, something beyond style magazines and latest trends, as it goes beneath the surface to the core of design-driven development. It wants ideas about design process and method, research data and its analysis, knowledge of the past for the purpose of building something appropriate to the present or future, and such resources and their integration and use can be or are explicit.

While design's newer contribution shifts to earlier stages, it is at such stages where the practice of design exhibits the most "complexity, uncertainty, instability, uniqueness, and value conflict," to use Donald Schön's (1983) terms. Design is a situated activity with all the messiness that its reputation implies. Taking these terms individually, how is design handling complexity—does it have research to develop methods that do so? How does design deal with uncertainty? Does it ask pertinent questions that can be answered through research, thereby reducing uncertainty? Does it access existing research? Or does it use its best judgment, and what is this based on? What about instability? Is the context of development so dynamic that particular strategies are called for? And if so, can we identify them? Is uniqueness true or a cover-up for lack of historical knowledge or investigation of the state-of-the-art? Certainly not all aspects of a design problem are unique. Finally, consider value conflict—are stakeholders identified and their values acknowledged? How are value conflicts explored and resolved? These few derivative questions, drawn from the changing context of practice, indicate the scope and intensity of the work ahead if design is to become a discipline.

What is a Discipline?

A distillation of aspects of discipline, drawn from several dictionaries, reveals the following: it is training to act in accordance with rules, activity, expertise, or a regimen that develops or improves a skill; it is a branch of instruction or learning. It also refers to punishment or consequences resulting from failure to follow the rules. Here, discipline refers to a branch of learning or instruction directed to the development of processes and sensibilities that result in *skillful performance*; this is the outcome of studying the discipline. These notions require further explanation.

Beginning from the discipline itself, there are systems of classification or taxonomies that reveal similarities or differences and that enhance identification of aspects of the discipline. Theories are developed, and confirmed or denied, based on study and evidence. Research develops questions of importance to disciplinary development or professional practice. Such research also depends on evidence based on an assembly of cases and their analyses, textual analyses, comparison of methods, quantitative or qualitative results. Histories examine the trajectory of disciplinary evolution, changes in technology or social/cultural need, the impact of large cultural systems, cross-cultural idea transfer—the list could go on and on. Processes and methods to improve performance change as they are developed and put into play. Useful methods evolve, and the others fade away.

Further, the discipline reveals itself through its discourse. Publishing and using research results in practice, and scaffolding new research on previous work provides a lively criticism that demonstrates that involvement in domain development is important and worthy of comment. In this way, the growing body of disciplinary knowledge is disseminated and becomes available for further action whether through research, criticism, application, or reflection.

Formal structure for a discipline is parsed at the university level by domain and degree: the bachelor's degree prepares for entry into professional practice; the master's prepares for advanced professional practice or disciplinary development and dissemination through teaching; and the doctoral degree prepares for research and teaching. These degrees differentiate what is studied, with each providing the scaffolding for the next higher level. Increasingly there is an expectation of continuing education—lifelong learning—as the discipline, its related technologies, and social/cultural context continue to evolve.

Expectation for those teaching within a discipline is also a factor as it is their role to pass along the context of the domain, its new knowledge, and its best practices, its research needs and achievements, as well as its changing practice opportunities. This requires an active engagement with disciplinary ideas as mentioned above, as well as attention to emerging ideas or controversies in the active role of a shaper of the domain.

Disciplines support professions. Again drawing on aspects identified by several dictionary sources, profession or its conjugates refers to someone who is expert at his or her work, is distinguished from an amateur by standing, practice, and methods, and has acquired knowledge of some department of learning. If there is a direct and formalized relationship between discipline and profession, licensing, performance standards, and ethical codes result.

Why is Disciplinary Development Resisted?

Two of the most prominent reasons to resist disciplinary development in design are the value placed on creativity, and the specificity and messiness of design practice. Methods for designing, as well as research development and use, appear to be the antithesis of intuitive and creative work. Yet such an impression is based on polarizing knowledge embedded in method or development through research in relation to artfulness and creativity. Development of knowledge through research is mistaken as a dry, unimaginative exercise. One only needs to read accounts of scientists at work (Shasha and Lazere, 1998; Greenstein, 1998) to understand the creative role of imagination and the excitement of discovery supported by deep knowledge of a domain. If the biographies of scientists are not appealing, collected analyses of a broader range of creative people (Csikszentmihalyi, 1996) with an analysis of their attributes may help to erase the mistaken notion that systematic knowledge and creativity are at odds.

Design practice is messy and specific, but perhaps in dealing with these characteristics and the details of getting to a solution, we have failed to grasp the repetitive actions—similar if not identical, patterns of function, form, sensory stimulation, invitations to action, etc.—that mark the work. Identification of recurrence is a first step toward building models and theories of practice. These ideas invite further exploration to better understand their limitations or context of use. Problem-solving processes rarely move smoothly within a diagrammatic representation of a generic process; however, the model remains useful as a touchstone, delivering a needed overview of process, helping to locate participants in an unfolding situation.

Together, these two reasons to resist disciplinary development, the need to support creativity, and recognition of the specificity of design action, lead to a fear of formulaic results. I am reminded of Christopher Alexander's *Pattern Language* (1977); this was not an invitation to simply replicate known architectural/social use configurations much like an old pattern book, but an acknowledgment of what is typical with an implied opportunity to modify and invent. Perhaps what is important is the designer's mental frame of reference. Jerome Bruner (1971, 116) in the context of education quotes Joseph Agassis; "...in any body of men who use their minds at all, one usually gets a sharp division between...'knowers' and 'seekers.' Knowers are valuers of firm declarative statements about the state of things. Seekers regard such statements as invitations to speculation and doubt. The two groups often deplore each other." Design has attracted seekers, but now it also needs knowers if it is to develop as a discipline. Best of all are designers who are both knowers and seekers.

Like other disciplines, biology, for example, has sub-disciplines of vertebrate or microbiology. Such classification focuses knowledge and makes it accessible for extension. Design is a term that encompasses many sub-forms or specific sub-

Table 1.1
Comparison of sub-disciplines of design according to their different or shared focus*

Urban/Regional Planning	Architecture	Environment	Product	Communication
Aesthetics	*Aesthetics*	*Aesthetics*	*Aesthetics*	*Aesthetics*
	Building materials			
Commercial use	Building types			
	Business investment		Business investment	Business investment
	Climate	Climate		
	Construction	Construction	Distribution	Distribution
Energy	*Energy*	*Energy*	*Energy*	
	Engineering	*Engineering*	*Engineering*	*Engineering*
		Flora/Fauna		
	Function	*Function*	*Function*	*Function*
	Human factors	*Human factors*	*Human factors*	*Human factors*
Industrial use		Interpretation	Interaction	Interaction
			Manufacture	Information
	Material science		Material science	
Meaning	*Meaning*	*Meaning*	*Meaning*	*Meaning*
Parks		Parks		Media
Patterns of use	*Patterns of use*	*Patterns of use*	*Patterns of use*	*Patterns of use*
		Public services		
Recreation		Recreation		
Residential use	Structure	Shelter	Shelter	
	Style	*Style*	*Style*	*Style*
Tax investment		Tax investment		
Transportation				
Waste disposal				
Water supply				
Zoning plan	Zoning compliance			

*Aspects shared by four or all sub-disciplines are presented as bold italic.

disciplines, but unlike biology, design is not well organized. The following table (see Table 1.1) lists the design disciplines that are typically found within many universities where disciplines largely develop. Design sub-disciplines tend to be isolated from each other and to look only internally at their own development. A larger concept of design would strengthen its specific parts, much like biology encompasses and locates many areas of related knowledge that benefit from association and exchange. Returning to the table, the list goes from large scale on the left to smaller toward the right. But even this depends on how scale is interpreted, on the left it could be one very large building or regional plan, while on the right it could be millions of copies of an original item, or millions of eyes and minds interacting with a website or software product. Concerns of the individual sub-disciplines often overlap, yet each envisions itself as distinct. There is also considerable variability in their disciplinary development and discourse. Those to the left are better organized than those to the right.

It is instructive to look across the table. The form-giving aspect of these sub-disciplines is evident in the fact that they are all concerned with aesthetics, even though their material concerns—objects, digital media, landforms, or buildings—are quite different. Their communication aspect is evident in the fact that they all develop meaning through form-giving. Another aspect of concern to all is patterns of use or what people do with the object or environment. Variation on finance is also an aspect crossing all, even though its manifestations are somewhat different, including tax investment (city planning and environment), or business investment (architecture, product, and communication). Other aspects cross over between two, three, or four sub-disciplines, and some are unique. Focus has been on the material concerns of the sub-disciplines that tend to separate them; this table shifts the focus to concerns they share.

The attributes of a sub-discipline within design are not a mystery, and there are numerous disciplines whose history and development are well documented. Enumeration of what constitutes a discipline has also been contributed from many viewpoints. Some have detailed the relationship between a profession and its discipline. Charles Owen (1998) has looked comparatively across several professions and their disciplinary underpinnings to identify differences in their metrics and sources of value. The differences among the disciplines are revealing as they underscore epistemological orientation. Owen maps the disciplines based on whether they are largely analytic or synthetic, and whether largely symbolic or real. Yet despite observations calling for disciplinary development over decades, design as an overarching idea with connections among its various practices has not emerged. There have been some general philosophical discussions of purpose and process in design (Simon, 1969; Schön, 1983; Cross, 2002), compendiums of methods within design and beyond (Jones, 1970; Jones, 1991) development of specific methodologies (Alexander, 1964; Owen, n.d.), discussion of teaching, but very little substantive research, and little impact on professional practice.

Some traditional habits that impede scholarly progress in design are as follows: isolation from others, disconnected information, traditional craft education that neglects contemporary challenges, and location in art schools in many universities. Prominently missing is an understanding of the process of knowledge building. Science is often misconstrued or ignored; varieties of research are unknown, and their possible role in design problem solving is unexplored.

Why Research and Collaboration?

Interdisciplinary work for significant design projects requires designers to be practically rooted in their own knowledge. The ability to fully participate in such a setting requires the confidence born of knowledge. Such knowledge can be based on experience and/or a critical synthesis of theory from other disciplines, but powerful knowledge that can be accepted by others with different disciplinary underpinnings is based on research. In this regard, Klaus Krippendorff (1995) states:

Most designers find themselves confronted by sophisticated research methods from other disciplines whose reality they are unable to relativize, analyze, and put in place. The reality of markets, profits, much like the reality of engineering products is rarely doubted precisely because language makes this compellingly obvious and their institutions back it up. When outsiders can veto a design without being confronted in an empirically grounded language, designers have lost the debate over the reality of their ideas.

Research gives rhetorical strength to interdisciplinary arguments or decisions. As will be argued later in the first chapter (7) in the section on Collaboration, current interest in innovation often requires interdisciplinary work in which designers are disadvantaged by their lack of disciplinary grounding. Bernd Meurer (1999, 27) states:

> Design activity, or put differently, innovation which squares up to such tasks [social and ecological product-process systems]—and they are contextual in the largest sense—entails not simply interdisciplinary design, but a cross-disciplinary complex of activities involving cross-fertilization by science, technology, design, economy, and politics.

Innovation is receiving more and more attention from design as well as from business and technology. In relation to innovation, knowledge production can be identified by three models (Foray, 2004, 67–68):

- The first major trend concerns the increasingly scientific nature of research methods. In more and more sectors, the "epistemic culture" of science for knowledge production is growing in importance.
- Users' increasingly marked engagement in knowledge production represents a second trend.
- Finally, the increasing complexity and modularity of industrial architecture make it more critical than ever to produce "integrative knowledge," such as standards, norms, common architecture, and platforms.

In an even stronger sense, Ken Friedman (1997) calls for a science of design that discloses its methods of inquiry and substantiates its facts through critical examination. Such an approach underscores the building of a discipline. Here, research is not used in a casual sense as is often the case in design education, including, for example, secondary research and its synthesis, politically correct and predictable design case writing, or formal visual exploration without analytical assessment. Research, as used here, seeks to answer timely questions that will contribute new knowledge to design performance; it generates empirical evidence, substantiates theory, and proposes reasoned processes and definitions; it is self-critical and open to debate.

Research is used here in a formal sense. It is not experimentation in a purely exploratory sense nor is it necessarily divorced from a project. It is not a scientific search for truth or certainty, but developing from evidence, it identifies substantial patterns in the interface and interaction between people and objects, communications, and environments created by design. As used in this book, research refers to investigations undertaken to develop formal knowledge through quantitative, qualitative, or comparative studies—project, theory, method, or tool creation that goes through cycles of development and revision based on some form of assessment. The goal of such research is to enhance design performance in a practical sense. The common designations of basic, applied, and clinical are reliable designations depending on what the research question is and how it is positioned. Basic research asks fundamental questions, the answer being unknown at the time of asking. An example of a basic research question in design is: do people assign the same meaning or interpretation to abstract motion on screen? Applied research examines a class of problem or possibility that moves research into useful, instrumental realms. An example of this is an application of technology, such as adapting global positioning systems for ordinary human use in automobiles or hand-held devices. Clinical research asks a practical question that can be answered in a specific project space. An example of a clinical research question is: should people archive their medical records, and if yes, what form of capture and access is useful, private, and easy to maintain? Because research is undertaken, not for itself, but to enhance design performance, to build a disciplinary foundation, or to solve some human or technical problem, design practitioners benefit from accessing appropriate design research and reporting back on its usefulness or difficulties, thus influencing research development. Design research can transform design action, but the transformation of research into action requires both understanding and creativity. Creating a meaningful feedback loop between design practice and design researchers in academia is not an easy task. Yet this is an important collaborative goal that can help to sustain a fundamental activity essential to discipline building.

While the university is known for its public sharing and presentation of knowledge, it is important to understand that design practice is not without its own research activities. And this presents another problem, because much of this research is proprietary and not sharable. Consequently, false leads and blind alleys are investigated over and over again for lack of common understanding of a research need, its history of investigation, and its false starts or movements toward success.

Design researchers will ask different questions than those in other fields. For example, regarding visual phenomena, they will likely originate questions that seek to identify patterns of meaning for form or motion that are significantly different from those asked by perceptual psychologists. Design research more readily translates into design action, because it emerges from questions designers care about and understand as important to improved practice. Design researchers will also likely examine the design process itself, which is not an incontrovertible given. No one but a designer would ask for such research; its relationship to practical use is obvious, and deeper examination of design practice will necessarily call into question performance standards.

Why Discourse?

Varieties of research results can propel disciplinary development and enliven practice if they are shared, accessed, used, and yes, even criticized. They are a contribution to discourse, revealing what serious designers think and talk about, the lively ideas that challenge them and how to open new avenues for investigation and performance.

In 1995, an article by Klaus Krippendorff in *Design—Pleasure or Responsibility* sought to redesign design from the standpoint of a profession. In it, he defined the importance of discourse to the viability and vitality of a discipline. He critically cited design's lack of discourse and the colonizing trends of other discourses (business, engineering, human-computer interaction, etc.) to usurp design's domain. Lacking a well understood and accepted core idea unique to itself, he observed that design was extremely vulnerable to colonization. This is intensified by the fact that there are many perspectives on design's core competencies and the extent of its domain. Increasingly, it poaches on other domains for ideas and methods. Because other disciplines are well organized and design is in disarray, the field is not level in competition with others. Writing from the perspective of industrial design, Krippendorff offered an axiom with which to ground design and its discourse: "Accept as axiomatic that humans act not on the physical qualities of things but on what they come to mean *to them*." Thus, meaning is core to human experience with, in this case, the artificial world of design, in which designers actively mediate meaning.

While his writing is also a call to action and ends positively, it does so only after dissecting some of design's positions that impede the development of a meaningful discourse. What follows draws from his list (Krippendorff, 1995), but adds others; it risks alienating some, but the presumptions and strategies designers use to reify their own position, derail discourse, and stonewall community-building necessarily need to be stated if change is to be entertained. Here goes.

Designer as lone genius creating an (auto)biographical design. This denies history and precedent, while it undercuts teamwork, collaboration, or even the contributions of the hired help. Some refer to this as the "star" syndrome or the cult of the personality.

Designers tend not to be broadly analytical. They don't ask interesting questions about design or design activity. They resist subject matter decomposition, preferring to work holistically to develop understanding and solutions to a problem. Most design education favors creation and reproduction rather than other system aspects such as distribution, reception, acculturation or consumption of ideas/products by culture. Designers are unable to criticize research or apply it effectively, because their education is largely in the craft tradition. They don't see the issues.

Designers, when they write or present, avoid attribution. There are few, if any, citations in what they write, and their design performance lacks recognition of seminal ideas or prototypes that provide the foundation for their work. Literature and reflection on design is disconnected and spotty; one cannot take a deep and interesting journey through it.

Designers avoid writing and reading. This allows their discourse, or what could be their discourse, to be colonized and defined by others.

Designers endlessly search for the "new." Without documentation of idea development, much time and effort is wasted in the repetition of ideas, whether they are successful or not. What is apparently new gets old very fast these days; horizons are short and ever-changing. This impedes not only development, but also the accumulation of design knowledge.

Designers' competitive posture is evident both privately and publicly. Categorically putting other designers down succeeds in marginalizing them as the speaker rises in stature. This makes community-building impossible.

Designers focus on practice with high interest in the doing of design. They have little interest in analyses of how and even less interest in why—they do what they do.

Designers often misunderstand science. They think that science provides a final truth or certainty rather than understanding science as an evolutionary process.

There is a need for various communities of practice in design. If one's focus is history, then identification of key historians for critique, collaboration, and community becomes important to an ongoing sense of intellectual and disciplinary development. Several colleagues from other disciplines have observed that designers do not argue. Perhaps we are too polite, or perhaps we are insecure because we lack the textual depth or clearly articulated knowledge resident in other domains. Rendered mute, positions on ideas remain unsaid because too much background material would need development. The critique of ideas, when it occurs, is often limited and dismissive. Articulate and ongoing criticism demonstrates the importance of the content and activity. Design needs this.

As a discipline, design requires a discourse that is responsible to history, uses scholarly apparatus (definitions, references, bibliographies, footnotes, etc.), reports research intelligently, supports dialogue between academia and practice, opens issues critically for examination, and builds knowledge, not only for its own purposes, but also to share with others with different disciplinary perspectives.

Object or Action?

As the preceding discussion demonstrates, perspectives on design vary. There has been a bias toward design object over design action. This may be a result of following trends established by art history and museum acquisition that treat design from an aesthetic standpoint as a commodity. Just as the social sciences have tried to one degree or another to take on the mantle of the physical sciences, design has followed the lead of fine art to justify itself. Often, design objects are considered solely from an analytical and expert distance based on aesthetics and originality as the dominant qualities; use-value and fittingness to human life are less important. This book seeks to shift the perspective from the object of design to the act of design. Do not misunderstand what unfolds here as a change of perspective that necessarily denigrates aesthetics or originality. The sensory qualities of objects and information that trigger pleasure, surprise, or profound and lasting enjoyment by those that use them is not trivial, but it is not isolated from other dimensions.

Two Paradigms?

Two classic books are important to understanding design more deeply as a process: *The Sciences of the Artificial* by Herbert Simon (1969) and *The Reflective Practitioner* by Donald Schön (1983). The two design paradigms presented in these books have played off of each other in recent years: Simon's rational problem-solving approach, and Schön's reflective practice. A thorough empirical study of these two dominant design perspectives was constructed (Dorst, 1997) and, like the book you're reading, Dorst's book also focused on design-as-experienced from the inside in an action sense, as a designer perceives the doing of design. Selection of a point of comparison was critical as each paradigm seemed to exclude the other. A fundamental issue in design-as-experienced, namely integration, is an issue not directly addressed in either paradigm—this became the point of comparison. The study identifies these two approaches as operating from different philosophical perspectives and at different stages in design process. Simon's approach operates in the information phase of design, in which the designer becomes informed; positivism is the basis. Schön's approach operates in the conceptual phase when meaning and value are explored; constructivism is its basis. The study concludes that these two paradigms are not either/or propositions, but are complementary.

From another perspective, Stephen Toulmin in his book *Return to Reason* (2001) argues that the sciences with their search for certainty and truth have distorted what was formerly a more holistic approach to human knowledge. The dominance of science has diminished the significance of disciplines that deal with less predictable and messy issues of human behavior and creation. Schön and Simon, respectively, represent artfulness and science in design—they exemplify the balance that Toulmin addresses. Too often we are caught in a polarizing situation that seems to require a limiting choice. Like the tacit and explicit discussed earlier, design action includes both intuition and fact. Successful design is not lopsided, all intuition with no fact, or all fact with no intuition. In redressing the balance in design and in seeking integration, we necessarily emphasize what is missing and can be made explicit such as the role of research or collaboration in design's disciplinary growth.

Why These Two Themes?

Research is present for three reasons: it is instrumental to creating a discipline; it moves ideas and actions to more explicit territory; and it is often overlooked by traditional approaches to design. Collaboration is the situation in which designer's knowledge limitations are transcended, and collaboration is a vital opportunity for design to learn from others and share its own knowledge in meaningful ways.

The importance of technology and human-centeredness in contemporary design situations underscore the need for collaboration and its importance; technology has complicated and expanded development and control of the artificial. Technology alters every aspect of our lives. It has been socialized into rules, roles, relationships, and patterns of action—these are now changing because of technology:

> We take for granted the workings of banks, schools, markets, meetings, the news, street traffic, visits to the doctor, and a thousand other arrangements. The weirdness and brilliance of information technology is that all of those arrangements are liquefying. Many of them existed to solve informational problems, or were limited by informational problems. They depended on a stable assignment of activities to places. But with information technology they are all suddenly renegotiated. (Agre, 2000)

Technology has become more reliable (from a technical perspective), but more challenging (from a human use perspective). Designers are among those who make sense of technology, mediating between technical possibilities and people's understanding and use of them.

> The design space is exploding, and so design must change. Information technology has few opinions of its own. It is plastic, malleable. Design means reconciling constraints, but now fewer of the constraints are dictated by intrinsic properties of technology. It need no longer be heavy, or to sit in one place, or to be connected by wires. It can be woven into the artifacts and patterns of daily life in unbounded ways. (Agre, 2000)

The presumption that technical means are hard to achieve, that once things "work," that is the conclusion, is no longer reasonable. Hidden within this technological focus is the understanding that people will adapt to the technical means available. Yes, people are very adaptable; they develop work-arounds and use things in creative ways, because the objects in question fail to meet their needs. A change in design orientation is called for, one that questions how people actually live their lives and how they use information, objects, and environments. What is needed is a focus on people.

 This brings us to human-centeredness. There is a fundamental indeterminacy of the people we design for—they are not one kind with universal desires. Who are we designing for? Not our surrogate selves or some ghostly composite, but real people in all their complexity and variation. Understanding and investigating what people actually do, how they understand things, how they value things, what features are desired in what context of use, becomes part of the designer's activity as they become advocates for users. This moves them beneath the surface forms and issues of aesthetics to work with sociologists, psychologists, anthropologists, computer scientists, material engineers, and others to see more clearly the interaction between people and their relationships to the objects, environments, and message systems that are technically possible. Design becomes a form of social practice, and this is not a practice that takes place in isolation.

The intensity of interaction between individuals with diverse intellectual perspectives brings both creativity and interpersonal strife as they collaboratively grapple with a problem, its solution, and practical development. Beneath goodwill and team spirit are the disciplines with their different epistemologies and ontologies. What constitutes legitimate knowledge or process can become an issue that supports or diminishes various disciplinary contributions. It is in this context that design's shortcomings are revealed and what may be valuable design contributions are called into question for lack of research, inability to argue for method, or the fairly pervasive idea that design is based on intuition alone—the designer awaits the "big idea."

Why Now?

Why is this the time to consciously build a design discipline? Two significant factors influence the timing. The interdisciplinary work in design just discussed is increasingly common, requiring team skills and sensitivity to different epistemic styles; doctoral programs in design are growing worldwide with increasing opportunity for research to be accomplished and openly reported. Increasingly, designers work in collaborative cross-disciplinary teams and participating in a team is different than performing as a solo practitioner or as a sub-contractor to someone who has delineated the extent of one's work. Cross-disciplinary team participation requires an ability to negotiate team process and participate in decision-making. Such participation calls into question the context behind one's participation—disciplinary research and knowledge, or what is known and how it is known, particular skills and perspectives—all of which go beyond one's individual experience to depend on the contribution of others in the form of discourse and knowledge in order to form a productive collaboration.

In Conclusion...

That design aspires to be artful is a well-understood goal with a long history. Artfulness refers to form giving sensory and cognitive dimensions in its material, whether two-, three-, or four-dimensional—it is often largely tacit. Positioning design only in relation to artfulness ignores its other attributes like function, social interface, or business enterprise. Science alone is not sufficient either. Thus a broader integration is needed, one that includes recognition of the limits to facts, principles, knowledge, and the necessity of creative leaps, exploration of alternative form, and synthetic judgment that pulls many-faceted ideas and contributions into an integrated whole. Design is opportunistic in borrowing knowledge from many sources and shaping such knowledge to its own action-oriented purposes; however, it has been slow to develop its own transferable information and knowledge. This is the primary issue addressed in this book. The disciplinary problem is identified; in subsequent chapters we elaborate on its challenges and opportunities in terms of research and collaboration.

This book is a collection of papers in two sections, each confined to themes that are timely and important to the development of a design discipline: research and collaboration. The two themes move us from an object orientation to one of idea and process. Each section develops some history, but its purpose is not historical per se; rather it seeks to set a context. It discusses the limitations of knowledge in the theme area and its overlaps with other themes as the limitations themselves give rise to suggested investigation. It searches for strategies and actionable ideas through the introductory challenge essay to each section with the articles that follow demonstrating cases or deeper investigation that suggests opportunities and alternatives for future development. Drawing an analogy to Thomas Kuhn's (1962) explication of normal science as opposed to revolutionary science, we seek to delineate advanced normal design as understood in its current context. Paradigm shifts come later.

References

Agre, Phil. 2000. Notes on the new design space. http://polaris.gseis.ucla.edu/pagre/design-space.html (Accessed 12 February 2009).

Albers, Josef. 1963. *Interaction of Colors*. New Haven, CT: Yale University Press.

Alexander, Christopher. 1964. *Notes on the Synthesis of Form*. Cambridge, MA: Harvard University Press.

Alexander, Christopher. 1977. *Pattern Language*. New York, NY: Oxford University Press.

Bruner, Jerome. 1971. The Relevance of Education. New York, NY: W.W. Norton & Company.

Buchanan, Richard. 2001. Design Research and the New Learning. *Design Issues*, 17.4, 3–23.

Cross, Nigel. 2002. Design as a Discipline. *Proceedings of the Inter-disciplinary Design Quandary Conference*. De Montfort University, February 13.

Csikszentmihalyi, Mihaly. 1996. *Creativity, Flow and the Psychology of Discovery and Invention*. New York, NY: HarperCollins.

Dorst, Kees. 1997. *Describing Design, A Comparison of Paradigms*. Delft, Netherlands: TU Delft, doctoral dissertation.

Foray, Dominique. 2004. *The Economics of Knowledge*. Cambridge, MA: MIT Press.

Friedman, Ken. 1997. Design Science and Design Education. In McGrory, Peter (ed.), *The Challenge of Complexity*. Helsinki, Finland: University of Art and Design Helsinki UIAH, 54–72.

Genet, Jean. 1962. *The Screens*. Translated by Bernard Frechtman. New York, NY: Grove Press.

Gerstner, Karl. 1974. *Compendium for Literates*. Cambridge, MA: MIT Press.

Gibson, J.J. 1979. *The Ecological Approach to Visual Perception*. Boston, MA: Houghton Mifflin.

Greenstein, George. 1998. *Portraits of Discovery, Profiles in Scientific Genius*. New York, NY: John Wiley and Sons, Inc.

Habermas, Jürgen. 1998. On the Pragmatics of Communication. Cambridge, MA: MIT Press.

Jones, J. Christopher. 1970. *Design Methods: Seeds of Human Futures*. New York, NY: John Wiley.

Jones, J. Christopher. 1991. *Designing Designing*. London, United Kingdom: Longman Group.

Krippendorff, Klaus. 1995. Redesigning Design: An Invitation to a Responsible Future. http://www.asc.upenn.edu/usr/krippendorff/REDESGN.htm (Accessed 12 February 2009).

Kuhn, Thomas. 1962. *The Structure of Scientific Revolutions*. Chicago, IL: University of Chicago Press.

Meurer, Bernd. 1999. New Design Challenges and Concepts. *Design Issues*, 15.1, 26–30

Owen, Charles. 1998. Design Research: Building the Knowledge Base. *Design Studies*, 19.1, 9–20.

Owen, Charles. n.d. Structured Planning. http://id.iit.edu/papers/Owen_theory/just.pdf (Accessed 26 April 2006).

Polanyi, Michael. 1983. *The Tacit Dimension*. Gloucester, MA: Peter Smith.

Schön, Donald. 1987. *Educating the Reflective Practitioner*. San Francisco, CA: Jossey-Bass.

Schön, Donald. 1983. *The Reflective Practitioner*. New York, NY: Basic Books.

Shasha, Dennis and Cathy Lazere. 1998. *Out of Their Mind*. New York, NY: Copernicus.

Shulman, Lee S. 2004a. *Teaching as Community Property*. San Francisco, CA: Jossey-Bass.

Shulman, Lee S. 2004b. *The Wisdom of Practice*. San Francisco, CA: Jossey-Bass.

Simon, Herbert. 1969. *The Sciences of the Artificial*. Cambridge, MA: MIT Press.

Toulmin, Stephen. 2001. *Return to Reason*. Cambridge, MA: Harvard University Press.

Weingart, Peter and Nico Stehr (eds.). 2000. *Practising Interdisciplinarity*. Toronto, ON, Canada: University of Toronto Press.

Zwicky, Fritz. 1969. *Discovery, Invention, Research—Through the Morphological Approach*. Toronto, ON, Canada: Macmillan.

DESIGN
RESEARCH

2

PERSPECTIVES ON DESIGN RESEARCH

Keiichi Sato

Design Questions—Research Questions

Is design research useful for improving quality of design? Does it help design innovation? Does it help business? Can design research solve societal problems? These are examples of somewhat naïve, but very fundamental questions anyone interested in improving the quality of design, design practice, or design education would ask. In some areas of design practice, the answer is obviously "yes," but in some areas it is less obvious. As we practice design, we face numerous design problems and generate many design questions. Whether personal or organizational, we experience many obstacles in our design processes as we work on a design project. Let us assume that these problems, questions, and obstacles in design practice can all be translated into research questions. These research questions define the space in which design research develops its activities.

Let us look at a simple and common design problem many designers often have—designing a button on a physical product or on a screen display as shown in Figure 2.1. How many design questions can we generate about this simple button? For example, what shape, size, color, stroke, material, texture, symbol, function, used by whom, on what, how, when, and where (see Figure 2.2)? Each question leads to many levels of factors affecting design decisions ranging from human factors concerning individual users such as ergonomic or cognitive factors, to factors concerning groups of people such as social and cultural factors. Furthermore, as we look into relationships between different questions and different factors, the number of questions grows exponentially.

Figure 2.1
A button to think, a button to
design, a button to hit

Figure 2.2
Who uses the button, for what, where,
when, and how?

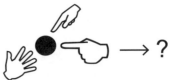

Looking at this flow of questions we can easily predict that a flood of design questions can be generated ranging from pragmatic to philosophical questions.[1] How long and stiff should the button stroke be to get appropriate tactile feedback? How would we feel about it? What does it mean in our life? The design of one simple button could affect our work, life, culture, business, and more.

The complexity of our design problem does not remain at the one button level. The problem extends to many buttons that are inter-related and, in some cases, geographically distributed. As we add more questions around the button design problem, the design problem becomes better defined; the nature of the design problem becomes apparent. Answering those questions shapes a button design that embodies the concerns and issues addressed in those questions. Some questions are answered by designers' intuitive insights without externalized rationale. Some questions are answered with well-formed rationale based on scientific knowledge.

The fast changing conditions of our physical, technological, economic, social, and cultural environments affect our views and, consequently, the way design problems are shaped. This trend of rapid change and increasing complexity of design problems imposes heavy demand for new design knowledge beyond the capacity of traditional design practice. Design as a discipline is entering a historical phase of structural change in its intellectual foundation, i.e., from empirical practice to knowledge-intensive practice. In order to achieve this ambitious change, design needs effective mechanisms for the accumulation, transfer, and generation of knowledge. This is probably a widely agreed upon statement in spite of possible disagreement on how we respond to the need. Other well-established disciplines such as medicine, engineering, and business have experienced similar transitions at different points in their historical development. The development of knowledge is the main mission of design researchers; however, the task of transforming the disciplinary foundation involves all stakeholders in design, e.g., educators of different levels, researchers in academia and industry, practicing designers, corporate management, public system planners, governmental policy makers, collaborators with design, and users of design.

This section, Design Research, (Chapters 2 – 6) explores broad perspectives on design research and their relationship to design practice, and provides examples of research areas and issues. The primary intent is to introduce different design research perspectives as *knowledge generating activities*. The question, "Why do we need design research more than ever?" is the core concern for discussion throughout the chapters in this section.

Defining Design Research

Definition of the Term

Before we start our argument on the nature of research in design, it is necessary to distinguish between two types of design research. Without this distinction, our discussion will be confused and obscured in our attempt to compose perspectives on design research as the knowledge-generating foundation for the design discipline.

One use of the term "design research" is the practice of developing information for a particular design project. This research typically includes information gathering about user needs, social issues, markets, competitive products, and related technologies. In recent years, "design research" in this sense has been becoming increasingly important because of a particular focus on understanding users' needs for human-centered system development. In the attempt to produce insightful human-centered design directives, interdisciplinary groups, consisting of professionals such as anthropologists, psychologists, and designers, are often involved in this class of activities. In this chapter, we will use the term "project information development" for these types of activities (practical design information development).

The other use of the term "design research" indicates the practice of developing a generalized and structured body of knowledge that is commonly applicable across different design cases as well as commonly verifiable or acceptable by general academic standards. The types of knowledge developed by this class of activities include theories, methods, principles, and tools that become resources for future cycles of knowledge development or for practical applications (academic research).

In this chapter, the latter meaning for the term "design research" is used unless specifically noted. Although these two types of design research have distinctively different goals, they have many common interests and activities, and mutually beneficial relationships.

General Design Research and Domain-Specific Design Research

Design research has two distinct areas of interest. One is the scientific study of the acts of design called "general design research," and the other is the study of the subjects of design called "domain-specific design research." In either case, research produces scientific knowledge about design. Though design is not a science, design research is a scientific engagement; its goal is to understand the nature of design and demonstrate how the resulting scientific knowledge can be applied to the design of artifacts in practice (Sato, 2000).

General design research leads to general design theories and methodologies that provide general models of design processes and knowledge. Most research in this category intends to develop methodologies or methods that contribute to improvements in the practice of design. Few attempts have been made to develop general theories of design, because design is considered to be too ill-defined as a subject for theories. General Design Theory (GDT), the first elaborate research effort to establish a theory of design, takes an axiomatic approach to establish its theoretical structure (Yoshikawa, 1987). In Chapter 3, Tetsuo Tomiyama gives an overview of GDT and its recent development. Research in GDT has been also extended to mathematical and philosophical research. Another example of an axiomatic approach is known as "the principle of design" that develops axioms and theorems about qualities of design based on patterns of function embodiment (Suh, 1990, 2005).

Domain-specific research leads to the development of knowledge about specific domains of design concern. Examples of such domains include human-artifact interaction, economic assessment of design value, universal accessibility, and environmental performance of artifacts. Most of the research questions generated for the button design problem mentioned earlier would apply to this type of research. Knowledge produced by this type of research needs to be further translated into forms that are applicable in design practice, e.g., design methods, information frameworks, guidelines, and design principles that are specific to the domain.

General theories and methodologies from general design research are not intended to be directly applicable to design practice; they provide frameworks and models of design for further research to develop domain-specific knowledge and methodologies applicable to actual design projects. The practical value of design research emerges when knowledge from general design research and knowledge about subject areas from domain-specific design research merge and are integrated into an actionable framework of domain knowledge and design methodologies. Kari Kuutti (in Chapter 4 of this book) points out that the crucial qualities of knowledge used in designing an artifact are local, particular, and timely. These qualities make knowledge fit for the purpose and determine if the design will succeed. One role of design research is to provide mechanisms and foundations that effectively support the process of acquiring and generating knowledge specific to the unique circumstances of individual design projects.

Design Knowledge and Its Lifecycle

Research on Design Knowledge

Design in practice seeks to identify problems in various aspects of people's lives that inspire creative generation of artifacts. People's needs and problems change as their social, technological, and economic living environments change. Design, being responsible for forming artifacts, therefore continues to face new questions that respond to new environments and needs. Every project has specific situations that create the need for new knowledge. Although every design project requires a unique set of knowledge, there is no need to produce anew the entire set of knowledge required for a project. A significant portion of required knowledge could come from personally or organizationally accumulated knowledge resources that are generic and reusable for different design projects. As the complexity of a design project increases, the amount of required project-specific knowledge also increases far beyond the practical capacity of the resources allocated to most projects. This indicates an increasing need for effective methods to manage the processes and knowledge at different phases of design activities throughout the course of the design project. The design discipline, therefore, needs formal mechanisms for developing knowledge and sustaining the knowledge lifecycle that provides operational and intellectual platforms for design practice. This is what we expect as the outcome from design research.

There are different categorization schemes of design knowledge. One categorization scheme is to distinguish between domain-specific knowledge about the subject of design and meta-knowledge about the nature of knowledge and knowledge manipulation. Domain-specific knowledge is tied to a design sub-category (environmental design or human-computer interaction, for example) that enriches the body of knowledge for the domain. General design research primarily deals with meta-knowledge to manage knowledge manipulation in the design process. Knowledge for combining multiple ideas, and knowledge for identifying relationships between elements of knowledge are examples of meta-knowledge.

Another categorization scheme is to distinguish between descriptive knowledge and tacit knowledge. While descriptive knowledge can be explicitly communicated in a form of language, tacit knowledge can be communicated only by ostensive means between the people who share it (Polanyi, 1966). It is knowledge that is experienced often through action. For example, knowledge about how to play a musical instrument can only be acquired through practice and communicated between performers by referencing similar experiences. There are many other categorization schemes that can be used for understanding the structure of knowledge. Differences in the ways we understand and define design knowledge set different orientations for framing questions and approaches in design research. For example, the notion of tacit knowledge could open a research area studying interactive mechanisms between descriptive knowledge and tacit knowledge to enhance creativity in the design process. Recently, many researchers in business and design management have adopted the term tacit knowledge to explain 'unexplainable' mechanisms of individual and organizational creativity.

Design knowledge intrinsically takes heterogeneous forms of representation reflecting the nature of the subject, personal patterns, and disciplinary conventions as depicted in Figure 2.3. For example, knowledge involved in button design is represented in various forms such as photographic images of use scenes, narrative synopsis of user experience, diagrams of causal relations between the button and its effect, drawings of the shapes, and symbolic description of the button behavior. While the heterogeneity of knowledge gives richness to design information and efficiency to operations within individual disciplines, it also causes major difficulties when integrating information in the course of artifact development. Communication and documentation of design knowledge across disciplines and activities of design projects have become critical issues in large corporate organizations because of the heterogeneity of knowledge representation and different disciplinary cultures.

Knowledge Lifecycle

Knowledge lifecycles do not occur only between research and the practice of artifact development, but also between artifact development and use of the artifact. Designers and researchers study users and usage of artifacts in order to develop better products and generate knowledge to be embedded into artifacts. Users also

Figure 2.3
Heterogeneous representation of the domain of concern

Figure 2.4
Knowledge cycle between artifact development and user

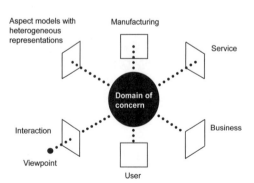

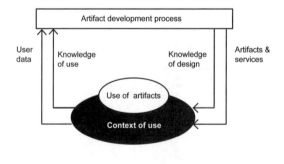

generate a significant amount of knowledge through interpretation of embedded knowledge in artifacts. Users need to position the product within the system of their daily life or work. This requires a significant amount of knowledge generation. In order for users to keep using an artifact beyond initial interest and understanding of its functionality, they need to understand the value, meaning, and ways to use the artifact in many different situations of their daily lives. Traditionally, product developers considered users only as data collection resources instead of knowledge-generating agents. The recent rise of human-centered approaches to designing artifacts has led to greater collaboration between users and artifact producers—including designers and researchers. This collaboration introduces another knowledge lifecycle between artifact producers and users (see Figure 2.4). The concepts of participatory design and collaborative design are based on the idea that the knowledge lifecycle between designers and users is a critical part of design creation and justification.

Knowledge Lifecycle for Human-Centered Design

The concept of human-centered design was introduced particularly to emphasize the importance of incorporating users' viewpoints and contexts of use into the process of design development. Because the process of system development involves a large number of disciplines, it is not a simple matter of collecting requirements through observation and following human factors guidelines. Human viewpoints need be reflected in fundamental aspects of the system solution in order to deliver its most suitable service to the intended users. In complex organizational activities and decision-making for developing artifacts, consistently maintaining users' viewpoints is not a trivial task. Often, somewhere in the process, technological and business viewpoints gain dominance in decision-making because of the clarity of their criteria for success. In order to profoundly establish the concept of human-centered design in the development process, design needs to offer perspectives and methodologies that interconnect rationales from different disciplinary viewpoints.

International Organization for Standardization (ISO) introduced a process guideline, ISO 13407 on "human-centered design processes for interactive systems," with an emphasis on user participation in the system development process (ISO, 1999). User participation in design process has its origin in Scandinavia in the 1960s as "participatory design." Yet full application of participatory design concepts and methodologies is relatively limited. Major problems come from the lack of effective methods for user knowledge elicitation and methodologies for bridging users' knowledge and designers' knowledge. Effective user participation cannot be achieved only by one-time participation in the development process. In order to establish continuing knowledge lifecycles between users and designers, user participation needs to evolve into a sustained social process of knowledge co-construction. While design

Figure 2.5
Knowledge cycle between practice, users, and research

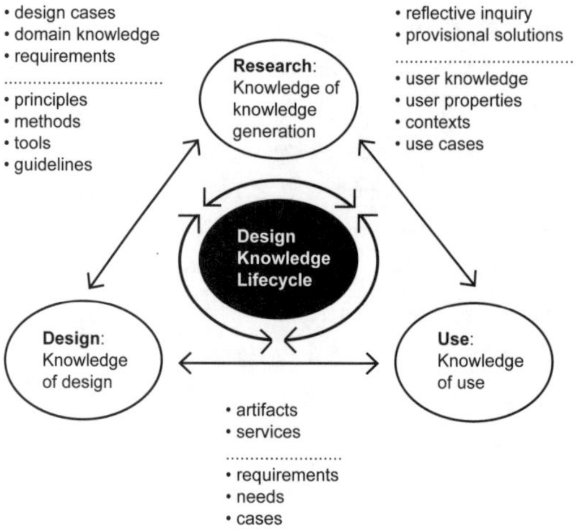

is a learning process for designers, artifact usage is a learning process for users. These two learning processes and the interaction between them form knowledge co-construction between users and designers throughout all knowledge acquisition cycles. Many design research questions must be answered with regard for users' knowledge, designers' knowledge, and their learning processes in order to enhance knowledge co-construction processes between them. Figure 2.5 shows a three-way knowledge lifecycle model involving users, designers/developers, and researchers.

Historical Perspectives

Early Development

After an introductory review of the nature of design research, an introduction of historical perspectives that illustrate how design research started and developed is useful for understanding its current state and to envision the future of design and design research. Although there are different categories of design research such as critical research, design theories, design methodologies, and domain-specific research, the perspectives in this chapter are limited to theoretical and methodological research that directly concerns design and its development of artifacts. Research in design history and criticism is not within the scope of this discussion.

Design practitioners have only started to more frequently refer to design research since computers started appearing on desktops. There are some causal relations that explain this emergent phenomenon in the field of design. Growing complexity and scale of the problems, environments, and technologies have been constantly inspiring design research from its earliest days. Paradoxically, designers seem to place themselves in an endless cycle of generating more complexity and produce more complex artifacts as a solution to the problems generated by increasing complexity.

Early research efforts in design methodologies in the 1960s and '70s addressed and focused on the complexity issue that emerged from the increasing problems of urban systems, the expanding scale of technical systems, and rapidly growing capability of information processing by computers. The first major milestone in design methodology research was achieved in the 1960s by researchers in design, architecture, and urban planning, who were focusing on methodologies for analyzing patterns of complex problems (Moore, 1970). In engineering and science, government agencies and industries devoted massive resources to developing methodologies for design and control of large-scale technical systems, e.g., space systems and industrial systems. Systems science and engineering made significant advances both in theoretical and methodological areas in the 1960s and '70s (Bertalanffy, 1968; Hall, 1962). Fast advances were also being made in related research areas such as operations research, cybernetics, and control theories.

System engineering research adopted the concept of Structuralism in its effort to model and simulate large-scale complex systems such as ecological systems, industrial systems, and societal systems. More conscious adoption of Structuralism as a research methodology emerged in an attempt to understand the emergent nature of large-scale systems where qualitative and structural nature is prevalent or quantitative modeling is premature (Mesalovic, 1971; Warfield, 1973). Interpretive Structural Modeling methodology was specifically introduced to support collaborative and participatory problem identification and decision-making processes among different stakeholders of large-scale complex system design projects (Warfield, 1976).

Structuralism as scientific methodology (Levi-Strauss, 1974; Pettit, 1977) also influenced design research with its attempt to develop rational methods to understand complex and ill-defined design problems that did not fit into conventional analytical methods in science and engineering. The primary outcome of these methods is qualitative understanding of the nature of the subject typically represented by structural diagrams (Alexander, 1964; Owen, 1970). Structured Planning methodology further extended the use of structural modeling beyond analytic methods toward synthetic and evaluative methods for developing large-scale system solutions (Owen, 1992, 2007). Design Rationale and Design Space Analysis, developed at Xerox PARC, have a conceptual base similar to Structured Planning, but the methodology was specifically developed for interactive system design (Moran and Carroll, 1996).

New Perspectives

Focusing on aspects of human-artifact interaction and human-environment relationships leads to another historical perspective. Ergonomics and human factors engineering, which address basic physical, physiological, and psychological issues of human-artifact interaction, have key roles in designing artifacts for human use. The notion of human-centered design introduced in the 1980s re-emphasized the humanistic roles of design as an advocate for the user's voice in the development of artifacts (Norman and Draper, 1986; Winograd and Flores, 1986). Ironically, the importance of the human-centered concept was widely addressed by computer science by its sub-discipline, human-computer interaction (HCI), when computer technology acquired sufficient capability for graphical user interface implementation.

Human-centered design is a more generic concept applicable to the general class of design concerns beyond human-computer interaction. Emergence of concerns about higher-level human factors and behavior, e.g., the meanings, values, and human-artifacts interaction in social contexts, led to the development of research in semiotics, communication theories, and sociological studies in design. Based on this, Klaus Krippendorff focuses on "meaning of artifacts" for his development of theoretical frameworks and conceptual approaches to the design of artifacts and human-artifact interaction (Krippendorff, 2005). The recent emphasis on field observation in design has been re-highlighted by collective efforts of HCI, social science, and cognitive science. Ethnographic methods that intend to understand human characteristics and behavior at individual and social levels have become an essential part of field studies in design practice and research. In spite of field studies' recognition in design, there is a significant gap between what social science-based methods intend and offer and what design practice expects. Because information used in problem-solving requires further interpretation, re-organization and viewpoint re-positioning on information gathered through field studies with sociological motivation, design research needs to bridge these two different intentions, viewpoints and activities through methodological development. Situated Actions (Suchman, 2007) and Activity Theory (Nardi, 1996; Kuutti, 1996) have been bringing new conceptual frameworks to design research, particularly by focusing on situations, contexts, and motivations that not only look into human-artifact relations, but also position them in the larger frame of social and cultural environments (Kaptelinin and Nardi, 2006).

Impeding and Challenging Factors of Design Research Development

Development of design research has been facing some impediments. One comes from the uncertain definition of domains of design concern. Since design's role is bridging human needs and technological possibilities, design concerns cross many disparate disciplinary domains such as social science, information technology, and material science. This makes the viewpoints, scopes, and approaches involved in design diverse and ill-defined. Furthermore, introducing clear criteria for design success is precluded by the excessively diverse dimensions that are inherent to the general design goal of producing the intended quality of human experience. Design research, still in the early development stage, has difficulty producing meaningful and verifiable results when it attempts to adopt conventional approaches of empirical or deductive research methods. Another impediment is the involvement of human cognitive systems both in design processes and in use processes of artifacts. Since the human cognitive process still does not have descriptive or predictive models, research in design processes, designed artifacts, and human use of artifacts suffers fundamental difficulty in retracing the course of research development in other well-established disciplines. These two challenging factors of design research, design as creative activity across different disciplines and criticality of human-oriented thinking for solving complex contemporary problems, have been motivating and attracting research interest from other research areas such as cognitive science, sociology, engineering, and business (Sato, 2004a). Design, as both disciplinary practice and as universal human activities across disciplines, is presenting numerous problems, needs, and opportunities for cross-disciplinary research collaborations.

Typology of Design Research

Since design research has some history, but has not yet established its standard research methods, it would be useful to provide an overview of a basic typology of design research.

Theoretical Research

Theoretical research aims to generate new theories, theoretical frames, and pre-theoretical insights. Theory has different meanings in different disciplines. Natural science in general uses axiomatic approaches to construct theories. Social science and other areas that engage in qualitative issues describe a logical construct of their claims using written language. Regardless of their representational methods and degree of rigor applied to the description, these theories offer models that explain and predict phenomena and can be verified by observed phenomena. Since the subject domain of design theories is not well-defined, there is a fundamental difficulty in developing theoretical research using conventional scientific approaches. In spite of this difficulty, General Design Theory (Yoshikawa, 1987; Tomiyama and Yoshikawa, 1987) and Nam Suh's Principle of Design (Suh, 1990, 2005) used axiomatic approaches with deductive mechanisms for constructing their theoretical models of design. Some research attempts to develop descriptive models of design processes and knowledge are important steps toward the construction of theoretical work (Pahl and Beitz, 1988; Cross, 1994). Some research uses more formal representation methods for simulating human cognitive processes by computer algorithms. Early artificial intelligence research introduced algorithmic models of human problem-solving drawn from simple design problems such as spatial layout generation (Simon, 1969; Eastman, 1975). Theoretical research can also be developed on a specific aspect, e.g., socio-cultural, or a specific subject domain, e.g., button design. When a socio-cultural model of user responses to button design is introduced, and if it is consistent with relevant theories and thoroughly verified in many different cases of observation, then the model is considered a valid and applicable theory.

Methodological Research

The goal of methodological research is to produce effective methods to improve the process and subsequent quality of design. Some of these methods are directly useful for practice. More generalized methods provide models for further development of practical methods specific to a particular domain. The scope of methods ranges from methods that support a very specific task in the design process, e.g., optimization of specific design parameters, to methods that help manage the overall design process. Resulting methods are usually implemented as a tool to demonstrate its applicability and effectiveness for its intended roles in design practice. In order to propose a method for improving qualities of design activities, research must identify the target functions that need to be improved by a new method within the scope of an assumed design process model.

Design research also has been adopting systematic, scientific, and algorithmic methods and frameworks from other disciplines. Application of statistical methods for profiling markets and products, neural net and genetic algorithms for parametric optimization, and Fuzzy Logic for design decision-making are some examples in this category of design research. In order to adopt a new method from other disciplines and establish its application for effective support of specific design activities, design research needs to introduce methods for formulating design problems and interpreting the original methods for the problems. Through this adoption process, design research can contribute to other disciplines by developing new application cases and by extending the original concepts and methods.

Because of recent emphasis on human-centered approaches, design practice and research have been adopting grounded theory, ethnographic methods, and other approaches from social science and cognitive science in order to understand users and contexts of artifact use. Situated Actions (Suchman, 2007) and Activity Theory (Nardi, 1996; Kuutti, 1996) provide conceptual frameworks for understanding human activities in a holistic perspective. A problem often faced in adopting new methods is misinterpretation of the original intention. The role of research is to interpret the original concepts, and develop operationally and conceptually appropriate methods for practical use. Design practice needs an easily accessible and rich toolbox that can offer appropriate tools for a wide range of design problems. The tool, however, should not dictate design approaches.

The problem most frequently encountered by the methodological research model is validation of the proposed methods. The effectiveness cannot be easily measured since it requires real use of the method in practice, and the evaluation involves many variables. This problem is common to all methodological research across disciplines including engineering design. There are several mechanisms that can be used as pragmatic alternatives to standard scientific validation procedures that use the cycle of hypothesis formation and logical or experimental demonstration. One mechanism is to set clear achievement goals and criteria prior to the development and evaluate the results against them. If the proposed method or concept consistently enables the specified function previously unavailable in the design process, the research result is considered valid. In order to help insure proper validation, it is critical to develop a structured argument that is made of a series of rationale or a commonly acceptable chain of logic, which explains how the original questions and final proposal are related.

Experimental Research

There are two types of experimental research. The first type intends to understand the nature of design subjects, and the second type intends to understand the nature of design processes and knowledge. Typical cases of the first type are experimental approaches for understanding human responses to perceptual and cognitive attributes of artifacts such as visual features and information structures. Intended outputs of this type of research are principles and guidelines for various design activities. Usability tests, user response tests, and design guidelines immediately benefit from the output of this type of experimental research. For example, many design questions generated about button design such as size, stroke, and shape, could be easily transformed into tasks for usability tests and a series of experiments.

The second type of experimental research sets up experiments with controlled design processes either in real work environments or in laboratory environments in order to understand how designers solve design problems (Cross, 1996). This class of experiments is called "design experiments" because of its inductive approach that holds a complementary relationship with the deductive mechanism of axiomatic approaches (Yoshikawa, 1992; Takeda et al., 1996). In order to observe cognitive activities in experiments, Protocol Analysis (Ericsson and Simon, 1988) is frequently used with other methods such as analysis of design documents produced through the experiment. Experimental research in general intends to identify significant patterns from observed data in experiments, or to validate a hypothesis established through other experimental research or derived from deductive methods. This type of research shares many research methods commonly used in other disciplines such as psychology and biology. Since the subject of investigation is often the cognitive process of problem solving, learning, and communication among subjects, data acquired through the experiment is not as accurate as in physical sciences. Even though reliability and repeatability of experiment is sometimes questionable, this method is still effective for capturing the qualitative nature of the subjects and introducing assumptive conceptual frames (Takeda et al., 1996).

Field Research

This approach investigates human actions in the field, much like field research in social science and natural science. It values observation of real situations in contrast with experimental approaches that control settings or conditions of observation. It uses many different methods and tools for data inquiry such as observation, interview, and note taking. In recent years, Ethnography and Grounded Theory added more consistent holistic approaches and conceptual foundations to this class of research.

When design questions and research questions significantly overlap, project information development and academic design research share common methods and activities. In some cases, field research for a specific project produces valuable case information for academic research. Particularly in the area of user studies, two types of activities, project information development and design research could effectively inform each other. Some cases of project information development in the book *Design Research: Methods and Perspectives* are examples that are informative to academic research (Laurel, 2003).

Statistical analysis of field data provides cross-population perspectives on a relatively small number of selected variables. On the other hand, research methods with emphasis on users' views, such as ethnography, closely examine human behavior and its underlying social and cognitive structures. This approach develops deep and holistic understanding of the subject of concern in a limited number of cases, instead of isolating specific variables for analysis. In other words, it produces cross-variable perspectives of situated human activities. In spite of frequent bipolar comparisons of these approaches in the design community, these two approaches can be used complimentarily for different aspects and purposes of design research.

Case Study

Case study is another form of empirical research with its origin in social science. It investigates a limited number of real-world cases bounded by time and place through detailed in-depth data collection (Creswell, 1998). Case studies are often conducted to investigate complex subjects that cannot be investigated by analytical or quantitative methods. It is a preferred method particularly when the researcher has little control over events, and when a focus is on a contemporary phenomenon within a real-life context (Yin, 2003). The primary goal of case studies is to find patterns that could lead to the formation of an hypothesis for further elaboration in research or problem solving. For comparison and accumulation of data for further research, standardized documentation formats are often used across cases. There are simultaneous studies that track and document ongoing events, and retrospective studies that investigate records generated in past events. Research in business often uses this method to identify significant patterns that manifest causal relations with consequences of actions, e.g., degree of business success or failure. Design research has not established effective ways of using this method. Although case study methods in social science and in business provide well-structured guidelines, design research needs to develop its own case study methods tuned for effective investigation of design specific problems.

Constructing Design Research: Two Examples

After describing various aspects of design research, we come to a practical question: how do we construct design research? A research project is framed with its defining information such as research questions, goals, conceptual and theoretical foundations, research methods, and constraints. The process of design research is not as straightforward as the logical arguments of a typical research paper. The process of research development involves uncertainty, inspiration, speculation, unexpected development, and faulty trials as well as normative research procedures. Following are two research examples developed by the author's group to examine how the research projects were initiated, framed, and developed. The outcomes of these projects became a core part of the Human-Centered System Integration methodology.

Research on Design Information Framework

The research was initiated with the question, "What characterizes human-centered approaches, particularly for complex interactive systems development?" Human-centered design involves a diverse range of information concepts representing different viewpoints and different contexts involved in various situations in people's daily life and work. Because many different concerns and information representation methods in different disciplines are involved in the human-centered design processes, misalignment of information between disciplines and project activities is a common problem in development organizations. Accommodating and bridging many different viewpoints in the development process is the key to the success of human-centered systems development. The research goal, therefore, was to develop a conceptual framework of a design information platform, and its software implementation, that can effectively facilitate multi-disciplinary design activities throughout interactive systems development.

The next research question that set the research strategy was, "How can such a design information platform be developed?" Conceptual inspiration for answering this question came from General Design Theory (GDT) that became the theoretical foundation for the development of the design information platform. The concept of the information platform, Design Information Framework (DIF), was introduced for representing and bridging a wide range of viewpoints, information concepts, representation frameworks, and design activities required for human-centered design (Lim and Sato, 2006). It provided mechanisms for defining concepts and frameworks of design information by combining a set of very basic types of information concepts such as entities, attributes, states, actions, and time. These information concepts, named Design Information Primitives (DIPs), cannot be conceptually decomposed further. All other information concepts are named Design Information Elements (DILs) and are represented by combining primitive concepts (DIPs). GDT provides the foundation to theoretically define these different information concepts and their relationships. DILs are higher-level concepts that can be defined by combining DIPs and other lower-level DILs. For example, a goal (DIL) can be defined as an entity's (DIP) desired state (DIP) at a particular time. Using this mechanism, every project can develop its unique set of information concepts that become the shared resource platform for communication across groups and activities, for developing and documenting chains of design decisions, and for generating and accumulating design knowledge. It also becomes an effective platform for the methods and tools that complementarily support activities in systems development. DIF does not impose any particular information framework. It provides a meta-level framework to accommodate information frameworks of different methods and viewpoints, as depicted in Figure 2.6.

DIF concept and related design support methods were implemented as a software system, DIF-based Knowledge Management System (DIF-KMS), in order to demonstrate and test its facilitating capability for human-centered design process (Jung et. al., 2005). The system supports a wide range of activities in the development process, starting from compiling multi-modal field data including four synchronized videos, notes and voice data, and tools for modeling. The core of the software is a data-encoding tool that formats field data into a spreadsheet with time codes and an information

Figure 2.6
Conceptual structure of Design Information Framework

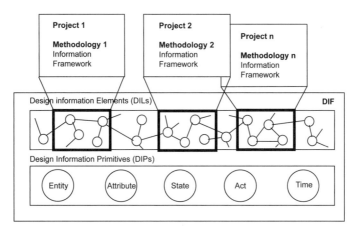

framework chosen for the project. By modularizing information on the structured format, DIF-KMS provides designers means for easy access to the complex and large-scale information for systematic analysis, problem-solving, and assessment, and a structured information platform for constructing new methods (Jung and Sato, 2005; Choi et al., 2008). The DIF-KMS software was successfully implemented, achieved the initially set goals, and demonstrated the potential usefulness of the DIF concept.

Though successful, several problems were revealed during the application testing. First, the user interface was not properly designed for easy access to the powerful design support functions. The second problem was the terminology used to represent the DIF concept—it was not familiar to practitioners. This is a critical impediment for the adoption of the methodology. The third problem was the scalability and adaptability of the methodology and the software system. The large-scale software does not allow partial use of the system, or phased introduction of the methodology. This inhibits a trial adoption of the DIF system. The experience and critical reviewing of the DIF implementation lead to the following strategy for further development: 1) improvement of user-interface and introduction of familiar terminology, 2) scalable and adaptive implementation of the DIF concept, and 3) enhancement of the tool kit of the DIF-KMS sufficient for effective use of the methodology and the software. Based on these guidelines, a new scalable and adaptive solution was introduced, the Modular Script Scenario (MSS) method. The word "scenario" was used and the MSS data format was changed to resemble the terminologies and conventions of scenarios and spreadsheets commonly accepted and used in many different disciplines. Development of new methodology was also planned using the DIF platform, in conjunction with further enhancement of the tool kit.

Human-Centered Product Architecture (HCPA)

What is fundamental knowledge for composing an artifact? What makes the artifact adaptive to a wide range of user requirements in different use conditions? These two questions initiated our research in product architecture. The term architecture has been used as a structural description of a system in some disciplines including systems engineering and computer science. While initiating our research in product architecture, mechanical engineering research was already using the term "product architecture," which is defined as a mapping scheme showing the physical arrangement of a product's functional elements grouped into physical chunks (Ulrich and Eppinger, 1995). In the product design perspective, product architecture is the structure that integrates components and subsystems of a product into a coherent mechanism that performs intended behavior and functions. It also reflects the rationale and intentions of the design from different viewpoints such as functions, methods of use, methods of maintenance, profit strategy, lifecycles, and production. As complexity of products and services increases, design needs to adapt with greater agility in order to accommodate fast-changing technologies, and an increasing diversity of user requirements and social concerns. Product design practice, therefore, needs to explicitly incorporate strategies and methodologies for designing a core structure for an artifact, i.e., product architecture.

Even though the basic functional, economic, and performance specifications exceed user requirements, there are many factors involved in the reasons why some products are

Figure 2.7
Mapping user requirements to product architecture

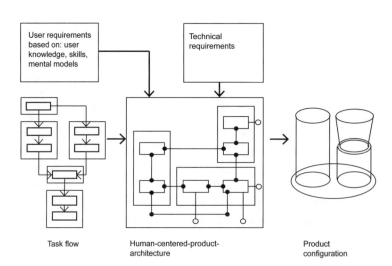

Task flow

Human-centered-product-architecture

Product configuration

Figure 2.8
Human-centered product architecture

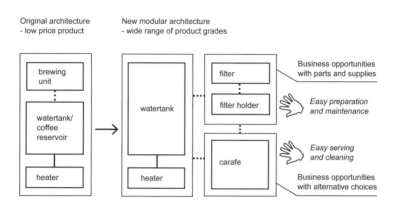

Original architecture
- low price product

New modular architecture
- wide range of product grades

well-accepted and some are not accepted by users and societies. Product architecture in engineering is primarily concerned with technical integrity, manufacturing costs, and model variation; these represent *internal* views and specifications of the product. On the other hand, *external* views and specifications reflect requirements from users and business for which the product is expected to provide its functions, use methods, meanings, and values. Therefore, the goal of our research in human-centered product architecture (HCPA) was set to develop a conceptual framework and methodology for developing architectural solutions from both internal views and external views, reflecting user and societal needs. HCPA methodology also addresses emerging issues in design and business such as platform-based product development, business strategy, human-centered design, service design, and sustainability.

In order to reflect, at deep levels, user needs on a product, reflection of user needs must be started from the early stage of product development, when product architecture is determined. For the first phase of our research on incorporating human-centered approaches to product architecture design, task flow and behavioral patterns were chosen as a primary basis for determining the product architecture (Teeravarunyou and Sato, 2001). Different cultures and social groups often develop different task flow and behavioral patterns reflecting their traditions, social protocols, and values, such as can be observed in tea-making and social interaction in meetings in different cultures. The research questions raised for the HCPA research were, "How to elicit users' intentions, knowledge, value systems, and rationale behind the behavioral patterns" and "How could the elicited information be effectively applied to generate product architecture that satisfies and resonates with the users' functional and cultural needs?" The Method for User Process-Based Product Architecture was developed to elicit users' knowledge related to the target activities and to reflect it on the product architecture design. The question for the second phase was, "What role does affordance have in the product architecture?" The concept of affordance was categorized into two types, functional affordance and informational affordance. Then, the Cross-Function Design Matrix was introduced for identifying function modules that require different types of affordances in user interaction for performing the function. This process was embedded in the product architecture design process as a part of HCPA methodology (Galvao and Sato, 2005; Galvao, 2007). Figure 2.7 shows the general process of HCPA approach and Figure 2.8 shows the concept and effects of HCPA for a coffee maker design. Yet, HCPA methodology still requires more extensive theoretical and methodological research and development to be readily accessible and effective in design practice.

Overview of the Research Chapters

This chapter started with simple questions about a button design. The subsequent discussion explored possible extensions of the questions and developed an overview of research issues and approaches. The following chapters in this Design Research section introduce different ways to set research questions and exemplify unique ways to frame and address issues of design research.

Chapter 3 gives an overview of Design Theories and Methodologies (DTM) research in engineering design. The author, Tetsuo Tomiyama, who has been developing General Design Theory (GDT), one of the most fundamental theories modeling the basic nature of design in a very broad sense, introduces a categorization scheme using the framework of GDT. This categorization gives a perspective of design theory and methodology research that provides ways to identify areas of research and determine research strategies.

Chapter 4 focuses on the nature of design knowledge and design activities in comparison to the nature of knowledge and activities of engineering and science. The author, Kari Kuutti applies Activity Theory to explain the mechanisms of design activities, i.e., the specificity of design knowledge—it reflects the different conditions where each project is situated. This contrasts with the universal nature of knowledge in science and engineering. Kuutti is one of the pioneers using Activity Theory to frame human-computer interaction in social and cognitive contexts.

Chapter 5 discusses design as *media*, an intermediate agent for embodying business plans by creating total user experiences that integrate products and services and offer additional value to users. Design is an intersection of business views and user views where users' expectation meets business offerings. In order to create innovative business-design-user relationships, Birgit Jevnaker argues that design needs to build its role as media that substantiate knowledge and methods to translate the value systems of users and business.

Chapter 6 introduces perspectives on managing the knowledge confluence between research and business in a corporate environment. User-centered research and development requires an interdisciplinary knowledge management platform where knowledge about users, technological possibilities, and business concerns merge and are transformed into tangible forms of research output. To accomplish this, highly interdisciplinary functions and different disciplinary viewpoints need to be understood to develop methodologies, culture, and organization in corporate environments. Tom MacTavish has extensive experience in leading and managing multidisciplinary and multi-national organizations in human-centered research and development.

Summary

These chapters show critical directions for design research that range from theoretical approaches to pragmatic approaches. Each chapter discusses a unique approach to explain how design knowledge frames design in different areas of design's extensive domain. Some chapters focus on how we define and construct design research, others focus on integrating different types of knowledge into a usable form. The fact that these discussions were drawn from outside traditional design, i.e., engineering design, HCI, business, and research and development management, collectively indicates emergent characteristics of the new generation of design research.

Notes

1. Svanaes conducted a thorough phenomenological study of a push button interface, starting with a single button to many buttons (Svanaes, 1997). Barbacetto explains visual syntax and morphology of key design through King and Miranda's conceptual exploration and design in Olivetti Design Research Projects (Barbacetto, 1987).

References

--. *ISO 13407: Human-centred design processes for interactive systems*. 1999. International Organization for Standardization.

Alexander, Christopher. 1964. *The Notes on the Synthesis of Form*. Cambridge, MA: Harvard University Press.

Barbacetto, Gianni. 1987. *Design Interface: How Man and Machine Communicate — Olivetti Design* Cambridge, MA: MIT Press, 17–44.

Bertalanffy, Ludwig von. 1968. *General Systems Theory*. New York, NY: George Braziller.

Choi, K., J. Choi and K. Sato. 2008. Socio-Cultural Factors for New Product Acceptance in Home Environment Design. *Journal of the Human-Environmental System,* 11.1, 65ñ71.

Cresswell, John W. 1998. *Qualitative Inquiry and Research Design: Choosing among Five Traditions.* Thousand Oaks, CA: Sage Publications.

Cross, Nigel. 1994. *Engineering Design Methods,* 2nd ed., New York, NY: John Wiley & Sons.

Cross, Nigel, Henri Kristiaans, and Kees Dorst. 1996. *Analyzing Design Activity.* New York, NY: John Wiley & Sons.

Eastman, Charles M. 1975. *Spatial Synthesis in Computer-Aided Building Design.* New York, NY: John Wiley & Sons.

Ericsson, K. Anders and Herbert A. Simon. 1988. *Protocol Analysis.* Cambridge, MA: MIT Press.

Galvao, A. and K. Sato. 2005. Affordances in Product Architecture: Linking Technical Functions and Users' Tasks. *Proceedings of ASME 2005 Design Engineering Technical Conferences and Computers and Information in Engineering Conference.* Long Beach, CA: September 24-28, ASME.

Galvao, Adriano. 2007. *Design Relationships: Integrating User Information into Product Development.* Saarbrücken, Germany: VDM Verlag Dr. Müller.

Hall, Arthur D. 1962. *Hall's Methodology for Systems Engineering.* New York, NY: Van Nostrand.

Jung, E. et. al. 2005. DIF Knowledge Management System: Bridging Viewpoints for Interactive System Design. Proceedings of 11th Human Computer Interaction International Conference. Las Vegas, Nevada: July 22-27.

Jung, E, and K. Sato. 2005. A Framework of Context-Sensitive Visualization for User-Centered Interactive Systems. *Proceedings of 10th International Conference on User Modeling.* Edinburgh, UK, : July 24-29. Berlin, Germany: Springer-Verlag, 423–427.

Kaptelinin, Victor and Bonnie A. Nardi. 2006. *Acting with Technology: Activity Theory and Interaction Design.* Cambridge. MA: The MIT Press.

Krippendorff, Klaus. 2005. *The Semantic Turn: A New Foundation for Design.* Boca Raton, FL: CRC.

Kuutti, Kari. 1996. Activity Theory as a potential framework for human-computer interaction research. In Nardi, B. (ed.), *Context and Consciousness: Activity Theory and Human Computer Interaction.* Cambridge, MA: MIT Press, 17–44.

Laurel, Brenda. 2003. *Design Research: Methods and Perspectives.* Cambridge, MA: MIT Press.

Levi-Strauss, Claud. 1974. *Structural Anthropology.* New York, NY: Basic Books.

Lim, Y. and K. Sato. 2006. Describing Multiple Aspects of Use Situation: Applications of Design Information Framework (DIF) to Scenario Development. *Design Studies,* 27.1, 57–76.

Mesarovic, Mihajlo D. et al.1971. *Theory of Hierarchical Multilevel Systems.* New York, NY: Academic Press.

Moore, Gary T. (ed.). 1970. *Emerging Methods for Environmental Planning and Design.* Cambridge, MA: MIT Press.

Moran, Thomas P. and John M. Carroll. 1996. *Design Rationale: Concepts, Techniques, and Use.* Mahwah, NJ: Lawrence CRC.

Nardi, Bonnie A. (ed.). 1996. *Context and Consciousness: Activity Theory and Human-Computer Interaction.* Cambridge, MA: MIT Press.

Norman, Donald A. and Stephen W. Draper. 1986. *User Centered Design: New Perspectives on Human-Computer Interaction*. Hillsdale, NJ: Laurence Erlbaum Associates.

Owen, Charles L. 1970. Decomp. In G. T. Moore (ed.), *Emerging Methods for Environmental Planning and Design*. Cambridge, MA: MIT Press.

Owen, Charles L. 1992. Contexts of Design Planning. *Design Studies,* 13.3, 216–228.

Owen, Charles L. 2007. *Structured Planning*. Chicago, IL: Institute of Design, Illinois Institute of Technology.

Pahl, Gerhard and Wolfgang Beitz. 1988. *Engineering Design: A Systematic Approach,* Berlin, Germany: Springer-Verlag.

Pettit, Philip. 1977. *The Concept of Structuralism: A Critical Analysis*. Berkley, CA: University of California Press.

Polanyi, Michael. 1966. *The Tacit Dimension*. London, United Kingdom: Routledge & Kegan Paul.

Sato, K. 2000. Constructing Knowledge of Design, Part 1: Understanding Concepts in Design Research. *Proceedings of International Conference on Doctoral Education in Design*. La Clusaz, France, July 8-12: Design Research Society and Norwegian School of Business.

Sato, K. 2004a. Perspective of Design Research: Collective Views for forming the foundation of Design Research. *Visible Language*, 38.2, 216–237.

Sato, K. 2004b. Context-sensitive Approach for Interactive Systems Design: Modular Scenario-based Methods for Context Representation. *Journal of Physiological Anthropology and Applied Human Science*, 23.6, 277–281.

Simon, Herbert. 1969. *The Sciences of the Artificial*. Cambridge, MA: MIT Press.

Suchman, Lucy. 2007. *Human-Machine Reconfigurations: Plans and Situated Actions: The Problem of Human Machine Communication.* New York, NY: Cambridge University Press.

Suh, Nam P. 1990. *The Principle of Design,* New York. NY: Oxford University Press.

Suh, Nam P. 2005. *Complexity: Theory and Applications*. New York, NY: Oxford University Press.

Strauss, Anselm L. and J. Corbin. 1990. *Basics of Qualitative Research*. Newbury Park, CA: Sage.

Svanaes, Dag. 1997. Kinaesthetic Thinking: The Tacit Dimension of Interaction Design. *Computers in Human Behavior,* 13.4, 443–463.

Takeda, H. et al. 1996. A Cognitive Approach to the Analysis of Design Processes. *Proceedings of the 2nd International Conference on Design Theory and Methodology*. Chicago, IL: September 10-13: ASME, 153–160.

Teeravarunyou, S. and K. Sato. 2001. User Process Based Product Architecture. *Proceedings of the 2001 World Congress on Mass Customization and Personalization*. Hong Kong. October 1-2:

Tomiyama, T. and H. Yoshikawa. 1987. Extended General Design Theory. In Yoshikawa, H. and E.A. Warman (eds.). *Design Theory for CAD*. Amsterdam, Netherlands: North-Holland, 95–130.

Ulrich, K.T. and S.D. Eppinger. 1995. *Product Design and Development*. New York, NY: McGraw-Hill.

Warfield, John N. 1973. *Structuring Complex Systems*. Columbus, OH: Battelle Monograph, Battelle Columbus Laboratory.

Warfield, John N. 1976. *Societal Systems*. New York, NY: John Wiley & Sons.

Winograd, Terry and Fernando Flores. 1986. *Understanding Computers and Cognition: A New Foundation for Design*. New York, NY: Addison Wesley.

Yin, Robert K. 2003. *Case Study Research: Design and Methods.* Thousand Oaks, CA: Sage Publications.

Yoshikawa, Hiroyuki. 1987. General Design Theory and Artificial Intelligence. In T. Bernold (ed.), *Artificial Intelligence in Manufacturing.* New York, NY: Elsevier Science Publishers.

Yoshikawa, Hiroyuki. 1992. Proposal for Artifactual Engineering: Aims to Make Science and Technology Self-Conclusive. *Proceedings of the 1st International Symposium on Research into Artifacts.* Tokyo: October 26-28: RACE, University of Tokyo.

3

DESIGN THEORY AND METHODOLOGY FOR ENGINEERING DESIGN PRACTICES

Tetsuo Tomiyama

Introduction

The scientific research field of design theory and methodology (DTM) has developed a variety of design theories and methodologies. Just like research in any field, design research has two aspects. One is fundamental research that aims at scientific understanding of design processes, design activities, design knowledge, and designed objects, contributing to further development of DTM. The other is application-oriented research that can be used, for instance, in design practices, better design support, and better design results. Many DTM results are taught in the classroom, experimented with in test cases, applied to practices, computerized for scaled-up applications, and are reported to have contributed to significant improvement of design quality and productivity. The former is often classified as design theory, while the latter is called design methodology. These two types of design research should enrich or even improve design practices.

However, many design practitioners seem to be unaware or even neglectful of the results of design research, under the assumption that in principle they are irrelevant to design practices, hence useless or powerless in design practices. Unfortunately, this is a commonly observed perception, and we can identify two reasons for it. First, designers can and do design without explicitly using any so-called design theories and methodologies. DTM may tell us why these designers could design, but they do not have to admit that they followed a particular method. Second, even if they use a design methodology, design solutions based on a design methodology are seldom vigorously compared with design solutions obtained "intuitively" based on experiences. Because of this lack of vigorous comparison, no one realizes the power of design theory and methodology. However, in engineering design, which uses analytical methods frequently, at least the power of analytical methods is rightfully recognized. It is less so in more synthesis-oriented design.

DTM lends itself not to scientific understanding of design alone. For instance, such scientific understanding helps researchers to identify what to research (research directions). It also helps design practitioners to correctly understand what can be done and what cannot with a particular type of design methodology. Without correctly knowing limitations of the design methodology, we will not be able to guarantee the correctness of design. In addition, correct understanding of design is a requirement to develop useful design tools and design support systems.

Any scientific understanding begins with appropriate positioning of past research work. This chapter attempts to establish a framework based on General Design Theory (GDT) (Yoshikawa, 1981; Tomiyama and Yoshikawa, 1987; Reich, 1995) to categorize design theories and methodologies that have been so far proposed. Of course, we cannot deal with all previously published theories and methodologies, and instead we focus on so-called descriptive and prescriptive theories and methodologies.

In 1989, Susan Finger and John R. Dixon published a landmark review of DTM in the mechanical engineering domain and categorized various theories and methodologies into six categories: descriptive, prescriptive, computer-based, representations, analysis, and Design for X (DfX) (Finger and Dixon, 1989). Although we will see these in more detail in the next section, the core components of DTM in this categorization are undoubtedly descriptive and prescriptive models of design processes.

It is interesting to note that while the publication of the development and advances of computer-based methods (computer-based, representations, analysis) and concurrent engineering related methods (DfX) has been significant over the last twenty years, very little has been reported regarding core DTM research, i.e., descriptive and prescriptive models. Almost no quantum leap has been reported regarding research in these categories. This implies that a) the core DTM research literally focuses on non-practical issues of design and does not lend itself to design practices, b) no significant effort has been put forward in these areas in recent years, and/or c) scientific methods of DTM are inefficient because of the nature (design being mostly psychological processes) and the complexity of the field.

This paper is motivated by this question. The first step to reduce such complexity is to provide a clear-cut view that helps researchers to understand essential aspects.

Recently, Imre Horváth (2004) published an extensive survey on DTM research work. While this work is extensive and covers the majority of the work done in this community, it does not provide a unified clear-cut view, which is the purpose of this chapter.

In the following section, the categorizations proposed by Finger and Dixon (1989) are briefly reviewed. Then, we will review GDT, which is basically a mathematical theory about how to operate design knowledge based on axiomatic set theory. GDT formalizes our knowledge about entities (i.e., design objects) with regard to functions and attributes of objects. It provides a knowledge-centric view of design in which design operations are operations about the entity set.

Based on this view, we will present an alternative systematic categorization framework for (especially) descriptive and prescriptive models of design. Note that the paper does not intend to serve as yet another survey paper of the current DTM. The intention is to provide the community with a scientific basis with which to compare methods.

The results of this paper can have educational implication. By clarifying relative positioning of various design theories and methodologies, it is expected that designers and students can obtain essential knowledge about how to correctly choose a right design method, understanding their advantages and disadvantages, and their limitations when applied in a particular type of applications.

Finger and Dixon's Review

More than 140 years have elapsed since Franz Reuleaux's work (1861, 1875); many varieties of design theories and methodologies have subsequently been developed and proposed. It is interesting that in that time, a clear definition of DTM has not been identified. Perhaps a classic view is that design theory is about how to model and understand design, while design methodologies are about how to design or how design should be done. However, the relationships among individual theories and methodologies are so poorly understood that designers are prevented from choosing a right method to conduct design processes and educators are unable to teach appropriate methods.

In their landmark review of DTM research (Finger and Dixon, 1989) that later became a community classic, Finger and Dixon categorized a substantial number of papers into six categories (see Table 3.1).

There are two things that need particular attention. First, we know that over the last forty years, the development and advances of computer-based methods were significant. This fact is reflected in the substantial number of papers in categories 3, 4, and 5. In

Table 3.1
Finger and Dixon's six categories of DTM research in 1989

DTM Research Categories	Types
1) Descriptive models of design processes (Descriptive)	Protocol studies (e.g., Ullman et al., 1988) Cognitive models (e.g., Gero, 1985) Case studies (e.g., Wallace and Hales, 1987) German (so-called) school of design methodologies (e.g., Pahl and Beitz, 1996; Hubka and Eder, 1982)
2) Prescriptive models for design (Prescriptive)	Canonical design process (e.g., Asimov, 1962; French, 1971) Morphological analysis (e.g., Pahl and Beitz, 1996) Prescriptive models of design artifacts (e.g., Yoshikawa, 1981; Tomiyama and Yoshikawa, 1987; Reich, 1995) Axiomatic Design (AD) (e.g., Suh, 1990; Taguchi, 1987)
3) Computer-based models of design processes (Computer-based)	Parametric design Configuration design AI-based methods for conceptual design Distributed agent-based design
4) Languages, representations, and environments for design (Representations)	Geometric modeling Shape grammars Behavior and function modeling Feature-based modeling Product modeling Integrated design support environments
5) Analysis to support design decisions (Analysis)	Optimization methods Interfaces to finite element analysis (or CAE) Decision-making support
6) Design for manufacturing and other lifecycle issues such as reliability, serviceability, etc. (DfX)	Concurrent engineering Design for X Tolerances Lifecycle engineering Computer-based design advisory systems

1989 (in which, coincidently, the ASME DTM conference series started), design and manufacturing had a national focus with regard to industrial competitiveness, a fact represented by concurrent engineering related methods (category 6).

In contrast, we must notice that there are not big differences between what we now know in the core DTM research areas, i.e., categories 1 and 2, and what Finger and Dixon listed. Of course, we now have Abstract Design Theory (ADT) (Kakuda and Kikuchi, 2001), meant as an extended version of GDT. Even so, theories that existed in 1989 are still considered valid and used without much modification. On the other hand, the review did not cover such important contributions as TRIZ (Teoriya Resheniya

Izobretatelskikh Zadatch, translated as the Theory of Inventor's Problem Solving) (Altshuller, 1984), Quality Function Deployment (QFD) (Mizuno and Akao, 1993), and Failure Mode Effect Analysis (FMEA) (McDermott et al., 1996), which should be included in category 2, although these existed already in 1989. This does not mean that the review was incomplete; it is impossible for any author to review all scientific research work even in a relatively narrow field. Perhaps their omission was simply because their values were not fully recognized, or even known by the community at that time.

More recently (since the 1990s), study has been directed at the introduction of soft-computing methods for design, such as genetic algorithms (e.g., Holland, 1975), artificial neural networks (ANN) (e.g., Dayhoff, 1989), and various learning algorithms (e.g., Shavlik and Dietterich, 1990).

Although the categorization given by Finger and Dixon might be still valid today, it has drawbacks as well. The authors explicitly warn that these categories are not mutually exclusive (Finger and Dixon, 1989), which implies that further sophistication is needed. In addition, the categorization was not based on a philosophical foundation that can justify the categorization.

If a research community does not share such a view backed up by a philosophical foundation, it can easily lead to diverse research efforts and advances in the field might be minimized. Of course, it is impossible to conclude that this is the reason why we see so few quantum jumps in the DTM core areas. However, we might expect an improved situation if a philosophically sound foundation that can categorize various ideas with a clear-cut view is provided. This is one of the motivations behind this research. The following sections define a philosophical foundation using GDT that results in a clear-cut view.

General Design Theory (GDT)

GDT's major achievement is a mathematical formulation of the design process (Yoshikawa, 1981; Tomiyama and Yoshikawa, 1987; Reich, 1995). GDT deals with concepts that only exist through mental recognition. GDT tries to explain how design is conceptually performed with knowledge manipulation based on axiomatic set theory. In this sense, GDT is not merely a design theory but an abstract theory about (design) knowledge and its operations as well.

Axioms of GDT

GDT begins with the assumption that our knowledge can be mathematically formalized and operated. This is represented by three axioms that define knowledge as topology and operations as set operations. GDT regards a design process as a mapping from the function space to the attribute space, both of which are defined over the entity concept set. Based on axiomatic set theory, we can mathematically derive interesting theorems that can explain a design process satisfactorily.

GDT makes a distinction between an entity and an entity concept. An entity is an existing concrete object, and an entity concept is its abstract, mental impression conceived by a human being. An entity concept might be associated with its properties, such as color, size, function, and place. These properties are called abstract concepts and include attributes and functions.

We should note here one particular set-up of GDT; i.e., in GDT, entities are elements of the entity (concept) set and properties of entity (including both attributes and functions) are defined as subsets in the entity set. The former extensional definition and the latter intentional definition can be contrasted in Figures 3.1 and 3.2. While these two are basically identical, there are some differences in philosophical and representational aspects (Tomiyama and ten Hagen, 1990).

GDT continues by defining its axioms as follows:

Axiom 1 (Axiom of recognition): Any entity can be recognized or described by attributes and/or other abstract concepts.

Axiom 2 (Axiom of correspondence): The entity set S' and the set of entity concept S have one-to-one correspondence.

Axiom 3 (Axiom of operation): The set of abstract concept is a topology of the set of entity concept.

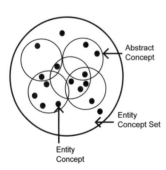

Figure 3.1
Extensional definition

Abstract
Concept

Entity
Concept Set

Entity
Concept

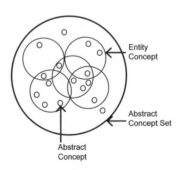

Figure 3.2
Intensional definition

Entity
Concept

Abstract
Concept Set

Abstract
Concept

We assume here that there exists a set S' that includes entities that existed in the past, exist now, and will exist in the future. This set, entity set S' or entity concept set S, represents a perfect database of knowledge about entities. Axiom 2 guarantees that S and S' are identical as well as the existence of a super designer who knows everything. Axiom 3 signifies that it is possible to logically operate abstract concepts as if they were just ordinary mathematical sets. Accordingly, we can use set operations, such as intersection, union, and negation.

Design in Ideal Knowledge

GDT now introduces ideal knowledge that knows all the elements of the entity set and that can describe each element with abstract concepts without ambiguity. Theorem 1 mathematically describes this situation.

Theorem 1: Ideal knowledge is a Hausdorff space.

In GDT, a design specification is given as an abstract concept to which the design solution must belong. Thus, specifications can be given by describing an entity with only abstract concepts (e.g., functionally). The function space is the entity concept set with a topology of functions, and the attribute space is the one with a topology of attributes. Therefore, a design specification is a point in the function space, and a design solution is a point in the attribute space. The most significant result of having ideal knowledge that can be further proven from the three axioms is that design as a mapping from the function space to the attribute space successfully terminates when the specifications are described.

Theorem 2: In ideal knowledge, a design solution is immediately obtained after specifications are described.

Because we know everything perfectly in ideal knowledge, when we finish describing specifications, they converge to a point in the function space. Because the function space and the attribute space are built on the same entity concept in the attribute space, this point (i.e., an entity concept) can also be considered in the attribute space. Thus, the design solution will be fully described by attributes; the design in ideal knowledge is a mapping process from the function space to the attribute space (see Figure 3.3).

GDT and Real Design

The situation in ideal knowledge does not apply to real design in many ways. First, ideal knowledge assumes three kinds of ideality: structural ideality, operational ideality, and analytical ideality (Yoshikawa, 1981). In addition, ideal knowledge assumes two kinds of infinity: memory capacity and operation speed.

Structural ideality refers to the assumptions that: 1) all entities existed in the past, exist now, and will exist in the future and are memorized as entity concepts; 2) these entity concepts have sufficient distinctions to be separately recognized (Axiom 1 and Theorem 1); and 3) these distinctions can be made both attributively and functionally.

Naturally, our knowledge cannot include any entity that does not yet exist. Even for entities existing before or now, we might not be able to think about sufficient descriptions to correctly distinguish them from each other. With regard to the ideality assumptions above, these imperfect states of our knowledge can result in: 1') some abstract concepts with no entity concept (vacancy in metallic crystal); 2') imperfect topology, i.e., insufficient separation of entities (dislocation); and 3') isolated entities existing without categorization (impurity).

Operational ideality refers to the assumptions that 4) any intersection operations of abstract concepts yield a non-empty set (filter condition) and 5) there exists a mapping function from the function space to the attribute space. If these idealities are violated, we may have such problems as: 4') no design solution (specifications designate an empty set) or no convergence (specifications diverge); and 5') no design solution because no corresponding point in the attribute space is found for specifications in the function space.

After we obtained converged specifications (in the function space to a design solution), we need to analyze the neighborhood of this design solution in the attribute space. Analytical ideality pertains to 6) this analysis process in order to obtain sufficient information to produce it. Due to imperfect memory about the neighborhood, 6') we might not able to obtain sufficient information to produce it.

Besides, GDT assumes 7) infinity in memory capacity, and 8) infinity in operation speed. Of course, these are limited, resulting in 7') no design solution because we don't have enough knowledge and 8') reaching design solutions in finite time.

In addition to the above-mentioned imperfections of real design processes, observations in design experiments (Takeda et al., 1990) tell us that design is not a simple mapping process, but rather a stepwise refinement process, where the designer seeks the solution that satisfies the constraints. This means that real design processes are more set operational, i.e., at every step of design, the designer actually performs a narrowing of the solution set. Furthermore, the ideal knowledge does not take physical constraints into consideration, and it can produce design solutions such as perpetual machines. Discussions that take these aspects into consideration have been developed by researchers (Tomiyama and Yoshikawa, 1987; Reich, 1995).

Design Processes as Design Knowledge Operations

As reviewed in the previous section, GDT sees design as design knowledge operations, i.e., set operational processes regarding the entity set and its subsets. This is clear in the following anecdote illustrated in the original GDT paper (Yoshikawa, 1981).

> Let us consider a primitive world, where only three kinds of meat are found, fresh meat, putrid meat, and dried meat; all natural entities, without any artificial processing. People of the world recognized and memorized them. Let S be a set, elements of which are natural entities;

> s1 = fresh meat,
> s2 = putrid meat,
> s3 = dried meat,

> Dogs or cats can also recognize and memorize them, but separately. On the contrary, human beings recognize and memorize them not only separately, but also with classifications. They construct concepts about peculiar characteristics abstracted from these entities, giving classifications or structures for them, that is the set S. For example, let T = {T1, T2} be a classification:

> T1 = {deteriorates with lapse of time}
> T2 = {not eatable}

> that have no one-to-one correspondence to each entity but to subsets of S. The subset generated by this classification has semantic significance from the viewpoint of function or value of the entity.

> Once the subset system T has been established, people can memorize the entities not only by their direct image but also by using the abstract character such as "not eatable and deteriorates, with lapse of time" which is equivalent to putrid meat in the present example. This means:

$$s_1 \in T_1 \cap \overline{T_2}$$

$$s_2 \in T_1 \cap T_2$$

$$s_3 \in \overline{T_1} \cap T_2$$

> It is assumed that people have the ability of logical operations such as disjunction, conjunction, or complement besides memory, abstraction and classification.

After achieving those abstract concepts, people started to think, memorize, and communicate by using them instead of the actual entities. Someday, a primitive man (or women) thought accidentally about;

$$\overline{T_1} \cap \overline{T_2}$$

that can occur without any difficulty if the combinations above are familiar to him (her). This idea, however, must have been drastic and dreadful to the primitive, because s/he had a concept having a correspondence to a thing that did not exist in the realistic world. $\overline{T_1} \cap \overline{T_2}$ had no correspondence to a real entity, but the value of it was higher than any existing entity. "Eatable and not deteriorate with lapse of time" had the highest value, and this conceptual combination was the necessary condition to invent smoked meat, which was the first artificial entity for human beings.

This anecdote illustrates the essence of design based on GDT.

First the knowledge about the entity must exist. For this knowledge to be usable, it must be categorized with abstract concepts (Figure 3.3, Step A). The region in which a new design solution exists can be designated as a result of logical operations of abstract concepts (Figure 3.3, Step B). The designer finds an entity that can fulfill these requirements designated with abstract concepts (Figure 3.3, Step C). If any design solution is not known (this corresponds to the imperfect situation 1, i.e., vacancy in knowledge), this becomes the core process of synthesis in design (Tomiyama et al., 2002). In this situation, a number of strategies are possible, if a design solution as "entity concept" is obtained. In this case, the solution is mapped from the function space to the attribute space and its neighborhood is analyzed to obtain attributive information necessary for production such as shape, geometry, material, etc. (Figure 3.3, Steps D and E).

Figure 3.3
Design process in ideal knowledge

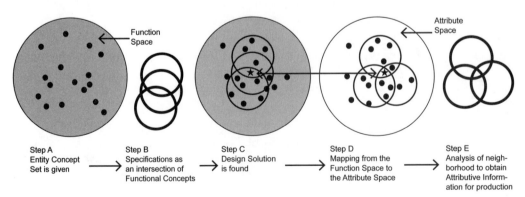

| Step A
Entity Concept
Set is given | Step B
Specifications as
an intersection of
Functional Concepts | Step C
Design Solution
is found | Step D
Mapping from the
Function Space to
the Attribute Space | Step E
Analysis of neigh-
borhood to obtain
Attributive Inform-
ation for production |

It must be noted that Step B is a necessary condition for any new design, because without such conceptual combination, even if we see "a naturally smoked meat from wild fire," we may not even notice its existence.

DTM to Generate a New Design Solution

Among those five steps of GDT, the most critical step is Step C. In case design knowledge is indeed imperfect and any existing entity is not known to satisfy the requirements, this requires a "synthesis" process to fill the vacancy with a new design solution. Some strategies that can be employed for this case are discussed below. Note that in the following categorization, one design method can be categorized in multiple categories.

Creativity-based Design

A new design solution is generated as a new element of the entity set. This case corresponds to invention, and not only to an artifact, but also to the creation of a piece of new knowledge. This is heavily dependent on human intuitive creativity, and few theories can rationally explain it in a general framework (Coyne et al., 1987).

A general formalization of this type of process with logic is abduction (Hartshorne and Weiss, 1931–1935; Burks, 1958; Schurz, 2002; Yoshioka and Tomiyama, 2000; Tomiyama et al., 2003). When design knowledge is well known and a design problem boils down to picking up a solution from a set of known entities, factual abduction can be used. At this moment, however, abduction cannot explain creative design, when a design solution is generated "out of the blue," but it can explain when multiple (known) theories are combined to produce a new solution that was unknown before. In other words, abduction can deal with creative design that comes from innovative, new combinations of existing well-known knowledge (Tomiyama et al., 2003).

Given a problem and a set of theories, if it is judged impossible to find a solution within the domain, abduction can introduce an appropriate set of relevant theories to form a new set of theories, so that solutions can be found with the new set of theories. For instance, as long as our knowledge is limited to the structural strength of materials of a given shape, we will never reach such an innovative design as "drilling holes" for lighter structure while maintaining the strength. This is only possible when we have a piece of knowledge that reveals that removing material that does not contribute to strength does not damage performance, but only makes the whole object lighter.

The importance of introducing multiple aspects to arrive at high quality products is pointed out by Stuart Pugh's total design (Pugh, 1991).

Emergent synthesis is a more recently developed methodology (Ueda, 2001). It typically uses such soft computing methods as genetic algorithm, simulated annealing, ANN, and a variety of learning algorithms. In the context of creativity-based design, for instance, ANN (Wang and Kusiak, 2001) can generate a design solution even for requirements that were not previously experienced. On one hand, this shows the robustness of the method and to some extent a kind of creativity, but on the other, its output is in one sense similar to past design experiences. The majority of learning algorithms applied to design exhibit more or less similar behavior (Wang and Kusiak, 2001), and ANN itself is a variation of learning algorithms.

Jami Shah (1998) points out two approaches to achieve creative designs: intuitive and systematic. Intuitive approaches increase the flow of ideas, remove mental blocks, and increase the chance of conditions perceived to be promoters of creativity, through such mental reasoning processes as association and analogy. By exposing designers to a collection of knowledge never before experienced, it is expected to stimulate their imagination. Examples of such collections of knowledge could be books and archives of past designs, other designers (i.e., a variety of methods for brainstorming), and some unrelated areas from which designers can be inspired (e.g., bio-inspired design).

Combination-based Design

In the latter of Shah's categorization, systematic approaches define methodologies to apply design knowledge and to arrive at creative designs more rationally and systematically. These methodologies make one important assumption: the existence of building blocks and rules to combine them to arrive at a new design solution. For example, a new machine can be designed by combining known components or units; combinatorial logical circuit design is an example. However, the question here is the level of those components.

Based on a definition of function as transformation of energy, material, and information, Gerhard Pahl and Wolfgang Beitz (1996) define rules to systematically model, decompose, and combine known "function carriers" at the physical principle level. In this method, the use of databases about known machine elements and physical principles and phenomena is highly recommended.

One thing common to Pahl and Beitz, TRIZ (Altshuller, 1984), and AD (Suh, 1990) is an explicit representation of functions with respect to entities (in the case of Pahl and Beitz, the function hierarchy and morphological table) or attributes (in the case of AD, the design matrix between function requirements and design parameters). By analyzing such representations, the designer can analyze and improve solutions. In this sense, these representations function more or less as a creativity stimulation method.

Modification-based Design

Modification-based design is perhaps the most often practiced method and begins with a solution close enough to the final solution. This near solution will be modified according to some rules. These modification rules can be that components are: 1) added (A -> A + B), 2) exchanged (A + B -> A + B'), 3) merged (A + B -> A'), and 4) removed (A + B -> A). These rules can be applied to the systematic method of creativity-based design.

The questions for this type of design relate to the function of judging how close a candidate is to the goal and the level of these components.

TRIZ (Altshuller, 1984) falls into this category. It primarily defines design problems as a process to remove barriers to achieve the goal from an existing (incomplete) solution. There are also rules to modify existing designs and a huge design database (built from Russian patents).

Other methods of emergent synthesis, such as genetic algorithms, simulated annealing, ANN, and a variety of learning algorithms, can also be seen as methods to derive "optimal" design solutions from close enough approximations (Ueda, 2001). In this sense, they are modification-based design methods.

DTM can enrich functional and attributive information in design solutions. Once a design solution is found in the area designated by the functional requirements, an analysis is conducted regarding its neighborhood, not only in the attribute space but also in the function space. The latter is carried out to achieve perfect design (e.g., to enhance customer satisfaction).

QFD is such a method. By building a house of quality, overlooked functional requirements regarding customer satisfaction and technical tasks will be identified. AD, its Axiom of functional dependence, is useful to enrich functional information with regard to technical solutions. FMEA also lends itself to identifying overlooked or potential problems to enhance quality. In this sense, FMEA is also a method to enrich functional information as well as attributive information from the design quality perspective.

Analyzing the attributive neighborhood of a design solution and enriching attributive information is equivalent to improving performance and eventually to generating sufficient information to physically build the design solution. A variety of engineering analysis techniques (typically CAE-related techniques) and optimization techniques fall into this category. DfX (Design for X where X stands for a variety of activities in the product lifecycle, such as manufacturing, assembly, disassembly, environment, serviceability, reliability, maintenance, recycling, etc.) lends itself to enriching the attributive information of a design solution (see Proceedings of ASME Design for Manufacturing Series). Taguchi method (1987) and AD (especially Axiom of information content) help designers to optimize design parameters.

Genetic algorithm is a method to pick out the most optimal solutions from a large problem space (Holland, 1975). Emergent synthesis based on genetic algorithm (Wang and Kusiak, 2001) can be viewed as a system to find optimal solutions as a combination of known components. In this sense, it is also a method to enrich attributive information of design solutions.

DTM to Manage Design and to Represent Design Knowledge

We can also identify two other categories of design theories and methodologies that correspond to Finger and Dixon's categories 4, 5, and 6. Since these are not the focus of this paper, they are not discussed in detail; however, short remarks are appropriate.

Design is a human activity largely driven by knowledge. A design process involves design knowledge and design information to be handled by a designer. This means that we need theories and methodologies to capture, represent, model, and codify design knowledge and information. At the same time, such knowledge has to be used appropriately.

This requires us to focus on two DTM areas. First, we must consider what theories and methodologies to capture, represent, model, and codify design knowledge and information about design processes, design objects, environments, and any other lifecycle issues. Examples of this category are theories of solid modeling and product modeling.

Second, we must address operations of knowledge. The scale of products is becoming increasingly bigger; the complexity of products as well as of processes is also increasing. Therefore, we need management perspectives. This second DTM area includes those theories and methodologies to manage design, such as design knowledge, design information, design process, and design complexity. Besides well-known knowledge management issues, we may add here AD (especially, Axiom 1 of functional independence) (Suh, 2005; Meijer et al., 2003), and DSM (Design Structure Matrix) (Browning, 2001; Dong and Whitney, 2001) to deal with complexity of design.

Conclusions

We have attempted to provide a clear-cut view that helps researchers to understand the essential aspects of various design theories and methodologies. Based on GDT, we proposed four categories: 1) DTM to generate a new design solution, 2) DTM to enrich information about functional and attributive information, 3) DTM to manage design processes, and 4) DTM to represent design information and knowledge. We focused on the first two categories and classified some existing theories and methodologies (Table 3.2 below summarizes the classification).

Two questions emerge here. First, where can GDT itself be categorized? Second, how different is this categorization from any previously published categorization such as the one by Finger and Dixon (1989).

GDT is not a design methodology, but it is a theory to model and understand design in a mathematical framework. In this sense, it is obviously a theory to capture, represent, model, and codify design knowledge based on axiomatic set theory, i.e., at a very abstract level. In this sense, it is not so different from design process modeling theories.

One answer to the second question can be that this categorization is not intuitive or empirical. It has at least justification, i.e., GDT.

Some final remarks about educational implications can be summarized as follows. In many engineering schools, various design theories and methodologies are taught, but they are mostly guided by a utilitarian point of view. There is nothing wrong with

Table 3.2
Proposed classifications for Design Theory Method

Design Theory Method (DTM) Category	Approach	Examples
DTM to generate a new design solution		
Creativity-based	Pure invention (intuitive) Stimulation methods	Intuitive invention Emergent synthesis Brainstorming Bio-inspired design
Combination-based design	Combining knowledge Systematic	Abduction Pahl & Beitz
Modification-based design		TRIZ Emergent synthesis
DTM to enrich information about functional and attributive information		Optimization Engineering analysis QFD, FMEA AD DfX Emergent synthesis
DTM to manage design process		AD DSM
DTM to represent design knowledge		GDT Solid modeling Product modeling

this viewpoint, but it does not give an organized view. For example, how different are AD and GDT? Both of them are based on a mathematical framework (but different ones). In which situation can the Pahl and Beitz method be used? Does this serve all purposes? According to this classification, it obviously does not. Pahl and Beitz is a good method only when students deal with functions that can be modeled in its specific way. It should by no means be mixed up with any intuitive method as is often the case when students need to come up with various options in morphological analysis.

In the same way, QFD and AD, are not "creative design methods." Although that doesn't mean that they cannot result in "creative design solutions," their strength stays with their capabilities to enrich primarily functional information with respect to attributive information.

References

Altshuller, G.S. 1984. *Creativity as an Exact Science*. New York, NY: Gordon and Breach Science Publishers.

Asimov, M. 1962. *Introduction to Design*. New York, NY: Prentice-Hall.

Browning, T.R. 2001. Applying the Design Structure Matrix to System Decomposition and Integration Problems: A Review and New Directions. *IEEE Transactions on Engineering Management*, 48.3, 292–306.

Burks, A. (ed.). 1958. *The Collected Papers of Charles Sanders Peirce, Vol. VII-VIII*. Cambridge, MA: Harvard University Press.

Coyne, R.D., M.A. Rosenman, A.D. Radford and J.S. Gero. 1987. Innovation and Creativity in Knowledge-Based CAD. In Gero, J.S. (ed.), *Expert Systems in Computer-Aided Design*. Amsterdam, Netherlands: North-Holland, 435–465.

Dayhoff, J.E. 1989. *Neural Network Architectures: An Introduction*. New York, NY: Van Nostrand Reinhold.

Dong, Q. and D.E. Whitney. 2001. Designing a Requirement Driven Product Development Process. *Proceedings of ASME 2001 DETC, DETC2001/DTM-21682*, Pittsburgh, PA, September 9-12, 2001.

Finger, S. and J.R. Dixon. 1989. A Review of Research in Mechanical Engineering Design. Part 1: Descriptive, Prescriptive, and Computer-Based Models of Design Processes. *Research Engineering Design*, 1.1, 51–67.

French, M.J. 1971. *Engineering Design, The Conceptual Stage*. London, United Kingdom: Heinemann.

Gero, J.S. and R.D. Coyne. 1985. Knowledge-Based Planning as a Design Paradigm. In Yoshikawa, H. and E.A. Warman (eds.), *Design Theory for CAD*. Amsterdam, Netherlands: North-Holland, 261–295.

Hartshorne, C. and P. Weiss (eds.). 1931–1935. *The Collected Papers of Charles Sanders Peirce, Vol. I-VI*. Cambridge, MA: Harvard University Press.

Holland, J. 1975. *Adaptation in Natural and Artificial Systems*. Ann Arbor, MI: University of Michigan Press.

Horváth, I. 2004. A Treatise on Order in Engineering Design Research. *Research in Engineering Design*, 15.2, 155–181.

Hubka, V. and W.E. Eder. 1982. *Principles in Engineering Design*. London, United Kingdom: Butterworths Scientific.

Kakuda, Y. and M. Kikuchi. 2001. Abstract Design Theory. *Annals of Japanese Association of Philosophy of Science*, 10.3, 19–35.

McDermott, R.E., R.J. Mikulak and M.R. Beauregard, 1996. *The Basics of FMEA*. New York, NY: Productivity Press.

Meijer, B.R., T. Tomiyama, B.H.A. van der Holst and K. van der Werff. 2003. Knowledge Structuring for Function Design. *Annals of the CIRP*, 52.1, 89–92.

Mizuno, S. and Y. Akao. 1993. *QFD: The Customer-Driven Approach to Quality Planning & Deployment*. Tokyo, Japan: Asian Productivity Organization.

Pahl, G. and W. Beitz. 1996. *Engineering Design: Systematic Approach*. Berlin, Germany: Springer-Verlag.

Poon, J. and M.L. Maher. 1997. Co-Evolution and Emergence in Design. *Artificial Intelligence in Engineering*, 11.3, 319–327.

Pugh, S. 1991. *Total Design: Integrated Methods for Successful Product Engineering*. Reading, MA: Addison-Wesley.

Reich, Y. 1995. A Critical Review of General Design Theory. *Research in Engineering Design*, 7.1, 1–18.

Reuleaux, F. 1861. *Konstrukteur*. Braunschweig: Vieweg and Sohn.

Reuleaux, F. 1875. *Theorische Kinematic*. Braunschweig: Vieweg and Sohn.

Schurz, G. 2008. Patterns of Abduction. Synthese. 164. 201-234.

Shah, J. 1998. Experimental Investigation of Progressive Idea Generation Techniques. *Proceedings ASME 1998 DETC*, DETC98/DTM-5676. ASME. Atlanta, GA, September 13-16, 1998.

Shavlik, K. and T.G. Dietterich (eds.). 1990. *Readings in Machine Learning*. Palo Alto, CA: Morgan Kaufmann.

Suh, N.P. 1990. *The Principles of Design*. Oxford, United Kingdom: Oxford University Press.

Suh, N.P. 2005. *Complexity: Theory and Applications*. Oxford, United Kingdom: Oxford University Press.

Taguchi, G. 1987. *The System of Experimental Design: Engineering Methods to Optimize Quality and Minimize Cost, Vol. 1 and 2*. Dearborn, MI: American Supplier Institute.

Takeda, H., S. Hamada, T. Tomiyama and H. Yoshikawa. 1990. A Cognitive Approach to the Analysis of Design Processes. *Proceedings of DTM'90*, DE-Vol. 27. ASME, Chicago, IL. September 16-19, 1990. 153–160.

Tomiyama, T., H. Takeda, M. Yoshioka and Y. Shimomura. 2003. Abduction for Creative Design. *Proceedings of ASME 2003 DETC*, DETC2003/DTM-48650. ASME. Chicago, IL. September 2-6, 2003.

Tomiyama, T., M. Yoshioka and A. Tsumaya. 2002. A Knowledge Operation Model of Synthesis. In Chakrabarti, A. (ed.), *Engineering Design Synthesis – Understanding, Approaches and Tools*. London, United Kingdom: Springer-Verlag, 67–90.

Tomiyama, T. and P.J.W. ten Hagen. 1990. Representing Knowledge in Two Distinct Descriptions: Extensional vs. Intentional. *Artificial Intelligence in Engineering*, 5.1, 223–32.

Tomiyama, T. and H. Yoshikawa. 1987. Extended General Design Theory. In Yoshikawa, H. and E.A. Warman (eds.), *Design Theory for CAD*. Amsterdam, Netherlands: North-Holland, 95–130.

Ueda, K. 2001. Synthesis and Emergence – Research Overview. *Artificial Intelligence in Engineering*, 15.4, 321–327.

Ullman, D.G., T.G. Dietterich and L. Stauffer. 1988. A Model of the Mechnical Design Process Based on Empirical Data. *Artificial Intelligence for Engineering, Design, Analysis and Manufacturing*, 2.1, 35–52.

Wallace, K.N. and C. Hales. 1987. Detailed Analysis of an Engineering Design Project. *Proceedings of ICED 1987*, Boston, MA., August 17-20, 1987. ASME, 86–93.

Wang, J. and J. Kusiak (eds.). 2001. *Computational Intelligence in Design and Manufacturing Handbook*. Boca Raton, FL: CRC Press.

Yoshikawa, H. 1981. General Design Theory and a CAD System. In Sata, T. and E.A. Warman (eds.), *Man-Machine Communication in CAD/CAM*. Amsterdam, Netherlands: North-Holland, 35–58.

Yoshioka, M. and T. Tomiyama. 2000. Model-Based Abduction for Synthesis. *Proceedings of ASME 2000 DETC*, DETC2000/DTM-14553. September 10-13, 2000. Baltimore, MD. ASME.

4

ARTIFACTS, ACTIVITIES, AND DESIGN KNOWLEDGE

Kari Kuutti

Introduction

The motto of the somewhat infamous Chicago World's Fair (1933-34), "Science finds, Industry applies, Man conforms," did not leave much room or role for the users of products coming from industry. Since then, the situation has changed and designers of all kinds of products and services are giving at least some consideration to the needs of the users. Expressions like user-centered or human-centered have become common in design literature, and there is even an ISO standard for user-centered design processes (ISO 13407). It is generally accepted that users have knowledge that is relevant and important for design. The nature of this knowledge and the best way to bring this knowledge to bear in design are not, however, so widely agreed upon. This has resulted in a variety of different methods for working with users, ranging from those that treat users just as passive objects of "requirements elictation," as in some forms of requirement engineering, to those that treat users as full partners in the design team, as in some forms of participatory design.

Working more closely with users has resulted in a better understanding of the complexity of the "user problem," and since the 1990s, attempts to find richer concepts to discuss users and their knowledge have increased. One such concept is "context," which during the last ten years has become a very popular expression in design literature. It has even invaded technical communities where using a term with such humanistic flavor would only a decade earlier have caused raised eyebrows. Recently, however, the 2004 Ubiquitous Computing conference had a workshop not only on context but on "Advanced Context Modeling and Management," and there is even a technically-oriented conference series devoted solely to "context studies," the fifth one held in Paris in 2005.

Like the popularity of the concept of context suggests, the enlargement of interest from isolated users towards ones within various contexts has made it easier to understand the knowledge needed and created in design, and it is clearly a step in the right direction. During the last few years, there have been increasing attempts to formulate a new conception about the object of design that is rich enough to deal with artifacts, activities, and contexts in a way that would satisfy the demands society is setting for design.

The issue is formulated by Richard Buchanan (2001, 14) in the following way:

> What I believe has changed our understanding of the problem of design knowledge is greater recognition of the extent to which products are situated in the lives of individuals and in society and culture. This has given us two areas of exploration that are, in a sense, mirror images of the same problem. On the one hand, we are concerned to place products in their situations of use. The product then is a negotiation of the intent of the designer and manufacturer and the expectations of communities of use. The product is, in essence, a mediating middle between two complex interests, and the processes of new product development are explicitly the negotiation between those interests.

Another prominent researcher within design research, Alain Findeli (2001, 5–6), has also been advocating a change of viewpoint regarding design knowledge; in a recent paper, he summarized the problem nicely:

> Indeed, all the drifts one is witnessing today in design can be attributed to one or all of these three central pillars: the already mentioned "effect of product engineering and marketing on design," i.e., the determinism of instrumental reason, and the central role of the economic factor as the almost exclusive evaluation criterion; an extremely narrow philosophical anthropology which leads one to consider the user as a mere customer or, at best, as a human being framed by ergonomics and cognitive psychology; an outdated implicit epistemology of design practice and intelligence, inherited from the nineteenth century; an overemphasis upon the material product; an asthetics based almost exclusively on material shapes and qualities; a code of ethics originating in a culture of business contracts and agreements; a cosmology restricted to the

marketplace; a sense of history conditioned by the concept of material progress; and a sense of time limited cycles of fashion and technological innovations or obsolecence.

One of the central questions Findeli is interested in is what is the epistemology that is compatible with design practices and how it can be connected with design methodology. He starts to develop an answer with two themes: "involvedness" and "visual intelligence." After Findeli's theories became well known, design has been dominated by two epistemological models; design has been seen as either "applied art" or as "applied science." In both cases the reference area for design has been outside design proper. Design has been seen only as straightforward application of knowledge and skill developed outside of design situations, and this is what Findeli wants to challenge. He believes that we should progress from "applied" to "involved" science, so that the scientific attitude should be brought into projects and practices, instead of being applied from outside, which will lead us to see a design problem as a change in the state of a system, when both designer and customer themselves belong to the system. A solution cannot be forced from outside; it has to be created within. Instead of a problem, one must understand the regularities and dependencies of changing the system. The change in the system changes the customer and the designer as well; taking this into account should also be part of the project. Findeli uses the term "visual intelligence" to describe the capablity of understanding such systems.

With visual intelligence, Findeli starts from Moholy-Nagy's maxim that "the key to our age is to be able to see everything in relationship" (Moholy-Nagy, 1938). Things are visible but relations are essentially invisible, and therefore the visual capability needed in design cannot be restricted to only the visible, but it must be able to grasp also these immaterial relationships within the system that require change.

> A contemporary anthropology will have to take into account the complex interplay and relationship of the various layers and subsystems which build up the inner world of thinking, feeling, and willing human being. Conversely, the outer world is much more than what even environmentalists and ecodesigners call the environment, usually reduced to its biophysical aspects. Here, we are also dealing with various interrelating subsystems, which function and evolve according to very different logics: the technical or man-made world, the biophysical world, the social world, and the symbolic world or "semiocosm." These inner and outer worlds interact with each other. As a consequence, before any project can be launched within such a complex situation, a designer indeed must make sure he/she has an adequate representation of the content, the structure, the

evolutionary dynamics, and the trends or "telos" of such a system. This is why future visual intelligence must be capable of penetrating into the invisible world of human consciousness (thoughts, motivations, purpose, fear, needs, aspirations, etc.) and into the intricate ecologies of the outer world (Findeli, 2001, 11).

Finally, Findeli considers the purpose of design and the ethical aspects of design. He believes it essential that a designer understands and also accepts the purpose behind the design. He criticizes the former idea, according to which it is enough to bring right ingredients, tools, and methods into the situation, and the goals will be reached automatically. He does not accept this, but believes that the purpose of the design must be understood differently:

> In the new perspective, however, the purpose of design must be considered as a horizon, as a guiding set of values, and as an axiological landscape to which one always must refer when taking a decision or evaluating a proposition within the design project, and not as an ideal goal to be reached in the more or less near future (Findeli, 2001, 13).

This chapter will make an attempt to promote Findeli's "visual intelligence" by outlining a first approximation of such a model consisting of interrelated subsystems, where "inner and outer worlds" can interact, and where "content, structure, dynamics, and purpose" are represented—knowledge about the artifact and use practice to be designed embedded in its context in a way that is also in harmony with Buchanan's ideas of the dual nature of this exploration area. Let us first consider the nature of design knowledge.

Nature of Design Knowledge

As recognized by Buchanan in the quotation above, design knowledge is distilled from the field where the artifact is going to be used, from the needs of the future users of the artifact, and from the possibilities and resources available in producing the artifact. Figure 4.1 is an attempt to illustrate this.

What can be said about this design knowledge? In fact, several interesting issues appear. First, we can say something about the sources of the knowledge, as pointed out in a comment by Nigel Cross (2001, 54–55):

> So design knowledge is of and about the artificial world and how to contribute to the creation and maintenance of that world. Some of it is knowledge inherent in the activity of designing, gained through engaging and reflecting on that activity. Some of it is knowledge

Figure 4.1
Major sources of artifact knowledge

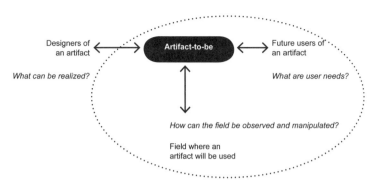

inherent in the artifacts of the artificial world (e.g., in their forms and configurations—knowledge that is used in copying from, reusing or varying aspects of existing artifacts), gained through using and reflecting upon those artifacts. Some of it is knowledge inherent in the process of manufacturing artifacts, gained through making and reflecting upon the making of those artifacts. And some of each of these forms of knowledge also can be gained through instruction in them.

Second, we know that artifact knowledge is different than scientific knowledge. This difference has been the source of heated discussion, and various explanations have been suggested. There is one rather simple and fundamental difference, however, that has not received much attention, and that may be one of the major reasons why designers have always been very reluctant to accept a "science of design." This difference is clearly indicated in a quotation from John Dewey (1938/1991, 52):

> A tool or machine, for example, is not simply a simple or complex physical object having its own physical properties and effects, but it is also a mode of language. For it says something, to those who understand it, about the operations of use and their consequences. To the members of a primitive community a loom operated by steam or electricity says nothing. It is composed in a foreign language, and so with most of the mechanical devices of modern civilization. In the present cultural setting, these objects are so intimately bound up with intentions, occupations and purposes that they have an eloquent voice.

The purpose of science is to produce general, global, and timeless knowledge, yet a part—and a crucial part—of artifact knowledge is always local, particular, and timely. In many cases, general, global, and timeless knowledge must also be used in the construction of an artifact, but in the end, it is the local, particular, and timely part that makes it fit for the purpose and decides if it will succeed or not. Artifacts are not built for eternity, but for immediate use. Despite that, they sometimes can show amazing longevity: when the last salmon dam was demolished at the Kiviranta rapids of the Tornio river between Finland and Sweden during the 1980s, it had served almost four hundred years of use with hardly any changes in its form or structure, with just a yearly replacement of outworn timbers. The dam, however, had not been designed for four hundred years but for the catch of the first year when it was used; its longevity was not a result of general and timeless knowledge, but of the stability of local conditions—no significant changes in the flood of the river, the shape of its bottom, nor in the instincts of salmons in a run upstream.

The importance of local, particular, and timely knowledge cuts deep when separating science and design. The scientific apparatus simply lacks the means to deal with such knowledge, and thus design has to develop means of its own. And this difference reflects in design research, too: if the purpose of design research is to understand what happens in design, and develop better tools for it, then local, particular, and timely knowledge must loom large also in design research. This is a rather solid foundation for the claim that design research is in a league of its own; there is only a limited amount it can borrow from other, existing approaches to research.

The locality, particularity, and timeliness are not, however, absolute; there is a certain variance. The Kiviranta salmon dam was necessarily unique, very local, and particular; it was handcrafted to utilize exactly the stones, waterways, and bottom forms of the most favorable position within a particular stretch of rapids. As such, it could not have been moved upstream or downstream without seriously hampering its function. Taking a more recent example, the traditional way of building information systems—in-house development from scratch—often leads to a rather unique artifact, useful only for a very limited group of users.

Of course, often the interest is in constructing artifacts for a broader group of users, and then design knowledge gets an interesting twist. We still have to get the local, particular, and timely, and then generalize this knowledge—but neither too little nor too much. Again, this is something at which science is not usually aimed.

Third, besides the importance of local, particular, and timely knowledge, we can say something about the constitution of the "whole" knowledge condensed into an artifact. In a way, we could call this "whole" a "hypothesis" covering some issues in a practical relationship between purposeful humans and the world where they are acting to fulfill their purpose. If the hypothesis is correct, the artifact will fulfill its purpose. This hypothesis is constructed during the design process and it contains at least three different "types" of knowledge (Figure 4.2).

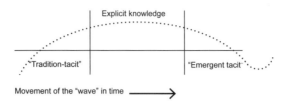

Figure 4.2
Types of explicit and tacit knowledge

One part of the knowledge is made explicit and reflected upon, and it may even be exactly coded into an artifact, like computer programs. Another part consists of issues that are taken for granted ("tradition-tacit") and not reflected on—tradition guides how some part of the construction is done. Existing infrastructures and resources are also used as ingredients in making the new artifact. Part of this knowledge may earlier have been explicit, but because of successful repeated use, it is not reflected on, but is instead taken for granted. Part may be a tradition that was learned as an element of a practice and has never been subjected to any reflection. But there is a third type, another kind of tacit knowledge, whose difference from the tradition-tacit knowledge is not always recognized. This knowledge, which could be called "emergent-tacit," remains implicit and tacit when the designer and other participants use their skill, judgment, and experience when responding to particular conditions in a situation— something that is so novel and unique that it cannot yet be subjected to reflection. And there is a certain "wave" movement between the types over time: emergent-tacit may become in time a part of explicit knowledge, and explicit knowledge may fall back to a tacit level after having been used successfully long enough, but this time it appears in the tradition-tacit form.

This is about the level of accuracy of descriptions that can be found within current design research. What would be needed for a serious analysis would be a more elaborate knowledge model of an artifact embedded in at least two contexts, use and design at the same time, and a possibility to connect in other, additional contexts. This is what we try to develop in this paper. Let us start with a general description of cultural historical activity theory; this will be used as the foundation.

Cultural-Historical Activity Theory

Cultural-Historical Activity Theory (CHAT) is a school of thought on the relation and interaction between human and material and social environments—a kind of theory of practices. Originally a psychological tradition, it has been expanded into a more general, multidisciplinary approach used in a number of other fields. Thus it would be more suitable to call it a framework, an approach or a research program. During recent years, CHAT has begun to be recognized within some specific subfields of design, in particular in Human-Computer Interaction design and research, but so far it has been largely absent from discussion within the broader community of design research proper. The first CHAT-oriented HCI design textbook was recently published (Gay and Hembrooke, 2004), but even within HCI it does not yet enjoy a wide popularity.

A potential reason for this slow acceptance is the unfortunate "theory" in the naming of the approach. People assume they will find a well-defined system of well-founded axioms, worked down to details, and are disappointed with what they find. Perhaps we should call the approach an "activity hypothesis" to better explicate the current completeness of the conceptual apparatus. As an integrative approach, CHAT is an important new opening against the specialization and narrowing of specific disciplines, but it is still a work in progress; it consists of a number of unevenly developed and detailed subareas, and unfortunately, the design area in which we are interested belongs to those that are even less developed.

To put it briefly, the following imbalance is one of the obstacles. Activities CHAT is interested in having a Janus-faced, two-sided nature: there is one side in the human psyche and another side in the world (CHAT does not accept the Cartesian divide between mind and world, so these are parts of the same phenomenon). The psychologists who founded CHAT were naturally most interested in the psyche side of activities; the process called for internalization, the assimilation of knowledge and experience and the formation of mind when participating in activities. Thus Lev Vygotsky, Alexei Leont'ev, Alexander Lurija, and their collaborators and followers laid a foundation for developmental psychology and educational research. The psyche and the movement "inward" was developed and explored, while the world side of activities and movements "outward" remained unexplored.

During the 1980s, a group of western researchers got interested in CHAT and they started to explore the world side of activities. One of them, Yrjö Engeström (1987), hypothesized a simple but rather powerful way to model the world side of activities (and thus also implicitly the psyche side of activities, assuming, as CHAT does, that they are the same). It has become a foundation for a large part of CHAT-oriented research "in the world." Engeström and his followers have been mostly interested in external activities and their change and development as such, and thus the connection between this model of the world side of activities and the Leontevian view of the psyche side of activities has not been much elaborated. Neither has the externalization process, the creation of the new in the world—understanding that would be crucial to the design research—really been worked out.

Several reasons make CHAT in its current form already an interesting approach for design research. Among social theories, CHAT is unique in that it puts human-made artifacts at the very center of the conceptual framework. CHAT is interested in purposeful human actions (in the context that makes them meaningful, which is called an activity, hence activity theory), and a basic idea is that those actions are mediated by material and linguistic tools and instruments. Design can thus be seen as a purposeful change in such mediated relationships.

It is possible to present here only a few major features of the framework relevant to the theme of this chapter. An interested reader is advised to explore a more complete overview of CHAT from the HCI point of view (Kuutti, 1996), and other papers in the same volume; papers from a selection of previous CHAT world conferences (Chaiklin et al., 1999); or a CHAT classic, like Leont'ev's book (1978).

Historical Background

The origin of CHAT is in work started in the 1920s by psychologists to establish a new approach in psychology founded on Marxism. The foundation of Activity Theory was laid by L. S. Vygotsky during the 1920s and early 1930s. His work was continued by A. N. Leont'ev, and A. R. Lurija who developed Vygotsky's ideas further and started to use the term "activity." (A good historical review of these early phases is Leontjev, 1989.) The Cartesian mind-body dualism could not be used as a base for a Marxist psychology; a monistic starting point was needed as a foundation. The major innovation of the founding fathers of CHAT was to assume that human thinking emerged and developed in practical actions and social interactions in the world, and thus there is no separate mind that could be studied isolated from these actions. A significant further finding was that an individual person is not the right unit of analysis of psychological phenomenon. To understand actions meaningfully, the purposefulness of actions must be taken into account, and thus it is necessary to include into the unit of analysis the minimal context of actions that make the actions meaningful for the acting subject. This context, a purposeful, social system of actions, is called an activity. A number of general principles in the framework are identified, e.g., object-orientation and mediation by culturally- and historically-formed artifacts (tools and signs); these are explained further in the next sections.

Object-orientation

The most central feature of CHAT is that activities are oriented towards a specific "object" and different objects separate activities from each other. The CHAT concept of object is complex and loaded. Activities emerge when human needs find in the world a possibility to become fulfilled. Object is the entity or the state of the world, the transformation of which will hopefully produce the desired outcome. An object has thus a double existence: it exists in the world as the material to be transformed by artifactual means and cooperative actions, but also as a projection to the future—the outcome. The object cannot be exactly given beforehand, but it unfolds and becomes concrete in the interactions with the material and the conditions. (If an end result is completely known beforehand, CHAT does not call it an object but a goal of an action, a construct of a next simpler level.) Being a constantly reproduced purpose for a collective activity that motivates and defines the horizon of possible goals and actions, the "sharedness" of the object is present only in social relations across time and space, and embodied also in terms of history. Locally, the sharedness of the object is a process of social construction with divergent views and creative uses of cultural and interactional resources. Activities are thus often multivoiced, and none of the existing perspectives on the object can be automatically assumed "right"—that can only be defined within an activity. The object of an activity is not a passive thing, only to be manipulated: Arne Raeithel (1992) has suggested that it would be more correct to call the object a "counterprocess," which does not easily subsume itself under the planned course of actions, but which has its "own will" and which can offer a strong resistance when formerly hidden connections and necessities are revealed in the process.

Mediation

The concept of tool mediation is another of the central features of CHAT. Human actions are mediated by culturally and historically constituted artifacts—something purposefully produced by human beings. Our relation with the world is thus shaped not only by our personal history and experiences from various interactions, but also by the history of the broader culture we are part of—where our tools have been shaped. The experiences from interactions with the world have been condensed into tools, symbols, and signs that we use in our activities. The world does not appear to us "uncontaminated," but as the culturally- and historically-determined object of

Figure 4.3
A model of the basic mediation (based on Engeström, 1987)

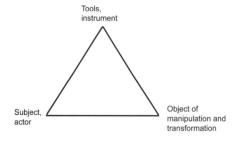

Figure 4.4
A model of an activity system (based on Engeström, 1987)

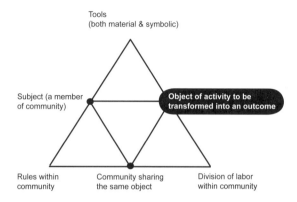

Tools
(both material & symbolic)

Subject (a member of community)

Object of activity to be transformed into an outcome

Rules within community

Community sharing the same object

Division of labor within community

previous activities. Humans project both these earlier meanings and those that arise from the current needs for their objects, and at the same time, we can see potential results that can be achieved. Language is an essential part of this toolkit, a "tool of tools." According to CHAT, all mediation has both language and material character; symbols and signs, and tools and instruments are both integral parts in the same mediation process. The basic mediational structure is depicted in Figure 4.3.

Overall Structure of Activities

After the founders of CHAT published their theories, new forms for depicting activity have been elaborated. The most influential attempt to model an activity has been done by Yrjö Engeström (1987), whose "model of activity system" aims at pointing to a historically- and concretely-constituted system that has a timespan and internal transformations of its own. The model is presented in Figure 4.4.

In Figure 4.4, the model of individual action from Figure 4.1 has been complemented to depict a collective activity system. The model looks at the activity from the point of view of one actor, the subject, but the fact that the object is shared by a number of subjects is indicated by the point in the model labeled "community." The relations between the subject and the community are mediated, on the one hand, by the group's collection of "mediating artifacts," and on the other hand, by "rules" that specify relations, the local culture, between members of the community, and "division of labor," the continuously negotiated distribution of tasks, powers, and responsibilities among the participants of the activity system (Cole and Engeström, 1993, 7).

In an activity, the relation between individual actions and the outcome of the whole activity becomes mediated and indirect. Leont'ev (1978) explains the relation between individual actions and collective activity with an example about primitive hunters who, in order to catch game, separate into two groups: the catchers and the bush-beaters who frighten the game towards them. When compared with the motive of hunting—to catch the game to get food and clothing material—the individual actions of the bush-beaters appear to be irrational unless they are put into the larger system of the hunting activity.

Although this "triangular" model may look too rigid to grasp the fluency of human life, it is only for the sake of representational simplicity and convenience. It is important to remember that CHAT does not consider activities as "givens" or static entities, but as dynamic ones: activities are always changing and developing. This development is taking place at all levels: new operations are formed from previous actions when participants' skills are increasing; correspondingly, at the level of actions, the scope of new actions is enlarging, but totally new actions are also invented, experimented with, and adapted as responses to new situations or possibilities encountered in the process of transforming the object. Finally, at the level of activity, the object/motive itself (and the whole structure of activity related to it) is reflected on, questioned, and perhaps adapted, reacting to larger changes and other activities.

Because activities are not isolated units but more like nodes in crossing hierarchies and networks, they are influenced by other activities and other changes in their environment. External influences change some elements of activities causing imbalances between them. CHAT uses the term "contradiction" to indicate a misfit within elements, between them, between different activities, or between different development phases of a same activity. Contradictions manifest themselves as problems, ruptures, breakdowns, clashes, etc. CHAT sees contradictions as sources of development; real activities are practically always in the process of working through some of such contradictions.

After this rather superficial glance at the origin and some central concepts of CHAT, let's consider its relation to design.

The Object of Design

The characterization of an object of activity answers very accurately to the demands for a "purpose of design" mentioned by Alain Findeli, quoted in the first section of the paper. It is, in fact, rather amazing how faithfully the description of the object of an activity, developed originally within a purely psychological research tradition and without any connection to design whatsoever, characterizes some of the central features of design: organizing the role of the thing-to-be for the whole enterprise, the unfolding of the object during the course of action, and the always locally limited horizon of possibilities, the existence of a counterprocess, and so on.

This similarity between the qualities perceived in design and those designated as an object of a general activity gives some credibility to the claim that "everything is design," expanding the scope of design to contain everyday actions and making it a most fundamental feature of human existence, as expressed, for example, by Herbert Simon (1969) and Harold Nelson and Erik Stolterman (2003). There is no need to explore that issue further here. My personal view, however, is that although this claim can be defended, and it certainly raises the status of design, expanding the scope that far would dilute the analytical and explanatory power of the concept of design, making it rather useless. I would prefer to limit the concept of design to situations where an artifact is purposefully created for others to use—which is the situation we are actually interested in.

After seeing the structure of one activity, and remembering the characterization given by Buchanan in the previous section, the first approximation for our model of a unit of design is not very surprising: it is made just to connect two activities—use and design activities—by the emerging artifact-to-be, which serves both as the object of the design activity and as the instrument in the use activity (Figure 4.5).

An object of design is thus something that is constantly oscillating between something to be created and something to be used, and neither of these views exists in a vacuum but instead in a real historical situation, where a multitude of dependencies and relationships is constantly influencing what can be done. I would like to suggest that the structure in Figure 4.5 represents the minimal model of an object of design

Figure 4.5
The minimal model of an object of design

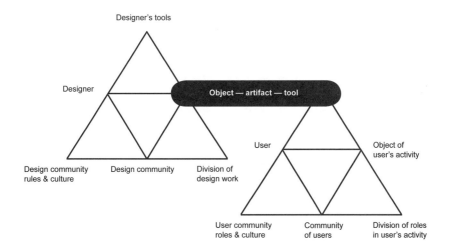

Figure 4.6
Adding activities to enrich the core model emerging new
activity versus the existing one

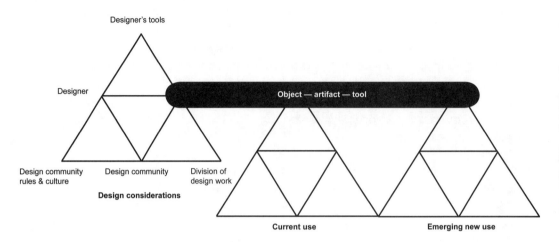

embedded in its network, where "enough" of the actual richness and complexity around the artifact-to-be involved in design is still preserved for it to be useful for analysis. It also obviously covers the Buchanan characterization given in the introduction of this chapter. Because the concept of tool or instrument covers also signs and symbols, we can also read that, instead of use, the other activity is signifying, or perhaps even think that both these interpretations can co-exist as overlays—but only as long as the object and community stay the same. Because that is not necessarily the case, this minimal model cannot cover all situations, but some enlargement will be necessary.

It is, however, relatively easy to expand the minimal core model to cover more aspects of a situation or more complex situations, and we will show a couple of examples of this. Let's first enrich the use activity. One of the typical distinctions in the use side is the separation between the current use and the future use, possible only with the emerging artifact-to-be. Taking this into account would lead us to the following network (Figure 4.6), by using, for example, the tensions between the old and new way of working. In a similar vein it would be possible to enrich the design side, where a typical distinction and a source of tension is the separation of design from actual fabrication of an artifact (this network is not depicted due to the space limitations).

Here, the right side of the model separates between old and new use activities, but this is not the only possibility. It is also possible to describe other potential activities where the new artifact has a role.

Figure 4.7
The design process used instrumentally by another activity

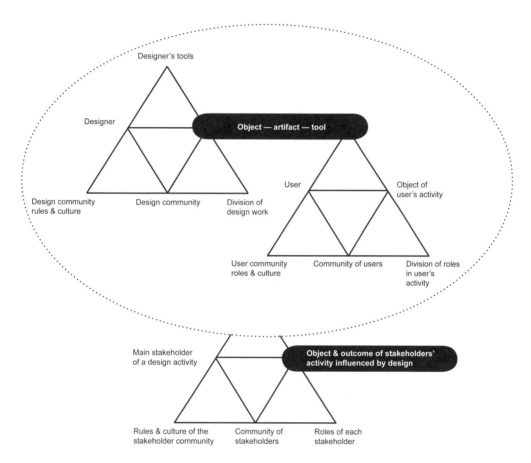

My other example of extending the core model deals with power and priorities. Why does the design process exist in the first place? What is the purpose? Again, it is possible to add more activities to the model, in this case in a hierarchical fashion. Some actor is using the design process instrumentally to transform some situation for benefit, and that can also be made visible (Figure 4.7). With this sort of enlargement, the power play by the community around the design can be discussed.

The two enlargements are only examples (and not necessarily very good ones) of how the core model and the activity structure can be used to describe different situations in and around design.

Discussion

The theme of this book is design integration, and the purpose of this chapter has been to contribute to understanding what kind of knowledges are integrated in design. It has been suggested in earlier discussion that what separates scientific knowledge from design knowledge is that the latter focuses on things artificial, although there are still different views on the nature of this artificiality.

In this chapter, the question is studied from the viewpoint that artifacts themselves are material expressions of condensed information, crystallizations of human experience with some aspects of the material world in some purposeful practice. One of the important characteristics of design knowledge embedded in artifacts is that it is local, particular, and timely. A design may use global, general, and timeless knowledge, but what really matters, what makes the difference between a successful and unsuccessful design, is the quality of local, particular, and timely knowledge collected and embedded in the artifact.

The ideal of science is global, general, and timeless knowledge. Thus, scientific knowledge has only a limited applicability in design. While this is the case with design proper, is it also the case with design research, which has to, for example, provide for design methods and conceptual tools, and thus has to take the problem of the local, particular, and timely in earnest. So design research cannot directly mimic science, but it has to carefully judge what to pick from existing areas of research and how what is borrowed must be adapted to form its own ways, methods, values, and norms.

Each artifact is a unique constellation of ways to take relevant issues into account, a core network of relations. This chapter has suggested that the concept of activity systems from cultural-historical activity theory could be useful in describing and mapping this network. A hypothesis that a network of two interconnected activities, design and use, is the minimal one that maintains enough complexity and richness to discuss the knowledge needed in design. This chapter has also suggested ways the minimal model can be amended to take into account increasingly complex and realistic knowledge.

Moreover, this chapter demonstrates that the conventional division between explicit and tacit knowledge may not be distinctive enough to grasp all the nuances of knowledge used in artifacts, and suggests separating two kinds of tacit knowledge: tradition-tacit and emergent-tacit. Tradition-tacit knowledge is taken for granted and without reflection, while emergent-tacit knowledge is not yet available for reflection, but is something brought forth by the instinct and intuition of a designer.

The framework is also capable to address a number of questions raised by prominent design researchers related to the nature of design and changes needed to our conceptualizations. Of course, the conceptual sketch presented above is not a solution to the tall order presented by researchers like Buchanan and Findeli, but I hope that even this short exploration is able to show that a number of important issues—such as novel epistemology, systemic relational complexity of design object, and integration of the purpose of design—can at least be adequately discussed within the suggested framework, and that is already a step forward.

The suggested knowledge model of an artifact sheds some light on why it has been so difficult to develop a comprehensive "theory" of design, despite long efforts. First, the knowledge necessary to embed into an artifact spans several levels of complexity, from the details of individual acts of using an artifact to the historical dynamics of socio-material activity system, when a new way of working emerges due to the use of a new artifact, and even beyond that, to the relations between different activity systems. Besides the "depth," the knowledge needed is also very "broad": it consists of elements and relations belonging to the realms of half a dozen already existing disciplines. Thus the knowledge must be interdisciplinary: it is somewhat obvious that any knowledge that has emerged within an isolated perspective of some individual element or relation of networks within design must be scrutinized and re-interpreted with respect to the whole network before it can have value for design. Thus, the best we can say is that the other contributing disciplines may only inform design—a suggestion which strongly supports Cross' idea of a "designerly way of knowing" (2001).

What does this mean for the discipline of research, as asked by Sharon Poggenpohl in the introduction of this book? It is indeed true, that if design wants to be a discipline, it has to adopt practices common to other academic disciplines. However, because of the nature of the unique object of design, those practices cannot be directly copied from existing disciplines. Design must be quite selective in selecting other disciplines' practices and deciding how they must be adapted to their new environment. As demanded by Alain Findeli in the quotation used in the beginning of this chapter, we must abandon the old idea of using natural science as the role model for our discipline. Instead, we must search for inspiration either in new, more practically-oriented approaches, like in engineering or decision science, as hinted by Buchanan (2001), or consult older, clinically-oriented disciplines like jurisprudence and clinical medicine, as suggested by philosopher Stephen Toulmin (2001). The nature of the object also dictates that the approach of design must necessarily be more synthesizing and integrating than that of most other disciplines. Even the most brilliant analysis of an isolated detail will be of little help if the results cannot be integrated back into the contextual network where the detail lives in real life. Finally, the importance of timely, local, and particular knowledge and limited possibilities to find global, timeless, and general foundations does not mean that design as a discipline is doomed forever to muddle through day-to-day details, without any wider vistas and general perspectives. On the contrary, to cope with the continuous change in different aspects of activities related to design, we have to better understand the origins, direction, and speed of such changes—the dynamics of human life in its material and cultural contexts, to put it succinctly—and one can hardly ask for a broader vista than that. Fortunately enough, we do not need to aim further than local, timely, and particular understanding of these dynamics, but that is still a challenge worthy of a discipline. Luckily, we in design have an extra arsenal of methods, beyond the reach of traditional disciplines bound to the position of an external observer. Besides observation, design can influence changes directly in the form of different design interventions, and it is easy to assume that these interventions will form the methodological core identity for the design discipline.

I'd like to conclude with a final remark. A theory of creativity was an area where polymath Arthur Koestler tried his hand (Koestler, 1970). While the details of his theorizing may be largely forgotten, his central conceptual foundation—the bisociative matrix—has stayed alive and is still often used and referenced. The principle of bisociation means that an issue of interest is brought under study at the same time within two frames of reference, which are in some ways incompatible, and the tension generated by this study is seen by Koestler as a major springboard for creativity. In the activity-based model of design, presented above, such a bisociative matrix is built into every object of design. This may be somewhat surprising, but it is also encouraging.

Acknowledgments

The writing of this paper has been supported by the Academy of Finland (grant #103114) and the Technology Development Agency (TEKES) as a part of the ÄES-project.

References

Buchanan, Richard. 2001. Design Research and the New Learning. *Design Issues*, 17.4, 3–23.

Chaiklin, S., M. Hedegaard and U.J. Jensen (eds.). 1999. *Activity Theory and Social Practice*. Aarhus, Denmark: Aarhus University Press.

Cole, M. and Y. Engeström. 1993. A cultural–historical approach to distributed cognition. In Salomom, G. (ed.), *Distributed cognitions: Psychological and educational considerations*. Cambridge, MA: Cambridge University Press, 1–47.

Cross, Nigel. 2001. Designerly Ways of Knowing: Design Discipline versus Design Science. *Design Issues,* 17.3, 49–55.

Dewey, John. 1938/1991. *Logic: The Theory of Inquiry.* In Boydston, J. (ed.), *John Dewey: The Later Works, 1925-1953. Vol. 12.* Carbondale, IL: Southern Illinois University Press.

Engeström, Yrjö. 1987. *Learning by expanding.* Helsinki, Finland: Orienta-Konsultit.

Findeli, Alain. 2001. Rethinking Design Education for the 21st Century: Theoretical, Methodological and Ethical Discussion. *Design Issues,* 17.1, 5–17.

Gay, G. and H. Hembrooke. 2004. *Activity-Centered Design: An Ecological Approach to Designing Smart Tools and Usable Systems.* Cambridge, MA: MIT Press.

Iacucci, G., A. Juustila, K. Kuutti, P. Pehkonen and A. Ylisaukko-oja. 2003. Connecting Remote Visits and Design Environment: User Needs and Prototypes for Architecture Design. In Luca Chittaro (Ed.): Human-Computer Interaction with Mobile Devices and Services, 5th International Symposium, Mobile HCI 2003, Udine, Italy, September 8-11, 2003, Proceedings. Lecture Notes in Computer Science 2795. Heidelberg, Springer,pp. 45–60.

Koestler, Arthur. 1970. *Act of Creation.* New York, NY: MacMillan Publishing Company.

Kuutti, Kari. 1996. Activity Theory as a potential framework for human-computer interaction research. In Nardi, B. (ed.), *Context and Consciousness: Activity Theory and Human Computer Interaction.* Cambridge, MA: MIT Press, 17–44.

Leont'ev, A.N. 1978. *Activity, consciousness, and personality.* Englewood Cliffs, NJ: Prentice-Hall.

Leontjev, A.N. 1989. The Problem of Activity in the History of Soviet Psychology. *Soviet Psychology,* 27.1, 22–39.

Moholy-Nagy, Lazlo. 1938. Why Bauhaus Education? *Shelter* (March 1938), 7–22. Cited in Findeli, A. 2001. Rethinking Design Education in the 21th Century: Theoretical, Methodological, and Ethical Discussion. *Design Issues,* 17.1, 5–16.

Nelson, Harold G. and Erik Stolterman. 2003. *The Design Way: Intentional change in an unpredictable world.* Englewood Cliffs, NJ: Educational Technology Publications.

Raeithel, Arne. 1992. Activity Theory as a Foundation for Design. In Floyd, Züllighoven, Budde and Keil-Slawik (eds.), *Software development and reality construction.* Berlin, Germany: Springer.

Simon, Herbert. 1969. *The Sciences of the Artificial.* Cambridge, MA: MIT Press.

Toulmin, Stephen. 2001. *Return to Reason.* Cambridge, MA: Harvard University Press.

5

MEDIATING IN-BETWEEN: HOW INDUSTRIAL DESIGN ADVANCES BUSINESS AND USER INNOVATION

Birgit Helene Jevnaker

Introduction

To understand design in action in real world enterprises we need to comprehend design and business practices, because both are in the making (evolutionary and/or breaking away) and not pre-given entities or processes. This is challenging because among designers, as well as among business managers, people tend to expect something pre-ordered (e.g., strategies, business directions) or almost ready-made (e.g., "design first," before its content)[1] from the other party. By contrast, reflective design and business practitioners, who are actually collaborating in dynamic, interactive ways over time, seem to acknowledge the value of their back-and-forth unfinished creative work. This chapter thus focuses on two themes.[2] The first theme involves the hidden potential of design/business collaboration, or how collaborative relations between design and business unfold and may affect the ways business and design are being done not merely once, but recurrently. The other theme is the potential value and critical activity for design and business collaborators to actually be moving about—enacting, interfacing or otherwise sorting out and refining—a number of issues and sentiments in the design and business use contexts and between something new and its realization.

Overcoming the many gaps of understanding between multiple users of everyday things is ever more difficult (Norman, 1988) if the change or flux of things is increasing in internationally transacting and communicating economies. Recent design, as well as management research, is emphasizing "the new complexities" of working with multiple specialists and critical interest groups that stretch their abilities in order to reinvent and differentiate offerings faster than before (Leonard-Barton, 1995; Hamel, 2002; Cagan and Vogel, 2002), or otherwise engage in designing new services with others (Thackara, 2005, 6–7). With this background, it seems fruitful to explore the gaps as well as potential "natural overlaps," as already understood by design pioneers Charles and Ray Eames when working with various agencies and corporate clients (Lipstadt, 1997, 151). Hence this chapter seeks to relate to this in-between phenomenon and thus move beyond some previous tendencies and blind spots in both design research and management research.[3]

Although design, such as industrial design, is sparsely researched (Dorst, 1997, 16 ff.) and still regarded as a neglected area within management (Bruce and Cooper, 1997, 3), designers and business collaborators can create and integrate ideas and visually manifest a networked vision that triggers new demand internationally as illuminated by the Apple design (Kunkel, 1997) as well as IKEA stories.[4] Yet most stories of how designers and other "creatives" actually help organize business and market offerings within and across industries are unknown or untold in spite of the growing interest in innovation and imaginative organization (Hamel, 2002; Nussbaum, 2005).

Despite the fact that a range of industrial products have been shaped successfully by designers since the 1930s or even before (Heskett, 1980; Sparke, 1986), businesses and organizations still tend to be "design-illiterate" (Kotler and Rath, 1984) and are also trapped by numerous product development failures (Cooper, 1993). More specific investigations are needed to capture how organizations build not merely "resource advantages" (Hunt, 2000), but also experiences and reputation among users. According to the knowledge-based strategy perspective (Nonaka and Teece, 2001), it is even more important to understand how enterprises—including design groups—build the capabilities to do so. Here I will address, in particular, how design/business relations contribute to these objectives.

Thus, the purpose of this chapter is to identify and examine how particular enterprises actually develop new practices through working with specialist designers such as industrial designers, and what types of benefits can be gained and replicated over time through a dynamic design collaboration between diverse design and business expertise. First, I propose a tentative framework that may sensitize us towards the multiple dynamics of design/business developments, which need to be further explored in tandem. Then drawing on my own field studies of design/business relations, a set of capability gains and related processes of industrial design are presented. Finally, I briefly reflect on how and why designers can act strategically although they seldom are formally included in strategic management (Blaich, 1993, 33).

Method and Material

This chapter is based on real-world case research from working relationships between industrial designers and business enterprises. As Starbuck (1993) recommends, the chapter draws mainly on the study of particular cases or "outliers" to gain new insight on enterprises and allied designers that have excelled in product design. It is not focused as a success story; both failures and successes are retold or can be observed in the particular cases.

The research draws on several primary data sets. First, we will look at an in-depth study of five small- and medium-sized product companies that have pursued new product design approaches collaborating with industrial design consultants over time and on more than one project. In order to provide some constancy of backgrounds, the companies were selected from similar kinds of industrial settings—from either form-intensive furniture industry or more engineering-based traditions where form and aesthetic design are not common knowledge[5] (see Tables 5.1 and 5.2). The respective design consultants working with these companies were also researched. Second, a focus group and other pilot studies were initially conducted in order to identify the most critical issues between designers and business firms. The intent was to identify and understand "what happens and how," i.e., how a capability for

Table 5.1
Two Norwegian/Scandinavian export-oriented manufacturers of furniture

Product firms	Core products	Product/strategy	Reported results via design/business relations (selective summary)
HAG	Ergonomically designed office chairs (for the contract market). HAG is a pioneer in its field and emerged as a large-scale exporter in Scandinavia.	Product Innovation	• A range of profitable office-chair models and platforms. • Serial innovator in office-chair design including economic management action, deviant thinking, cross-disciplinary teams, dynamic ergonomics.
		Design scope	• Extended to early NPD, launch events, communication, identity, ethos, and art; learning programs, multiple network events.
		Design strategy	• From none to recurrent design innovation with 12 external design groups.
		Business strategy	• B2B transgression based on "Man is not created to sit still."
		Corporate strategy	• New strategic mission and philosophy co-created.
		Reputation	• Via everyday use, prestigious design excellence awarded chairs, exhibited in international museums, media coverage of its design/business philosophy.
Stokke	Ergonomically designed furniture (for the individual customer). Stokke is a pioneer in its special niche.	Product	• A series of innovative sitting-tools and children's products adopted or co-created.
		Innovation	• Serial innovator through its few designer relations.
		Design scope	• Extended to family of products and marketing links internationally.
		Design strategy	• From ad hoc to recurrent design innovation and relationships.
		Business strategy	• B2C transgression into niche-supplier re human need for movement and variation, entirely new marketing networks emerged.
		Corporate strategy	• New corporate and business strategy and philosophy.
		Reputation	• Via everyday use, design excellence awarded chairs, exhibited internationally and in museums, news coverage.

Table 5.2
Three Norwegian/Scandinavian export-oriented manufacturers in technically-based industries
(High and medium tech firms)

Product based firms	Core products	Product/strategy	Reported results via design/business relations (selective summary)
HAMAX	Consumer-oriented plastics for leisure (bicycle childrens seats, helmets, and other bicycle accessories and children's sleds).	Product Innovation Design scope Design strategy Business strategy Corporate strategy Reputation	• A series of redesigned leisure products for children. • New product concepts in time-compressed developments, new technology and new links with approval authorities and suppliers via designers. • New models and package of less seasonal products for small children families, new packaging, and communication material. • From *ad hoc* to recurrent investments and relationships. • Design opened up for new dealer relationships in European markets. • Design became integral part of new corporate brand strategy. • Via everyday use, several design excellence awards, media coverage with designers allied, prestigiously awarded (the Dutch n|p|k).
TOMRA	Reverse vending machines for disposable beverage containers (TOMRA is a pioneer and the world's leading producer in its field).	Product Innovation Design scope Design strategy Business strategy Corporate strategy Reputation	• Co-created a range of recycling products, platforms, systems. • Continuous contributions including new materials, modular solutions, use interface experiments with R&D, and learning in shifting NPD teams. • Reinforced family of machines and identity via visual programs and graphic designs, design thinking regularly introduced to service system. • From none to 2 integrated industrial designers (one part-time). • Design contributed from the first export contract onwards. • Industrial design part of company strategy. • Via everyday use, excellence awards, sustained design advance, senior designer prestigiously awarded.
GRORUD Industries	Window and door metal-based fittings. (GRORUD was later shut down.)	Product Innovation Design scope Design strategy Business strategy	• Redesigned metal product, e.g., locking mechanisms easier to manufacture. • New design thinking and time-compressed development introduced in old metal-based firm. • 1st concept not introduced in market, in 2nd project company reappears on client's bidding list and wins decisive new contracts. • From none or *ad hoc* to one recurrent relationship. • New to involve designer in B2B, repeat commissions gained via design.

design advance of enterprises occurred in practice. The focus on design/business relationships and possible gains embedded in the relations were sharpened in the multiple-case study, because the initial focus group pointed to the critical importance of a dynamic collaboration among designers and business enterprises behind the design-related outcomes. The author, through repeat interviews and observations, collected the data. Genuine relational data (tape-recorded) from all five product-based companies (using several informants) and their design partners were analyzed, inspired by a grounded theory approach to provide insight and nuance.

To gain a broader understanding, complementary material was collected from both local design consultancies (in Oslo) and American and international design consultancies, most notably Fitch (London, Ohio) and IDEO Design (London, Palo Alto, Boston) and the Chicago-based Doblin Group (see Table 5.3). Moreover, the present study draws on collaborative research in product design cases in Nordic,

Table 5.3
Designers or Design Consultancies selected for the study of industrial design collaboration

I. Industrial designers working for the Norwegian firms	Position and background
Roy Tandberg from Tandberg Design, Asker.	Part-time employed designer at Tomra, free to work for other clients. Product design education from Art Center, Los Angeles, and work experience from the US.
Steinar Flo, Oslo	Independent industrial design consultant with metal design/industrial design education from Norway and Sweden.
Wolfram Peters from Ninaber/Peters/Krouwel, Leiden	Partner of one of the largest industrial design consultancies in the Netherlands. Industrial design education at TU Delft.
Peter Opsvik from Peter Opsvik Ltd., Oslo	Founder and alternative seating designer pioneer (Balans design solutions). Educated in furniture design in Norway and London, with further studies in ergonomics from Germany. Work practice from Tandberg Radio Factory where he worked as an industrial designer.
II. Additional international design consultancies	Characteristics
IDEO Product Design & Development (Bill Moggridge, Ingelise Nielsen, Alison Black, Tim Brown), Palo Alto and London	Industrial/product design and engineering design with multiple complementary disciplines. Offices on three continents: Tokyo, San Francisco, Palo Alto, Chicago, Grand Rapids, Boston, London.
Fitch (Deane Richardson, Sandra Richardson, David Clare), Columbus, Ohio and London	Multi-disciplined design and branding consultancy; the British Fitch is famous for its strengths in retail design and branding, and the American Fitch merging with RichardsonSmiith in Columbus, Ohio has a special strength in industrial product design. Offices on three continents: Columbus, Ohio, San Francisco, Boston, London, Paris (through Peclers) and Singapore.
Doblin Group (Larry Keeley, Erik Kiaer, Jeff Tull, Jeremy Alexis), Chicago	Strategic design and innovation focused consultancy rooted in cross-disciplinary strategic design planning, industrial design, interaction design, information design, graphic design as well as corporate orientation.

European, American, and cross-national settings, allowing the search for similar patterns and contrasts (Yin, 1984/1989) as well as more conceptual discussions. Both within-case analyses and cross-case analyses were conducted through a systematic iterative, multiple-case logic. The research base is more fully explicated elsewhere.[6]

Since design and design relations are complex and ambiguous phenomena (Heskett, 1980; Lawson, 1990/2006) and research of design-in-business is at an early stage (Kristensen, 1998), the first step is to briefly introduce design and position the research in current theories and debates.

Exploring Design/Business Relations

How do industrial designers with transdisciplinary[7] and creativity-based expertise not only belong to the emergent network era (Castells, 2000), but engage themselves in deep and recurrent creation with other organizations? Bringing a traveling or nomadic expertise to selective settings and companies, industrial designers also seem to become a particular kind of creative insider contributing to corporate innovation, as we shall learn more about. Although designing relations have not been explicated much until now, designers appear to connect and mediate in multiple ways that may provide new insight to the current focus on more interactive or co-creating relationships between businesses and users (Prahalad and Ramaswamy, 2004). Interestingly, design and designers can also be related to and extend how enterprises and their core groups actually come to sense and seize business opportunities, and renew their organization's distinctive competencies, which have been coined "dynamic capabilities" (Teece, 1998). Because industrial designers are often located outside their client firms and work across organizational boundaries (Sparke, 1983, Bruce and Morris, 1998), we need to explore design-making also in connection to external or partly independent partners (design consultants). This extension may provide insight into, not merely the creative people-factor of development efforts (Hart, 1995), but concerns for actually projecting "what can be" that currently are called for within new theory building on managing industrial knowledge (Nonaka and Teece, 2001).

Exploring design/business relations may also help us move beyond the current polar debate on open versus closed innovation. Here it is worth noting the previous empirical research by MIT professor Eric von Hippel (1988), who found that innovation can emerge from multiple sources including lead users, and he recommended further research on this "distributed innovation process" rather than focusing simply on a focal firm. In contrast, the Berkeley economist David Teece (1998, 72) often highlights the significance of firm-related dynamic capabilities, but he comments that "it is relatively easy to define dynamic capabilities, quite another to explain how they are built."

In this chapter, I propose that the transdisciplinary educated and experienced industrial designers and their relationship with business enterprises represent a compelling, yet mostly unexplored or insufficiently understood, in-between source of building innovation and competitive advantage (Blaich, 1993). Industrial transdisciplinary design can be conceived in a variety of ways, although most definitions miss significant aspects (see Chapter 1). Here I refer to design mainly as a potentially creative and human-centered, projecting expertise to configure/reconfigure[8] and visualize something that did not exist before, at least not in exactly the same form (Walsh et al., 1992), place, or meaning. Moreover, design may gestalt something with identifying character and charge[9] the emotional aspect in products and services, which may in turn trigger consumers. In short, design (whether professionally or amateurly performed) can transform products and services—for the better or worse—and may have long-term user consequences (Norman, 1988; Moggridge, 2007).

Multiple design disciplines exist. Industrial design is a profession, rooted in humanistic-artistic and technology-based disciplines as well as cultural and marketing practices, thus context matters (Heskett, 1980; Sparke, 1983, 1986). Put briefly, industrial designers conceive and "draw" as well as digitize future products or systems for industrial and use purposes in a rich variety of ways (Heskett, 2002). In fact, "one of the main difficulties and fascinations of designing is the need to embrace so many different kinds of thought and knowledge" (Lawson, 1990/2006, 5). Nevertheless, designers need to convince their industrial partners of the potential design-related benefits, which can be highly challenging (Blaich, 1993, 37). As next outlined, multiple chasms exist on the road towards actually making new designs work.

Gaps in Current Knowledge

Debating what tends to be absent in design theorizing is relevant in a sparsely researched area such as creative design/business relations. This may include naming[10] of what people find interesting or valuable to attend to during the making and framing of something new. Naming or otherwise framing is a recurrent challenging activity when designers and business collaborators are generating something new for others. How are we to find words or ways of expressing something not-yet-born? According to IDEO Tim Brown's recent presentation in World Economic Forum in Davos,[11] "Changing the frame of the problem is the first thing people do in being creative."

Opening up for new or alternative ways of looking at resources, problems or solutions through a design-creative approach resonates with my previous conversations with Tim Brown[12] and numerous other designers. Yet based on numerous interviews and conversations with experienced designers, a possible unlocking through design still seems to be a somewhat deviant practice, not much known or reflected upon. Even though there is a vast social science and management literature that may orient us towards the rich potentialities of various resources as well as image constructions,[13] development of something new still tends to be related to a rather instrumental efficiency and technology-oriented management focus.[14] This leaves a recurrent gap between generating something new from resources—often seen as technical resources—on the one hand, and idea visualizing-cum-expression, or what can become an image-creation, on the other, which appears to become a chasm for reflective practitioners as well.[15] Last but not least, designing from the viewpoint of users' experiences may not be explicitly coordinated across the turfs that may exist between research and technical development, and communication, brand, and image-construction respectively.

Nonetheless, what tends to be undocumented, such as the visual and aesthetic organization of companies (Strati, 1999), can trigger our further exploration. As Donna Haraway (2003, 88) notes: "Anyone who has done historical research knows that the undocumented often have more to say about how the world is put together than do the well pedigreed."

In fact, as understood already by Ouchi (1981, 85), it is not so easy to understand what an organization is. In short, while becoming sensitized by the various practice-oriented strands of management and organization literature, it is critical that these can make us explore real-world actions while *not taking anything for granted*. This relates, for example, to so-called calculating entities such as business firms or other actors' working through associations or collectives (Latour, 2005).

Creative Ensemble, Assembly or Something Else?

If we recognize that design-making is more than putting together a group of specialists, then how do we understand dynamic relations such as the potentially tension-rich one between designers and directors of established firms? The industrial designers coming from "outside"[16]—or being recruited to in-house positions to serve in design-oriented work and in so doing being highly dependent on collaborating with the firm's core-groups—seem to encounter multiple and fragmented concerns, including neglect of design issues as well as high involvement and even possible rivalry (Lorenz, 1986/1990; Blaich, 1993; Svengren, 1998). As underlined by one experienced designer in my initial focus group study (Jevnaker, 1996, 268):

> … you need to take care, for example, in relation to a product developer/ engineer, which they have already in advance (in the client firm), then you have to make clear that it is not the designer that now shall take over his job…all depending on the product type one has to make clear that we can contribute so much, and then you contribute so much, for example, and this makes them relax somewhat more, they see that no-one is coming to take something away from them.

Previous design management texts tend to stress organizing for order and visual coherence, a clear identity, and so forth (Olins, 1989; Gorb, 1990). I do not deny this possibility, but a close rereading of design-in-context oriented texts reveal another reality of observed high internal inconsistencies and what appears to be a syndrome of multifaceted and messy challenges for design-making—in addition to the external expected uncertainties of technologies or markets. As reflected by Robert Blaich (1993, 110), former design director of Philips:

> John Thackara in a review (…) comments that design consultants learned to their dismay during the 1980s boom of design consultancies that "the crucial business of implementation, whether of corporate identity, or a new product range entailed complex and messy processes and involved people and organizational matters, not just the rational production of a manual."

I could not agree more that design processes are often messy and complex, with multiple considerations going beyond the specific project in question.

Arguably, firms may be lagging rather than leading in their design approaches, as proposed by Dumas and Mintzberg (1989, 40). As one highly experienced industrial designer underlined during my fieldwork: "It is first when they see that this goes in the wrong direction that they come to the designer." One manager stated that "our use of designers is very product-related and related to one product."[17] This seems to fit to the *ad hoc*, incremental, and perhaps reactive or mixed innovation orientation found by previous research in various established organizations (Burns and Stalker, 1961/1994; Henderson and Clark, 1990).

It is never easy to break new ground. Extending theorizing by Henderson and Clark (1990), I suggest we may examine "architectural innovation" at the relational and expressive levels in an industrial design and business enterprise context. Interestingly, bringing design to business organizations may open up a broader human-centered approach (Heskett, 2002). This includes designing in relation to the broader scope of real use and interaction experiences (Moggridge, 2007). As already hinted at by Philip Kotler (1973–1974, 48) long ago:

> One of the most important recent advances in business thinking is the recognition that people, in their purchase decision-making, respond to more than simply the *tangible product* or service being offered. The tangible product—a pair of shoes, a refrigerator, a haircut, or a meal—is only a small part of the total consumption package. Buyers respond to the *total product*. It includes the services, warranties, packaging, advertising, financing, pleasantries, images, and other features that accompany the product.

The French-American design pioneer Raymond Loewy understood this broader design-scope early on in his passionate work for American corporations. However, he created mythical objects by also streamlining the tangibles—from jukeboxes, Greyhound buses,

Table 5.4
Preliminary sketching of designing relations — with who and what?*

Design/Business Relations		Industrial Designing Concerns What?		
		Enterprise products and technology processes	Character and image-building of augmented products and services	Business concept creation or other capabilities for innovation
Designing Relations — what qualities?	Core competent insiders	Tendency towards focusing technical resources and existing development methods (Henderson and Clark, 1990).	Possible tendency of distinctive competence (Selznick, 1957), or alternatively neglected? (Kotler and Rath, 1984; Dumas, 1993; Olins, 1989; Pilditch, 1990).	Possible tendency towards valuable rare resources (Barney, 1997), or 'integrate what is not good enough' (Christensen et al, 2004), or alternately inadequacy? (Selznick, 1957).
	Mobile specialists	Possible tendency of relations with crossover but 'silent' industrial design consultants (Sparke, 1983).	Possible tendency of *ad hoc* outsourcing to advertising or other design agencies (Rand, 1993; Pilditch, 1990).	Not much studied.

*Source: Based on Jevnaker (2009)

car bodies, to Lucky Strike cigarette packages—many of which shaped our current impression of the 1950s American Dream (Trétiack, 1999). In short, this concerns design reconfiguring capacities and the dynamic aspect of value creation within the business of relationships, which depends on the actors concerned, their ability to connect (Ford et. al., 1998), work together, or enable a value-creating practice that cannot be fully anticipated (Normann and Ramirez, 1998). This is an important "fusion field," which may also expand the meaning and value of design into the possible strategic domain of innovations, says Larry Keeley, president of the innovation-oriented design consultancy Doblin Group in Chicago. Yet he admits that designers are still "almost never" on the boards of American corporations,[18] which suggests that we need to explore design from other angles than traditional corporate governance.

How then can enterprises expand with new or unfamiliar approaches that are emanating at least partly from outside the business firm's inherited resources or cumulative strategies and, furthermore, involve relatively uncommon dynamics? Previous and contemporary research and my own initial conversations with company management and designers suggest that this points to a fundamental problem in design/business relations.[19] Gaining insight into design-creation in connection to a variety of business enterprises that were *collaborating recurrently* with partly independent and externally working industrial designers, I propose to extend our orientation beyond a firm-centric view. As previously discovered, the dynamics of industrial design-making turned out to unfold through specific relations with somewhat rare but still mobile experts; this was puzzling (Jevnaker, 1997). How to understand designer relations within an expanded management framework is demonstrated in Table 5.4. In line with the foregoing descriptions, there appear to be gray or even white areas of design/business relations that were not much theorized in existing literature.

The position of allied designers "at a distance" (Aldersey-Williams, 1996) of firms—yet becoming sufficiently familiar[20] with their core competencies (Prahalad and Hamel, 1990)—offers an interesting entry point from which to understand not merely what dynamic capabilities of firms exist (Eisenhardt and Martin, 2000), but how they are constituted, expanded, and enabled. Firms tend to have biased information of user needs (von Hippel, 1988) and master only parts of the innovation process (Tidd et al., 1997/2005, 79). Previous research into product development teams suggests that teams may be too narrowly specialized or inward looking, and self-referential community practices may co-exist even in the cross-disciplinary product development processes (Henderson and Clark, 1990; Svengren, 1998). Jones (2002) claims that organizations still only pay lip service to user needs and desires. As noted by Philip Kotler (1973–1974, 48), "Men of business tend to be practical and functional in their thinking; if they were poetic they probably would not be businessmen. Therefore they have neglected the aesthetic factor in consumption."

In contrast, transdisciplinary and experienced designers may see the not-yet-embodied product or service from *multiple* possible angles,[21] which can leave room for a dialogue—not only between "what is desired and what can be realized" (Lawson 1990/2006, 272) but exploring *with* others when turning conventional ideas on their heads or probing ideas used elsewhere. During my fieldwork, practitioners gave telling examples of how collaboration with external industrial designers had created new product and service architecture that could meet more sophisticated needs and entice even the pragmatic industrial buyer. One example is the telecommunication company NERA's experience when exhibiting the company's redesigned satellite transceivers for a fair in Germany:

> The product had major new technology embodied but what was evoking a triggering interest was the smart new design, which also had significant use installation benefits providing a snap-on solution inspired by the industrial design consultant's long-term work for Rottefella (source: conversations with both industrial designer and former CEO of Nera, Spring, 1996).

Rottefella is the world leader in nordic bindings (for skiing).[22] This example illuminates what can be gained by relationships with hands-on designers—often termed "creative cross-pollination"—that unfolds even within more technically-oriented product innovations, when ideas move across industries and product categories. Previous literature suggests that product development and marketing efforts tend to lack such fresh reconfiguring and expressive coordination of their resources and activities in their various communicative contexts, and firms often have problems with making their mission visible and updated (Blaich, 1993; Olins, 1989). More often than not, firms fail to build unique products (Cooper, 1993) or create sufficient attraction forces among otherwise fragmented resources (Hedberg et al., 1997). Although identity- and brand-building are not new (Keller, 2003), ample evidence suggests that there is a lack of coordination between the firm's and its partner's various input-related activities and their output-related marketing, communication, and customer relations. In particular, visual and other sensory markers and symbols are neglected or misused,[23] which appear to relate to the lack of skilled marketing aesthetics (Schmitt and Simonson, 1997) as well as the lack of managing or integrating design issues (Olins, 1989; Blaich, 1993; Svengren, 1998).

This is a paradox in our highly visual and knowledge-intensive economy. On one hand, there is a rich supply of specialized resources in factor markets and networks that the firm and its collaborative partners seek to mobilize and combine in new or more efficient ways (Hedberg et al., 1997). On the other hand, products, services, messages, and brand promises are offered in product markets and networks through a plethora of marketing and customer-focused activities (Keller, 2003).[24] Networking processes hold or fail to hold the arrangement of associated elements in place, as pointed out by Ford et al. (1998).

The missing links accord to what network sociologist Burt (1992) calls "structural holes," which can offer opportunities for entrepreneurial linking. A production facilitator, a broker, or another connecting body can create value by fostering enriched activity-links, which again may affect resource-ties and actor bonds—to use the terminology developed by industrial marketing purchase research on business relationships. However, this dynamic coordination often relates to "non-tradable" or less tradable assets, warns economist David Teece (2003) in a conceptual paper. How then can some form of unifying attraction or common engagement be created? One major conclusion in previous research on business relations is "that the way a company creates economic value is to a large extent dependent on its relationships" (Ford et al., 1998, 261).

Yet potential strategic action within the frames of business relationships regarding those between designers and their clients is not sufficiently delineated. Previous network research focuses on issues such as trust and relational norms, investments, adaptations, and learning (Pettigrew and Fenton, 2000; Ford et al., 1998). The creative combination and synchronization of the creativity-based and expressive side of business are seldom sufficiently delineated. This is a mixed-motive situation. The current exchange process between, for example, new technology providers and marketing people is not only about cooperation. It involves working with other specialists, managers, and supply companies, but it also involves working against them, through them, and often in spite of them (Ford et al., 1998). How this actually happens and can be understood must be taken out of the shadow of the mystery of creative relationships or secret interactions behind the scenes.

Just any designing will not do; it needs relevance and creative leverage, i.e., to be capable of advancing the actual business and its stakeholders to a point where a distinct but also moving performance of offerings can be enjoyed. The field material suggests that design is more than creatively staging something novel. Perhaps even more crucial are the efforts to find ways to reinvent and improve a variety of users' real-life experiences. My aim here is to identify and delineate how this multifaceted dynamic capability is constituted through design/business relations.

Strategic Gains Identified

As introduced, industrial design is interdisciplinary, often tacitly emerging and involves multiple interfaces, trade-offs, and layers (Heskett, 1980, 2002). How do enterprises gain a dynamic capability in this creativity-based and not well understood field through their design-supply relations? Based on the five SME design/business cases, I found seven elements, each of which made a distinct contribution to the companies' product innovation and commercialization processes, though to varying degrees. Some design/business relationships exploited only a few elements; others made design relevant to ever-larger audiences so that design became more or less suffused in the firm's task environment. The findings are elaborated more fully elsewhere[25] so I will only briefly summarize the seven elements in the following section.

Dynamic capability gains

Contrary to seeing design as a "creative flair" to be bought as part of marketing late in a generic value chain (Porter, 1985), all five cases told a rich story of more specific paths of innovation over time (Mowery and Rosenberg, 1998). Interestingly, partly independent designers at work with corporate developers, managers, and others in intensive interaction around new product designs concretized new promising paths for the here-and-now as well as future work. Design in these companies often started small, but over time, designers and some entrepreneurial business collaborators became strategic in conceiving, assembling, and making sense of the new or redesigned products. As in core product-innovation projects when new crossroads of such paths are created (Håkansson and Waluszewski, 1999), there were possibilities to find new combinations (Schumpeter, 1928), or in fact, co-create them. Designing emerged as both separate and joint collaborative endeavors encompassing multiple stages of the product creation process, some of which revealed a high intensity of interaction to assemble new and more profitable products for commercialization (Belliveau et al., 2003). The parties typically needed to actually work together intensely over periods[26] to make design tailor-made and valuable to the particular enterprises, their settings, and stakeholders. The elements gained, found in these interactive processes, are summarized in Table 5.5 and elaborated below.

Reconfiguring-and-Mediation Gains

Designers were used in all five cases to come up with new ideas and reconfigure existing concepts. The reinvented or reconfigured concepts were made visible and observable mainly through prototypes (3D and digital) together with associated sketches, renderings, instructive and explanatory comments on drawings, etc. Interviews with development and management teams repeatedly told the same kind of story. The mediation by design created "shared space" (Schrage, 2000; Weick, 1979) for constructive probe-and-learn through which development teams gained visible experience of what they were constructing. To see how a new product model functions, for example, fosters further scrutinize-and-improve activities between designers and their collaborators from technology, marketing, project management, corporate directors, and other stakeholders. In short, it helped illuminate experimentation as well as implementation.

Opportunity Foresight Gains

In all five cases, but to a different degree, designers also provided new, alternative thinking about products and their uses that opened up new markets, new customer relationships, or set new standards in existing ones (Jevnaker, 1995). For example, the two furniture-makers gained access to new opportunities via the independent design group, "Balans," and its alternative sitting-concept that eventually put dynamic ergonomics on the agenda within the Nordic furniture industry and beyond (Jevnaker, 1993, 1995; Cranz, 1998, 170 ff.). Designer Peter Opsvik and his collaborators were especially significant in transforming this ergonomic-design experimentation into a more coherent innovative product/user philosophy that could be realized in office furniture and children's chairs, and expressed to customers and dealers (Jevnaker, 2005).

Table 5.5
Dynamic capability gains of design relations identified from
five Norwegian/Scandinavian product-based firms*

Component capability gains of design	Characteristic design processes
Reconfiguring and mediation gains	Visualizing and reassembly.
Opportunity foresight gains	Empathic designing for users and imagining user futures.
Creative integrity gains	Providing new ideas and alternative paths while also mobilizing knowledge of existing or previous paths.
Scope gains	Enhancing an attractive coherence of product character, product support, marketing communication, and stakeholder networking through visual coordination.
Knowledge expressive gains	Making sense of new designs through creative dialogues, analogies, storytelling, use of signs, and symbols.
Replicate dynamic innovation gains	Staging replicate dynamics of resources and activities.
Credible reputation gains	Fostering and assembling reputational assets (awards, media coverage, design-signatures, etc.).

* Source: Jevnaker, 2006

Creative Integrity Gains

Designers in these enterprises proposed ideas that did not all end at the ideation stage, which often happens in corporate creativity processes (Robinson and Stern, 1997). Rather, ideas were adopted, projected, edited, tested, transformed or modified, improved, and refined within both a close and also a wider network of product design and development relationships, where ideas "rubbed against" each other and could enable new solutions (Leonard-Barton, 1995, 89). Briefly, design was creatively integrated. New product designs were also eventually made commercially viable through close collaboration with the producer's respective marketing networks. For example, Stokke, with new-design models and their special philosophy, and not to forget, with assistance by some creative partners, has been able to establish entirely new international networks of committed dealers in Germany, the Netherlands, and elsewhere.

Scope Gains

In some of the enterprises, efforts were made to enhance the basic new or reconfigured products with appropriate package, marketing material, internal and external communication, and identity-building visual profiles, whereas this broader scope for design was *underexplored* in other companies. Design-oriented connections were also made to a varying degree with external experts, suppliers, dealers, customers, investors, and other stakeholders that in some cases eventually enacted a dynamic community for co-creating and appreciating those innovative efforts that could lead to value in a broad sense, i.e., both commercial and well-being. The "packaged" products and broadened design thinking could foster and enrich many relationships, even internationally. These scope gains helped leverage the new products to deliver value within the firms' target markets, albeit liabilities of newness were also observed. Thus certain stamina and replication efforts were needed over time to accumulate the desirable scope.

Knowledge Expressive Gains

When providing new design ideas and models, some of the design teams took great effort in finding the right arguments (in Greek: *inventio*) and formulating them (*elucito*) in an appropriate "true" persuasive way that made sense. The designers, inventors, and creative managers adopted metaphoric analogies such as sitting "in balance" as a small child, as a horse-rider, etc. This verbal-expressive ordering typically followed the visual-expressive one and was part of a design-related sense-making far beyond a top-down image-building. For example, the key terms "balans" and "movement and variation" were not planned *a priori*. Rather the vital words emerged while refining and talking vividly around prototypes and problematic product-human interfaces (Jevnaker, 2005).

Replicate Innovation Gains

Several factors influenced innovation processes in these firms, as pointed out in the previous literature (Burgelman and Sayles, 1986; Tidd et al., 1997/2005). Yet designers and design processes—including some entrepreneurial collaborators—were significant in mobilizing, recombining, and transforming manifold resources and activities into a smaller number of critical ones that could express an attractive competent approach that made sense to stakeholders. As also found by Karl Weick (2001, 68) initial small steps can become "stabilized into repetitive sequences that then become a new emergent structure" such as at Tomra, which, following the designer's initiative, adopted a modularity principle as a design rule (for its recycling machines' development), which has facilitated an innovation platform with reduced uncertainty.

Credible Reputation Gains

All five enterprises and their partly independent designers were granted several design awards in Norway and/or internationally for their new or reconfigured products embodying new knowledge and meaning about the product's user benefits and attractiveness. Supporting processes by managers, designers, or other ambassadors in even a larger network (e.g., of physiotherapists), probably also helped to build this credible reputation. Numerous articles in the national and international press covered the Balans group[27] and their designs for HÅG and Stokke. And designer Peter Opsvik's follow-up product creations have repeatedly received awards and are also exhibited internationally. The design-inspired exploration and philosophizing that continued for more than three decades in and around HÅG and Stokke, and ongoing even longer among some notable designers and an inventor, seemed to also inspire some younger design groups. For example, K8 Industridesign, and later Eker Design, working with Stokke-people and Formel Industridesign, at work with HÅG, have contributed to further design innovation that has recently lead to important international awards and much media coverage—for Stokke's Xplory stroller (launched 2003) and HÅG's Sideways chair (launched 2008). Interestingly, the younger design groups, in close collaboration with corporate teams, have innovated by attending to the active user's (or better, user-to-user) physical movement-and-variation *as well as* human interaction needs—when sitting in meeting chairs or strolling around. Also, the Dutch design group npk design and its work for Hamax has received several awards and attention internationally for new bicycle accessories, e.g., reclining bike seats for sleeping children (Jevnaker, 1995, 2009).

Briefly summarizing this section, I have stated that dynamic capability in design consists of a set of processual elements ranging from mediation/reconfiguring of resources and activities to evoking reputation and a corporate credibility. These elements were all potentially strategic since they honed an often overlooked user need (Norman, 1988), created unique offerings (Cooper, 1993), expressed innovative architecture (Henderson and Clark, 1990; Kay, 1993), and fostered beneficial reputation (Fombrun, 1996). In accordance with criteria for strategic capabilities within evolutionary economics (but moving beyond the firm-centric tendencies) (Teece, 1998) and resource-based theory (Barney, 1997), the design/business relationships also encompassed "difficult to replicate" expertise (Teece, 1998),[28] since ideas and possibilities often emerged through an intricate blend of personalized imagination or know-how and joint activities within highly interactive relationships. It was thus sometimes difficult to judge which party contributed what in the design development process, but every manager interviewed acknowledged the significant inputs from, and constructive interplay with, designers.

All of the above elements were gained within industrial design relations, but they were achieved to different degrees. Yet all lead to at least temporary strategic advantages for the firms involved, according to management. Gemser and Leenders (2001) found similar impacts of design innovation within the product development process investigating a Dutch sample of manufacturing firms in two industries (home furniture and precision instruments).

Taken together, the seven elements constitute a partly visible and partly hidden treasure, contributing beyond the visible form of new product offerings. The term "hidden treasure" does not necessarily refer to something mystical. Rather, it is a metaphor that can illuminate the potential richness of collaborative design/business efforts including designing experiences, models in use, and creative encounters of contacts and alliances that were accumulating in the shadow of the respective design and business development processes.[29]

Discussion

Kao (1996) reminds us of the need to build and secure a place, or "hot zone," to nurture disciplined creativity at work. Yet this study shows how design sketches, prototypes, or models also need to be exposed and expressed to selective target customers for creative interaction and for commercial reasons. In the five enterprises, communicating new designs evoked an interest in business-to-business networks, but as pinpointed by one product development manager, sustained efforts are often needed to sort out, test, and improve possible technical weaknesses—before triggering too much demand and delivery. This indicates a complex *temporality* in designing innovation that can be staged with more or less practical wisdom—and I found that both creative dialectic and friction occurs. According to industrial designer Wolfram Peters from Dutch consultancy npk design:

> What was quite difficult at XX [a firm] sometimes was the commitment of the production team. It is not easy…they gave the idea … for them it was quite new to work with external people. They had done all of that job many years themselves, and then it is not easy to work such a big project with externality (interview December 22, 1994).

In fact, people from diverse disciplines and functions can have continued problems to fully share or fuse their views. Yet people can be inspired or creatively coordinated to perform well. This study suggests that design can become a mediating and transforming force, not merely recombining (Schumpeter, 1928; Kogut and Zander, 1992) existing resources with subtle new ones, but transfiguring them into new offerings and innovative experiences. Grounded in firsthand accounts of the companies' design-related experiences, I propose that design can build a platform for further engagement that may develop new possibilities for enterprise. This new understanding may bring us toward a more dynamic framework for how design partners can contribute strategically to a particular business and its networks.

The present study illuminates how even "design-illiterate" firms (Kotler and Rath, 1984) can take part in new ideas and designs. To take advantage of the meeting of new and old ideas or know-how, the repeated constructive interplay within mutually creative design/business relationships seems significant, and leads to what we may call relational design-making or just design alliance. The parties experiment and discuss within the frames of productive relationships valuing "thick" design/business experiences and their spillovers. In all five enterprises, this also implied creative breakings—and surprising results—when designers and some entrepreneurial managers strived to create alternative methods and enhance coherence of "the whole product experience," i.e., of the firm's product architecture, use interfaces, or how this was exposed and communicated. In sum, design/business relations can invite not merely some attractive visual renderings, but enriched perspectives of what the enterprise and its networks actually have to offer.

This seems important within global markets when product or service concepts need to be exposed and literally sold in persuasive ways—sometimes before any physical industrial products or system service solutions are actually made. Moreover, if climbing quality ladders is crucial, as often is the case in industrial markets and when communicating peer-to-peer with complex product services, this study suggests that productive design/business relations need to be sustained, at least temporarily, as concerted innovation action. Concerted action among diverse design/business experts, crossing previous boundaries, can be found even in large resourceful corporations such as Novo Nordisk (insulin-pens), LM Ericsson (mobile phones), Ingersoll-Rand (construction tools), and IBM (creation of its previous Thinkpad PCs) (Bruce and Jevnaker, 1998). This accords to recent claims within network marketing research (Möller and Halinen, 1999), although design relations are hitherto not much explored.

How then was this creative and concerted action actually sustained (or not)? What I find striking, but also easy to overlook, is how the experienced designers studied constantly engaged-in innovation-oriented activities everyday—in what economists would call micro-level experiments—which were not always commissioned but which nevertheless could benefit their business clients. This seemed to foster a mixed sensibility that is both self-reflective (Schön, 1983) *and* productively creative. I suggest that the deep pleasure of these micro experiments, including little innovations and "small d" designed experiences (Kelley, 2001, 44, 217), may help the designers to sustain their passion and abilities for constantly improving products—even embracing more ambiguous latent or unarticulated user needs—while also being aware of the dilemma of constantly reconfiguring new products for an affluent world.[30] In fact, some of the designers and also some of their corporate management collaborators were highly articulate about making "something more," for example, more sustainable products. They spoke about meeting both significant end user needs and, perhaps even as challenging, effectively communicating the new concepts throughout the marketing channels and in connection with other kinds of specialists.

Figure 5.1
Children on the move with Hamax's
bicycle children's seat, designed by
npk design
Credit: Hamax

Figure 5.2
Tomra invented the first system for automatic
recognition of container types. This is their
reverse vending system for deposit return for
recycled beverage containers.
Credit: Tomra Systems

Figure 5.3
Stokke Xplory, designed by K8 industrial
design, developed with Eker design and
Stokke.
Credit: Stokke

In these cases, design innovation, included the sensing of and interaction with tangibles, retained their significance for design development and marketing efforts, in contradiction to recent theorizing that attends mainly to intangibles (Barney, 1997) or invisible assets (Itami, 1987). Hence, I would rather draw attention to the interesting dynamic between tangibles and intangibles, which is an aspect of all aesthetic stage-setting, but seemed especially critical to designing viable innovations. This tangible/intangible double aspect was important already in the fuzzy early efforts, when teams were quickly building unfinished prototypes to imagine and test new user experiences. Even at this early stage, the tangible/intangible dynamic was probably essential to influencing customers and users. Recall the simplified and salient solution to an otherwise complex problem of putting bottles in the right manner into a high tech recycling machine, or being able to sit with some frequent small movement in a modern office chair—due to rocking wheels and knee support (although not yet being elderly). Or consider conveniently letting your kid fall to sleep in Hamax bicycle seats for children during daily commutes on bikes (common in several European cities).

In these cases, a combination of highly creative, partly independent design experts and their intensive interplay and collaboration over time with several corporate development and marketing groups created a new and attractive coherence of tangibles and intangibles. This way of innovating and advancing practice does not seem to be captured by the current literature on "communities of practice" (Wenger et al., 2002).

Conclusion and Implications

As expected, industrial design consists of visualizing matters and meaning, but there is more to it than an aesthetic ordering within otherwise often rough industrial contexts. Intelligent designers' creative focusing[31] and expressions regarding visuals can help multidisciplinary teams build unique value propositions for the customer and some sensory integrity for firm offerings, thus reaching beyond fragmented resources and activities. This was experienced in all five enterprises studied, though to different degrees. The case evidence also suggest that industrial designers' constant scanning and way of recombining ideas from multiple sources (see also Hargadon, 1998) can expand the dynamic capabilities of enterprises (and design groups), thus escaping potential "traps of specialization" and preferred ways of problem-solving and interpretation in organizations (Knudsen, 2003; Dougherty, 1992; Leonard-Barton, 1995).

However, experienced and creative design is not merely correcting previous organizational narrowness. Rather, intelligent industrial designing may contribute to—or actually create—the expressive character and architecture of the augmented products and service spaces. Industrial design is typically a fungible expertise and may help connect the relevant products[32] as well as eventually foster an improved profile or integrity for the enterprise (Olins, 1989). As identified in the five cases, and also found elsewhere,[33] this is highly challenging, but may be positively experienced when it occurs, such as at HÅG, which appears to have become reborn. At best, perhaps, designing weaves resources and activities into unifying or engaging themes, and links with—or creates—deeper values that mobilize networks and relationships encompassing more than one single organization. This sets the scene for further beneficial action and leveraged expertise (Leonard-Barton, 1995) that can accumulate into a dynamic value-creating capability or underlying "hidden treasure" (Jevnaker, 1995, 1998a). Ample evidence suggests that design relationships provide new mediating "glue" and link the enterprise and its product and market development groups to innovative themes (see Svengren, 1998; Freeze, 1998; Jevnaker, 1998b). Although not an easy process, industrial design-making may contribute to our understanding, more generally, of the art of continuously creating new imagination and energy around innovation and renewal efforts of networking firms. Creating an engaging design seems to contribute not merely to increased sales in the short term, but by providing something to flock around and advance for the longer term.

The cases clearly indicate that this dynamic is created over time; initial projects may not be successful. It is thus worth noticing how designers and their collaborators actually moved new ideas and product innovations forward from often fairly weak initial situations. The new concepts or specific design approaches were seldom reflected in the firms' strategies at the outset, but several of the firms were striving for economic survival or recovery (Jevnaker, 2000a). Only a few of these companies appeared a *priori* especially design-competent (Kristensen, 1998); industrial design actually had to establish its relevance perpetually to dominant competence groups and management. A consistent finding in comparison to other internationally competing firms is that creative incorporation of design in business can take considerable time and effort and tends to happen through somewhat fragile personal and collaborative efforts (see Freeze, 1998; Svengren, 1998; Jevnaker and Bruce, 1999). Thus design becomes strategic within design/business relationships in a variety of contexts (Bruce and Jevnaker, 1998), and indeed, recurrently so when design/business relations enable serial innovations such as happened at both Tomra and HÅG (Jevnaker, 1995, 2000a, 2009).

Practical Implications

An important implication for design management and research is to include and further explore actual experiences of developing new imaginative perspectives such as those brought forward by industrial design alliances. Moreover, creative and reputation-winning design capabilities typically need to be co-created and experienced over time, while also repeatedly expressed and vividly explained by live agents. Indeed, both design and enterprise seemed to become potentially recreated at every presenting. This can help management to start seeing design as a possible *strategic interface* rather than merely an operational issue. From a management perspective—familiar with the time and effort needed in asset and brand building—it is perhaps most effective to expand and extend design innovation in order to capture broader scope gains and propel accumulation of assets with increasing returns such as reputation.

I started this chapter by pointing to the diffuse and little-researched design management background. How then can mobile specialist designers still become important to business? I propose that this is not confined to product development in a narrow traditional sense, although specialized industrial design relations have left a number of interesting product models, prototypes, or other cues over time in product innovation (Heskett, 1980, 2002; Flinchum; 1997). Interestingly, Alan South,[34] former head of IDEO Europe, recently reflected:[35]

> Design thinking and design methods can be used not just to do great communications, or great products, but also to design experiences or to design businesses using exactly the same methods.

This needs further research and it may fruitfully be done in between new as well as established enterprises and design actions, because challenges, tensions, and also creative transgressions appear to unfold in the elusive in-between as found in the present study. Furthermore, we need more research about new enterprises using the infrastructure of the internet and an increasing variety of media and engaged activists in relation to their design action, because this is a difference *in kind*, not just scale or scope. Throughout this chapter, I have sketched how even some established enterprises via their design/business alliances develop not merely architectural product innovations (Henderson and Clark, 1990) or new market offerings, but broader capacities, or in fact, a dynamic collaboration for a continuous building of sustainable resource advantages and engagements. Since this is done with a dramaturgical sensibility as observed at the two enterprises who originally were furniture-makers, but now are delivering active seating solutions and other "movement"-oriented products in the context of recently restructured business enterprises, we may call this strategy an ongoing way-finding as well as "stage-setting," keeping in mind that the metaphor should not be stretched too far (expecting to stage every customer experience). For management it is important to notice that the actual recurrent stage-setting via design/business relations was, in fact, elaborated and tested through constant inquiry modes and empathic immersion in order to improve and dynamically fit the product to its manifold use and market context. Thus, this concerns an expanded exploration, beyond the single product or project level, but simultaneously also a real world "implementation" or realizing of new designs that "go on forever," pinpointed MetaDesign's Holger Volland.[36]

In conclusion, if we want to understand how expressive resource-advantage actually is generated, we need to recognize both creative specialist talents at work *and* the highly interactive creation efforts enabled through particular design/business relationships, which became significant for the five companies' design developments and indeed, how their new innovating and industrial marketing were actually constructed. This relational design-based creation of new paths for the enterprise emerged over time by entrepreneurial or design-championing initiatives, often from both parties (Jevnaker, 2000b). Hence interacting parties constituted the new paths for both design groups and their corporate clients.

This chapter has explored and expanded the relational perspective between business and design by identifying how designers and their collaborating parties—through some fundamental capabilities gains and relational dynamics—are actually shaping what the organizations have to offer and express. This seems significant since design talks to multiple audiences (Gorb, 1988). Interestingly, the particular design/business collaborations explored recurrently both helped create and communicate the new or unfamiliar product/service possibilities and they engaged in the broader philosophizing. And it is precisely this *expanded* in-between design mediating that seemed to foster access to ways of breaking away, as well as sustaining potentially value-creating innovation in the enterprise networks. The cases reveal that there are varied practices, but at best, designers interacting with managers embedded in strategic action may develop "something more."

Notes

1. This is grounded in a firsthand account from a previous Innovation Master of Science student at the Norwegian School of Management, who worked in an ICT-business in London at the time of our conversation (April 16, 2006). It resonates with other of my field encounters including numerous design/business learning forums from 1988 onward (Jevnaker, 1996, 2009).

2. This is based on Jevnaker (2009).

3. See Bruce and Docherty (1993), Freeze (1998), Bruce and Jevnaker (1998).

4. See the presentation and personal conversation with Lars Engman, IKEA's Design Manager, at the Design Day in Oslo, November 25, 2004. See also the 2006 *BusinessWeek*-Boston Consulting Group survey where IKEA is ranked nineteen among the top twenty-five companies (*BusinessWeek* magazine issue April 24, 2006, see also http://www.businessweek.com/magazine/toc/06_17/B3981magazine.htm, accessed April 23, 2006).

5. During my fieldwork, and a previous comparative study (of 12 furniture-makers), it turned out that—even in a form-intensive industry such as furniture—many firms were little aware of the expertise of industrial designers (Jevnaker, 1993, 1996). For example, HÅG had not used professional designers before the collaboration with designer Peter Opsvik beginning in 1973, according to the former CEO and key owner. This slight awareness of professional design has also been found by others (Sparke, 1983, 1986; Kotler and Rath, 1984).

6. See Jevnaker (1995, 1996, 2000a, 2000b, 2009).

7. Relatively young disciplines, like industrial design and interaction design, are not only interdisciplinary (covering more than one area of study) but appear to be transdisciplinary, i.e., moving in areas across and beyond established disciplines (Jevnaker, 2008). For illustrations, see Heskett (1980, 2002) and Moggridge (2007).

8. Design historians also highlight redesign as fundamental in designing (Michl, 2002, but still someone has to figure out the difficult question of what to keep—and perhaps even strengthen—and what to take away, which is a basic challenge of creative combinations and reconfiguring (Jevnaker, 2001). This relates to a fundamental dilemma recognized within practical knowledge philosophy (Molander, 1992).

9. This notion is grounded in the present study and coined in a previous article (Jevnaker, 2000c) but resonates with other research. For a further exposition, see Donald Norman's 2004 book that focuses on emotional design.

10. This also accords to what Schön (1983) mentions in relation to problem setting.

11. Source: Bruce Nussbaum's Design Blog, February 2, 2006, *BusinessWeek* online (http://www.businessweek.com/innovate/NussbaumOnDesign/archives/davos_design/index.html, accessed February 17, 2006).

12. See my conversations with Tim Brown in London (May, 1997) and also in Ålesund (May, 2000); Tim Brown and Ingelise Nielsen were also present in the author's workshop on Design Innovation during the first Innotown conference.

13. Interestingly enough, some scholars re-examine the dynamics and intricacies of identity building that can reorient us towards what particular resources, design and mediation can do in organizations. For example, Hatch and Schultz (2004) debate the complexities of brand communicating and identity-construction as an ongoing practice. This is not only about the prescriptive views on how to succeed in the reputation, fame, and visibility games of business (Fombrun, 1996; Fombrun and van Riel, 2004), but explores issues that are often taken for granted.

14. See a further exposition in Jevnaker (2009); see also Thackara (2005, 3 ff.).

15. For example, this emerged as a core theme in my long conversation with Anita Krohn Thrane, at BI Nydalen, February 22, 2006. Thrane is former managing director of Simula Innovation AS at Fornebu outside Oslo, and our conversation was focused on, and grounded in, her fresh on-going ideation and commercialization experiences at SIMULA Innovation and its research and business partners. For further validating, see also case-description of the technical product versus brand/ image-creation of Ericsson mobile phones in Svengren (1995).

16. This emerged recurrently in field encounters, e.g., in my long interviews with the Formel industrial designers, 26 August 2008, and also in my conversation with design consultant and industrial design professor Per Farstad at Design and Architecture Centre in Oslo, October 15, 2008. Industrial designers in Norway tend to be located outside of their client firms and thus commonly work from the "outside-in" in terms of their work relationships with business and other organizations (Jevnaker, 1995, 1996, 1997; Rismoen, 1998).

17. Source: My long focus group, February 20, 1991; see also Jevnaker, 1996, 268.

18. Source: My interview with Larry Keeley at Doblin, Chicago, May 27, 2003.

19. Previous literature suggests that managers, key developers, and designers can have difficulties with communicating and learning about each other's background knowledge, as well as the nature of their specific design and business expertise respectively (see Sparke, 1983; Dumas, 1993; Jevnaker, 1996).

20. This "familiarity knowledge" even by outside designers was identified early in my fieldwork; see focus group (fully recorded and transcribed discussions) among designers and corporate representatives from February 20, 1991 (Jevnaker, 1996).

21. I observed this in recurrent presentations by transdisciplinary designers such as industrial/interaction designer Birgitta Cappelen, co-founder of Interaction Design in Oslo, now Creuna. See her guest-lecture at Norwegian School of Management, October 11, 1999.

22. Rottefella's range of products covers cross-country, backcountry and telemark. Their military bindings are "preferred by NATO," according to their website (http://www.rottefella.com/english.cfm, accessed April 23, 2006).

23. This emerged in a presentation by Holger Volland, head of MetaDesign's Brand Communication, at the Norwegian Design Council's Business Day, Oslo, October 15, 2008.

24. With reference to marketing professor Philip Kotler, strategic brand management-author Kevin Keller (2003: 4) notes that competition within many markets now "…essentially takes place at the *product augmented* level because most firms can successfully build satisfactory products at the expected product level" (emphasis added).

25. See Jevnaker, 1998, 2000b, 2009.

26. Formel Industridesign recently worked intensively with HÅG—including letting some of HÅG's key construction suppliers spend days each week in the design studio for several months—when designing and developing the new Sideways chair. Source: my interviews with Formel industrial designers Alexander Borgenhov, Geir Eide, and Sigbjørn Windingstad and HÅG's current Vice President and R&D director Hilde Britt Mellbye and new design manager Anders Ramstad, at Formel and HÅG respectively, Oslo, August–September, 2008. Mellbye is also directing the research, design, and development of the new Scandinavian Business Seating (established autumn 2007 as a Nordic HÅG/RH/RBM Group of three branded manufacturers, from December 2008 named Scandinavian Business Seating). 27 The 'Balans' design group was not a fully integrated designer-group, but rather a temporary, loosely collaborating group of three designers, one inventor, and some companies eventually participating in various concerted efforts that became significant for alternative views on sitting (see Jevnaker, 1993; Cranz, 1998).

27. The Balans design group was not a fully integrated designer-group, but rather a temporarily, loosely collaborating group of three designers, one inventor, and some companies eventually participating in various concerted efforts that became significant for alternative views on sitting (see Jevnaker, 1993; also Cranz, 1998).

28. After a presentation by Berkeley professor David Teece at the Copenhagen Business School (September 2, 2003), he answered—after direct question by this author—that dynamic capabilities are built through internal resources (and he added) because of the need to know the many complexities involved as relates to the particular firm. The argument in this article is that dynamic capability-building for the enterprise may (also) be created or expanded through relationships with "external talents" over time. From a competitive advantage perspective, it is interesting to note that these long-term, innovating design/business relations are possible but tend to be rare, socially complex, and unique as all are genuine relationships (see Jevnaker, 2001, 2009). For the independent design-group, such collaborations may be challenging to "plan," finance and sustain over time. Whereas Peter Opsvik's studio has found ways to collaborate with a few selective enterprises for 30–40 years, the younger, cofounding designers of Formel, one of Norway's leading industrial design agencies have, after 12 years, decided to shut down in mid 2009 "when we are on top." Yet they do hope to continue their design/management work in other organizations (source: personal communication, March 2009), which illuminates design and designers on the move in-between organizations (Jevnaker, 2003, 2009).

29. See Jevnaker, 1993, 1995, 1996.

30. One of the designers, Peter Opsvik (b. 1939), particularly reflected on the ethical issues of designing and thus continuously facilitating a stream of new products, which might not be sustainable in either an environmental or economic sense.

31. IDEO's California-based co-founder David Kelley pinpoints "focused innovation" as the way IDEO design teams typically work. Source: Video from IDEO as recorded and presented by ABC Nightline in 1999 (see also Kelley, 2001).

32. The term product is here used in a broad, extended way as Kotler has suggested; see Keller, 2003, 4.

33. See Ericsson case as described by Svengren (1998).

34. Alan South has a BSc Engineering from the University of Bath, a DIC Product Engineering from Imperial College and a Master of Design from Royal College of Art in London. He joined IDEO in 1996 after 10 years at Cambridge Consultants, where he built and led the product design group (source: http://www.norskdesign.no/designdagen/2005/dbaFile11373.html, accessed January 24, 2006). South was head of IDEO Europe until Nov. 2006, when he became chief innovation officer at Solarcentury Ltd. (personal communication and LinkedIn).

35. Source: Author's recording (on MD) of Alan South's presentation to the Annual Design Day 2005 (Culture Church St Jacob, Oslo, December 5, 2005).

36. Presentation by the Berlin-based MetaDesign's Holger Volland, and personal conversation with him afterwards, when in Oslo, October 15, 2008.

References

Aldersey-Williams, Hugh. 1996. Design at a Distance: The New Hybrids. *Design Management Journal*, 7.2, 43–49.

Barney, Jay B. 1997. *Gaining and Sustaining Competitive Advantage*. Reading, MA: Addison-Wesley.

Belliveau, Paul, Abbie Griffin, and Stephen Somermeyer (eds.). 2003. *The PDMA ToolBook for New Product Development*. New York, NY: John Wiley & Sons.

Blaich, Robert with Janet Blaich. 1993. *Product Design and Corporate Strategy: Managing the Connection for Competitive Advantage*. New York, NY: McGraw-Hill.

Bruce, Margaret and Rachel Cooper. 1997. *Marketing and Design Management*. London, United Kingdom: Thompson Business Press.

Bruce, Margaret and Catherine Docherty. 1993. It's All in a Relationship: a comparative study of client-design consultant relationships. Design Studies, 14.4, 402–422.

Bruce, Margaret and Birgit H. Jevnaker (eds.). 1998. *Management of Design Alliances: Sustaining Competitive Advantage*. Chichester, United Kingdom: Wiley.

Bruce, Margaret and Barny Morris. 1998. A Comparative Study of Design Professionals. In Bruce, Margaret and Birgit H. Jevnaker (eds.), *Management of Design Alliances: Sustaining Competitive Advantage*. Chichester, United Kingdom: Wiley.

Burgelman, Robert and Leonard R. Sayles. 1986. *Inside Corporate Innovation*. New York, NY: The Free Press.

Burns, Tom and G.M. Stalker. 1961/1994. *The Management of Innovation*. Oxford, United Kingdom: Oxford University Press.

Burt, R.S. 1992. The Social Structure of Competition. In Nitin, Nohria and Robert G.E. Eccles (eds.), *Networks and Organizations: Structure, Form, and Action*. Boston, MA: Harvard Business School Press.

Cagan, J. and C.M. Vogel. 2002. *Creating Breakthrough Products: Innovation from Product Planning to Program Approval*. Upper Saddle River, New Jersey: Financial Times Prentice Hall.

Castells, Manuel. 2000. *The Rise of the Network Society*. Oxford, United Kingdom: Blackwell Publishers.

Christensen, Clayton M., Scott D. Anthony, Erik A. Roth. 2004. *Seeing What's Next: Using the Theories of Innovation to Predict Industry Change*. Boston, MA: Harvard Business School Press.

Cooper, Robert G. 1993. *Winning at New Products: Accelerating the Process from Idea to Launch*. Reading, MA: Addison-Wesley.

Cranz, Galen. 1998. *The Chair: rethinking culture, body, and design*. New York, NY: Norton.

Dorst, K. 1997. *Describing Design: a comparison of paradigms*. Rotterdam: Delft University of Technology. Ph.D.

Dougherty, Deborah. 1992. Interpretive barriers to successful product innovation in large firms. *Organization Science*, 3.2, 179–202.

Dumas, Angela. 1993. *The Effect of Management Structure and Organisational Process on Decisions in Industrial Design*. Ph.D. dissertation, London Business School.

Dumas, Angela and Henry Mintzberg. 1989. Managing design designing management. *Design Management Journal*, 1.1, 37–43.

Eisenhardt, Kathleen M. and Joan A. Martin. 2000. Dynamic Capabilities: What Are They? *Strategic Management Journal*, 21.10-11, 1105–1121.

Flinchum, Russell. 1997. Henry Dreyfuss, *Industrial Designer: the Man in the Brown Suit*. New York, NY: Rizolli International Publications.

Fombrun, Charles J. 1996. *Reputation: Realizing Value from the Corporate Image*. Cambridge, MA: Harvard Business School Press.

Fombrun, Charles J. and Cees van Riel. 2004. *Fame and Fortune: How Successful Companies Build Winning Reputations*. Upper Saddle River, NJ: Financial Times Prentice Hall.

Ford, David, Lars-Erik Gadde, Håkan Håkansson, Anders Lundgren, Ivan Snehota, Peter Turnbull, and David Wilson. 1998. *Managing Business Relationships*. Chichester, United Kingdom: Wiley.

Ford, David and R. McDowell. 1999. Managing Business Relationships by Analyzing the Effects and Value of Different Actions. *Industrial Marketing Management*, 28, 429–442.

Freeze, Karen with Earl Powell. 1998. Design Management Lessons from the Past: Henry Dreyfuss and American Business. In Bruce, Margaret and Birgit H. Jevnaker (eds.), *Management of Design Alliances. Sustaining Competitive Advantage*. Chichester, United Kingdom: Wiley, 205–215.

Gemser, Gerda and M.A.A.M. Leenders. 2001. How Integrating Design in the Product Development Process Impacts on Company Performance. *The Journal of Product Innovation Management*, 18.1, 28–38.

Gorb, Peter (ed.) with Eric Schneider. 1988. *Design Talks! London Business School Design Management Seminars*. London, United Kingdom: The Design Council.

Gorb, Peter (ed.). 1990. *Design Management. Papers from the London Business School, LBS Design Management Unit*. London, United Kingdom: Architecture Design and Technology Press.

Håkansson, Håkan and Alexandra Waluszewski. 1999. *Path-dependence: Restricting or Facilitating Technical Development. Paper submitted to the 15th Annual IMP Conference*. Dublin, Ireland, 2–4 September.

Håkansson, Håkan and Alexandra Waluszewski. 2001. *Co-evolution in Technnological Development: The role of friction. Paper presented at the 17th Annual IMP Conference*. Oslo, Norway, 9–11 September. Abstract with paper on CD in conference report. Sandvika, Norway: BI Norwegian School of Management.

Hamel, Gary. 2002. *Leading the Revolution: How to Thrive in Turbulent Times by Making Innovation a Way of Life*. Cambridge, MA: Harvard Business School Press.

Hamilton, Carl. 1994/2000. *Absolut Biography of a Bottle*. New York, NY: Texere.

Haraway, Donna. 2003. *Simians, Cyborgs, and Women: The Reinvention of Nature*. New York, NY: Routledge.

Hargadon, Andrew B. 1998. *Firms as Knowledge-Brokers: Lessons in Pursuing Continuous Innovation*. California Management Review, 40.3, 209–227.

Hart, Susan. 1995. Where we've been and where we're going in new product development research. In Bruce, Margaret and Wim G. Biemans (eds.), *Product development: Meeting the Challenge of the Design-Marketing Interface*. Chichester, United Kingdom: John Wiley & Sons, 15–42.

Hatch, Mary Jo and Majken Schultz. 2004. *Organizational Identity: A Reader (Oxford Management Readers)*. New York, NY: Oxford University Press.

Hedberg, Bo, Göran Dahlgren, Jörgen Hansson, and Nils-Göran Olve. 1997. *Virtual Organizations and Beyond: Discover Imaginary Systems*. Chichester, United Kingdom: Wiley.

Henderson, Rebecca and Kim B. Clark. 1990. Architectural Innovation: The Reconfiguration of Existing Product Technologies and the Failure of Established Firms. *Administrative Science Quarterly*, 35.1, 9–30.

Heskett, John. 1980. *Industrial Design*. London, United Kingdom: Thames and Hudson.

Heskett, John. 2002. *Toothpicks & Logos: Design in Everyday Life*. Oxford, United Kingdom: Oxford University Press.

Hitt, Michael A., Patricia Gorman Clifford, Robert D. Nixon, and Kevin P. Coyne (eds.). 1999. *Dynamic Strategic Resources: Development, Diffusion and Integration*. Chichester, United Kingdom: Wiley, 267–298.

Hunt, Shelby D. 2000. *A General Theory of Competition: Resources, Advantages, Productivity, Economic Growth*. Thousand Oaks, CA: Sage.

Itami, Hiroyuki with Thomas W. Roehl. 1987. *Mobilizing Invisible Assets*. Cambridge, MA: Harvard University Press.

Jevnaker, Birgit H. and Margaret Bruce. 1999. Design as a Strategic Alliance: Expanding the Creative Capability of the Firm. In Hitt, Michael et al. (eds.), *Dynamic Strategic Resources: Development, Diffusion and Integration*. Chichester, United Kingdom: Wiley, 267–298.

Jevnaker, Birgit Helene. 1993. Inaugurative Learning: Adapting a New Design Approach. *Design Studies*, 14.4, 379–401.

Jevnaker, Birgit Helene. 1995. *Den skjulte formuen. Industridesign som kreativ konkurransefaktor (The Hidden Treasure main empirical report)*. Report 36/95. Bergen, Norway: Foundation for Research in Economics and Business Administration (SNF), (in Norwegian).

Jevnaker, Birgit Helene. 1996. *Industridesign som kreativ konkurransefaktor: En forstudie (Industrial Design as a Competitive Factor)*. Report 54/96. Bergen, Norway: Foundation for Research in Economics and Business Administration (SNF), (in Norwegian).

Jevnaker; Birgit H. 1997. Competing through Mobile Design Expertise. In Eskelinen, Heikki (ed.), *Regional Specialization and Local Environment—Learning and Competitiveness*. Stockholm, Sweden: NordREFO.

Jevnaker, Birgit H. 1998a. Introduction. In Bruce, M. and Jevnaker, B.H. (eds), *Management of Design Alliances: Sustaining Competitive Advantage*. Chichester, United Kingdom: Wiley, 13–37.

Jevnaker, Birgit H. 1998b. Absorbing or Creating Design Ability: HÅG, HAMAX and TOMRA. In Bruce, Margaret and B.H. Jevnaker (eds.), *Management of Design Alliances: Sustaining Competitive Advantage*. Chichester, United Kingdom: Wiley, 107–135.

Jevnaker, Birgit H. 2000a. How Design Becomes Strategic. *Design Management Journal,* 11.1, 41–47.

Jevnaker, Birgit H. 2000b. Championing Design: Perspectives of Design Capabilities. *Design Management Journal Academic Review*, 1, 25–39.

Jevnaker, Birgit H. 2000c. Dynamikk mellom design og innovasjon i bedrifter. *Magma, Tidskrift for økonomi og ledelse,* 3.1, 21–39 (in Norwegian).

Jevnaker, Birgit H. 2001. Strategic Integration of Design and Innovation: Dilemmas of Design Expertise and Its Management. *International Journal of New Product Development & Innovation Management*, 3.2, 129–151.

Jevnaker, Birgit H. 2003. Exploring the Innovating Inbetween: Industrial Design as Boundary Work. *International Journal of New Product Development & Innovation Management*, 4.4, 339–358.

Jevnaker, Birgit Helene. 2005. Vita Activa: On Relationships between Design(ers) and Business. *Design Issues*, 21.3, 25–48.

Jevnaker, Birgit Helene. 2008. Corporate Design. In Donsbach, Wolfgang (ed.), *The International Encyclopedia of Communication, Vol. III*. Malden, MA: Blackwell, 1010–1014.

Jevnaker, Birgit Helene. 2009. *An Inquiry into Designer/Business Collaborations*. Oslo, Norway: Norwegian School of Management BI.

Jones, Tim. 2002. *Innovating at the Edge*. Oxford, United Kingdom: Butterworth-Heineman.

Kao, John. 1996. *Jamming: The Art and Discipline of Business Creativity*. New York, NY: Harper Collins.

Kay, John. 1993. *Foundations of Corporate Success: How business strategies add value*. Oxford, United Kingdom: Oxford University Press.

Keller, Kevin L. 2003. *Strategic Brand Management: Building, Measuring, and Managing Brand Equity*. Upper Saddle River, NJ: Prentice Hall.

Kelley, Tom. 2001. *The Art of Innovation: Lessons in Creativity from IDEO, America's Leading Design Firm*. New York, NY: Doubleday.

Knudsen, Christian. 2003. Pluralism, Scientific Progress, and the Structure of Organization Theory. In Tsoukas, Haridimos and Christian Knudsen (eds.), *The Oxford Handbook of Organization Theory: Meta-Theoretical Perspectives*. Oxford, United Kingdom: Oxford University Press, 262–286.

Kogut, Bruce and Udo Zander. 1992. Knowledge of the Firm, Combinative Capabilities, and the Replication of Technology. *Organization Science*, 3.4, 383–397.

Kotler, Philip. 1973–1974. Atmospherics as a Marketing Tool. *Journal of Retailing*, 49.4, 48–64.

Kotler, Philip and G. Alexander Rath. 1984. Design: a powerful but neglected strategic tool. *Journal of Business Strategy*, 5.2, 16–21.

Kristensen, Tore. 1998. The Contribution of Design to Business: A Competence-Based Perspective. In Bruce, Margaret and Jevnaker, Birgit H. (eds.), *Management of Design Alliances. Sustaining Competitive Advantage*. Chichester, United Kingdom: Wiley, 217–241.

Kunkel, Paul. 1997. *Apple Design: The Work of the Apple Industrial Design Group*. New York: Graphis.

Latour, Bruno. 2005. *Reassembling the Social: An Introduction to Actor-Network-Theory* (Clarendon Lectures in Management Studies). New York, NY: Oxford University Press.

Lawson, Bryan. 1990/2006. *How Designers Think*. London, United Kingdom: Butterworth Architecture.

Leonard-Barton, Dorothy. 1995. *Wellsprings of Knowledge*. Boston, MA: Harvard Business School Press.

Lipstadt, Hélène. 1997. "Natural overlap": Charles and Ray Eames and the Federal Government. In Albrecht, Donald (ed.), *The Work of Charles and Ray Eames: A Legacy of Invention*. New York, NY: Harry N. Abrams.

Lorenz, Christopher. 1986/1990. *The Design Dimension*. Oxford, United Kingdom: Basil Blackwell.

Michl, Jan. 2002. On Seeing Design as Redesign. An Exploration of a Neglected Problem in Design Education. *Scandinavian Journal of Design History*, 12, 7–23.

Moggridge, Bill. 2007. *Designing Interactions*. Cambridge, MA: The MIT Press.

Molander, Bengt. 1992. Tacit Knowledge and Silenced Knowledge: Fundamental Problems and Controversies. In Bo, Göranzon and M. Florin (eds.), *Skill and Education: Reflection and Experience*. London: Springer-Verlag, 9–31.

Mowery, David C. and Nathan Rosenberg. 1998. *Paths of Innovation: Technological Change in 20th Century America*. Cambridge, United Kingdom: Cambridge University Press.

Möller, Kristian K. and A. Halinen. 1999. Business relationships and Networks: Managerial Challenge of Network Era. *Industrial Marketing Management*, 28, 413–427.

Nonaka, Ikujiro and David J. Teece (eds.). 2001. *Managing Industrial Knowledge: Creation, Transfer and Utilization*. London, United Kingdom: Sage.

Norman, Donald A. 1988. *The Psychology of Everyday Things*. New York, NY: Basic Books.

Normann, Richard and Rafael Ramirez. 1998. *Designing Interactive Strategy: from Value Chain to Value Constellation*. Chichester, United Kingdom: Wiley.

Nussbaum, Bruce with Robert Berner and Diane Brady. 2005. Get Creative! How to build innovative companies. Special report. *BusinessWeek*, August 1, 2005.

Olins, Wally. 1989. *Corporate Identity: Making business strategy visible through design*. London, United Kingdom: Thames and Hudson.

Ouchi, William G. 1981. *Theory Z: How American Business Can Meet the Japanese Challenge*. Reading, MA: Addison-Wesley.

Pettigrew, Andrew and Evelyn Fenton. 2000. *Innovating New Forms of Organizing*. London, United Kingdom: Sage.

Pilditch, James. 1990. *I'll Be Over in the Morning: A Practical Guide to Winning Business in Other Countries*. London: Mercury.

Porter, Michael E. 1985. *Competitive Advantage: Creating and Sustaining Superior Performance*. New York, NY: Free Press.

Prahalad, C.K. and Gary Hamel. 1990. The Core Competence of the Corporation. *Harvard Business Review*, 68.3, 79–91.

Prahalad, C.K. and Venkat Ramaswamy. 2004. *The Future of Competition: Co-Creating Unique Value with Customers*. Cambridge, MA: Harvard Business School Press.

Rand, Paul. 1993. *Design, Form, and Chaos*. New Haven: Yale University Press.

Rismoen, Jon H. 1998. *Innføring av industridesign i småbedrifter (Introducing industrial design in small businesses)*. Trondheim: The Norwegian University of Science and Technology, (in Norwegian).

Robinson, Alan G. and Sam Stern. 1997. *Corporate Creativity: How Innovation and Improvement Actually Happen*. San Francisco, CA: Berret-Koehler.

Schmitt, Bernd and Alex Simonson. 1997. *Marketing Aesthetics. The Strategic Management of Brands, Identity, and Image*. New York, NY: Free Press.

Schrage, Michael. 2000. Serious Play: *How the World's Best Companies Simulate to Innovate*. Boston, MA: Harvard Business School Press.

Schumpeter, Joseph. 1928. The Instability of Capitalism. *The Economic Journal*, XXXVIII.151, 361–386.

Schön, Donald A. 1983. *The Reflective Practitioner*. New York, NY: Basic Books.

Schön, Donald A. 1988. *Designing: Rules, Types and Worlds*. Design Studies, 9.3, 181–190.

Selznick, Philip. 1957/1984. *Leadership in Administration: a sociological interpretation*. New York: Harper&Row.

Sparke, Penny. 1983. *Consultant Design: The History and Practice of the Designer in Industry*. London, United Kingdom: Pembridge Press.

Sparke, Penny. 1986. *An Introduction to Design & Culture in the Twentieth Century*. London, United Kingdom: Routledge.

Starbuck, William H. 1993. Keeping a Butterfly and an Elephant in a House of Cards: The Elements of Exceptional Success. *Journal of Management Studies*, 30.6, 885–921.

Strati, Antonio. 1999. *Organization and Aesthetics*. London, United Kingdom: Sage.

Svengren, Lisbeth. 1995. *Industriell design som strategisk ressurs. (Industrial design as a strategic resource.)* Lund, Sweden: Lund University Press (in Swedish).

Svengren, Lisbeth. 1998. Integrating Design as a Strategic Resource: The Case of Ericsson Mobile Communications. In Bruce, Margaret and Jevnaker, Birgit H. (eds.), *Management of Design Alliances. Sustaining Competitive Advantage.* Chichester, United Kingdom: Wiley, 159–178.

Teece, David J. 1998. Capturing Value from Knowledge Assets: The New Economy, Markets for Know-How, and Intangible Assets. *California Management Review*, 40.3, 55–79.

Teece, David J. 2003. *Explicating Dynamic Capabilities: Asset Selection, Coordination, and the Entrepreneurship in Strategic Management Theory.* Business and Public Policy Working Paper BPP-98. Berkeley, CA: University of California.

Teece, David J. and Gary Pisano. 1998. The Dynamic Capabilities of Firms: an introduction. In Dosi, Giovanni, David J. Teece and J. Chytrym (eds.), *Technology, Organization, and Competitiveness: Perspectives on Industrial and Corporate Change.* Oxford, United Kingdom: Oxford University Press.

Thackara, John. 2005. *In the Bubble: Designing in a Complex World.* Cambridge, MA: The MIT Press.

Tidd, Joe, John Bessant, and Keith Pavitt. 1997/2005. *Managing Innovation: Integrating Technological, Market and Organizational Change.* Chichester, United Kingdom: Wiley.

Trétiack, Philippe. 1998/1999. *Raymond Loewy and Streamlined Design* (translated from French). New York, NY: Universe Publishing.

von Hippel, Eric. 1988. *The Sources of Innovation.* New York, NY: Oxford University Press.

von Stamm, Bettina. 2003. *Managing Innovation, Design and Creativity.* Chichester, United Kingdom: Wiley.

Walsh, Vivian, Robin Roy, Margaret Bruce, and Stephen Potter. 1992. *Winning by Design: Technology, Product Design and International Competitiveness.* Oxford, United Kingdom: Blackwell Business.

Weick, Karl E. 1979. *The Social Psychology of Organizing.* New York, NY: McGraw-Hill Humanities.

Weick, Karl E. 2001. *Making Sense of the Organization.* Oxford, United Kingdom: Blackwell.

Wenger, Etienne, Richard McDermott, and William M. Snyder. 2002. *Cultivating Communities of Practice.* Cambridge, MA: Harvard Business School Press.

Yin, Robert K. 1984/1989. *Case Study Research. Applied Social Research Methods Series*, Vol. 5. Beverly Hills, CA: Sage.

6

THE SYNTHESIS OF DESIGN, TECHNOLOGY, AND BUSINESS GOALS

Tom MacTavish

This chapter introduces perspectives of managing knowledge confluence between research and business in corporate environments. User-centered research and development requires interdisciplinary knowledge management platforms where knowledge about users, technological possibilities, and business concerns merge and are transformed into tangible forms of research output. For these highly interdisciplinary functions, different disciplinary views and cultures need to be understood to develop methodologies. This chapter is organized around these three key perspectives that concern users, technology, and business valuation and addresses common methodologies used by each discipline to discover and evaluate information. The concluding section discusses the need for an integrated approach to enable project members' ability to easily review key information for multiple projects and multiple functions, and iteratively share information to reach an appropriate consensus that creates new product concepts by balancing design, technology, and business needs.

Knowledge about Users

There are many perspectives and methods used to collect knowledge about users of products, and the approach taken is very much dependent on what aspect or stage of the product development process is under consideration. Inquiries into human behavior, which are measured by their ability to discover incremental value for existing products or product concepts, are significantly different than unbounded investigations initiated for a product concept that is not yet formulated or a market that is not yet determined.

Incremental Improvement

Incremental improvement of existing products is based on a body of knowledge about the product, the users, and the market. If the initial product has achieved market success, there will be an inherently conservative approach to re-designing it, based on the assumption that the success elements are pervasive throughout the product. Introducing radically new ideas and re-designs will require significant justification. If the initial product has failed in the market, there will be an inherently dismissive approach to re-designing it, with a bias toward rejecting anything that looks like the former product. In any case, if the initial product has been in the market and has flowed entirely through the distribution chain, there will be an opportunity to collect, examine, and exploit large amounts of data associated with the product lifecycle.

For validation of existing product concepts or for determining incremental improvements in existing products, it is important to identify all humans that engage with a product in any manner, so that the designers, researchers, and implementers can assess all the possible opportunities for creating satisfaction and loyalty with the product. For example, if a product's user base is rooted in formal business enterprises and the goal is to design a computer-enabled product, one should consider the user population to include, not only the equipment operator, but also the purchasing officer, the IT department, the cleaning crew, and the facilities management staff. After determining the product's lifecycle and planned use, a careful review of each user's experience with the product would be useful input into considering the design, features, functions, color, finish, and materials. Successful product roll-outs can be extensively delayed or even terminated by making a product that the operator or consumer loves, but creates problems for the IT department, cleaning crew, or purchasing organization. One example illustrating this principle comes from Jim Adamson, the General Manager for NCR Corporation's [formerly known as National Cash Register] Self-Service Division during the period when Automatic Teller Machines (ATMs) were first created and then deployed in large numbers. In his role as a mentor to rising engineering managers (including me), he described how, in the early 1980s, great emphasis had been placed on ATM reliability, securely storing and issuing cash, and the ease of use for the end consumer. While these early machines were functional and met the acceptance criteria for reliability, security, and usability, they were not widely embraced by banking institutions. Upon deeper analysis and discussion with a wide variety of different functional departments within banks, Jim and his team of ATM product managers discovered that the IT department represented an area of significant purchasing resistance. They had been overlooked as a key user, and a major effort was needed to address their dominant concerns: that the ATMs needed to be more easily connected to their networks, network management tools were needed, and machine state of health notifications, cash replenishment alerts, and receipt paper replenishment alerts were needed. With the addition of a wide variety of networking protocols, remote alerts, remotely-accessed machine diagnostics, and myriad design changes to accommodate the new features, banks were much more inclined to deploy widely disbursed networks of ATMs and the ATM product roll-out began in earnest. The machines became essential products for anyone in the retail banking business and their ubiquity transformed users' expectations about the availability of cash.

Assessing users and determining what they value requires both a quantified and qualitative understanding of them. Too often, products succumb to the anecdotal experiences of the product manager in charge of the profit and loss statement when they express their intuition or "hunch" that a product needs a particular characteristic. Engineering teams, eager to please an influential decision maker, will implement new features based on the best of intentions, but with sparse supporting data beyond the product manager's hunch. While intuition is useful and popularly acknowledged by books such as Malcolm Gladwell's *Blink* (2005), more validation of consumer preferences with statistically significant indicators will prevent product misfires. The electronics industry's historical record of innovation is littered with products that misjudged the acceptability of new products because the process of understanding the entire population of users and their needs was never accurately measured. For example, pen-based computing has seen many spectacular failures due both to the technology and misunderstanding the various needs and abilities of their users. Arguably, inadequate technology contributed to some degree, but Wang's Freestyle, GridPad, Go, Momenta, and the Apple Newton all failed to sustain their market's interest beyond the early adapter phase, largely because they did not adequately understand their users, the tasks they were trying to achieve, and the role of other solutions (such as pen and paper). The first pen-based system to assess the user's needs with formal approaches was likely the Palm Pilot, which simplified the user experience to four key applications, "instant on" capability, and automatic data synchronization with the user's host device (their personal computer).

Quantifiable information about user behavior for product use can be collected according to many categories, but for task-oriented electronic devices, they usually include a formal study of task productivity as expressed by learning time, task initiation time, task completion time, task completion success rate, operator error rate, error recovery tasks, error recovery time, and various impacts on the user, such as fatigue level, cognitive workload, and emotional response. These data are collected by direct or recorded observation, logging various interaction aspects, or biometric monitoring.

Qualitative information can be collected based on observed or self-reported methods and usually includes states of user satisfaction, willingness to re-purchase, and expressed perceived value. A simple "cognitive walk-through," which compares the user's thought processes while using their current solution against their expressed intentions when using a prototyped new product, can reveal many qualitative differences between the old and new solution.

Unbounded Investigations

Unbounded investigations that are geared toward discovering new product concepts to serve either existing or new markets are more focused on understanding the unarticulated needs of the user at a more general level than are the techniques for incremental product improvement.

Common approaches for new concept discovery include ethnographic studies that directly observe peoples' behavior in their natural environment across a number of people or communities and over a period of time. This may include a range of techniques from unobtrusive "shadow visits," where behaviors are quietly observed, to recorded in-depth conversations including "think aloud" sessions, where the observed person states their thought processes and rationale for conducting a task or behavior. Whatever methods are used, the raw collected data will be analyzed from a number of perspectives to extract common themes, goals, or interests that may lead to new products or services to serve those new value proposition discoveries. One common technique for analyzing the data is to create a framework of polarized behaviors and map the observed phenomenon as part of a continuum across the resulting 'n' dimensional spaces. For example, one hypothetical pairing could consist of "active lifestyles" and "reflective lifestyles" that can be positioned as opposed end-points of one set of behaviors and represent an

Figure 6.1
Lifestyle framework for information products

X axis and another hypothetical pairing consisting of "community-centered lifestyle" and "personally-centered lifestyle" that can represent end points for a Y axis in a simple two dimensional visualization. Figure 6.1 depicts such a system being used as a framework to represent information concepts that traverse these axes. As more details are collected, the quadrants could be bisected to include more detailed aspects of related behaviors or, if needed, a third axis (Z) could be added to represent orthogonal behaviors of interest.

Scenario development and persona definitions are useful tools for better defining and realizing the experience of use in some future state. Scenario development entails describing likely environments of use, foreseen tasks, and suspected benefits within the context of a plausible story in a "day in the life" of targeted users. Persona definitions are descriptions of likely user affinity groups that would benefit from a new product. These techniques are especially helpful when the environment of use is heavily affected by some new enabling technology or combination of technologies that make it difficult for current users to image the future environment and some new tasks. One benefit of high-fidelity prototypes (such as physical appearance models or interactive simulations) is that they can be introduced into usage scenarios with reasonable credibility and they can be used (within the limitations of the simulated embodiment) by new users to see if they fit properly into their world view. For example, one easy litmus test for new wearable communication devices is to create a physical appearance model and then ask representatives from potential user groups to wear the product throughout their day. We soon learn what products are not fashionable, too heavy, too rigid, or too encumbering before proceeding beyond the simple foam or wood model. Also, we can test the user's interaction with a future communication device by creating a visual, virtual representation of the product on a touch screen based computer and ask users to directly interact with the virtual model presented on the screen. These two separate acts help us verify the physical and logical model of a new product well before committing significant development funding. When we surround these verification methods within the context of a new usage scenario, we can begin to really see how users will behave in the future environment with the conceptualized products.

Another helpful technique in understanding users is to assess their expressed and implicit goals in conducting a task so as to better understand how each incremental task performed contributes to the overall goal. This process of User Goal Determination can include self-reported statements of goals they are trying to achieve, direct observation of tasks and outcomes, and post-hoc analyses of an accomplished task.

Technological Possibilities

Assessing the potential of new technologies to create new products or services requires collecting and assimilating several perspectives that include, at a minimum, the environment of use, the technology infrastructure and ecosystem, and the business case. In major corporations, much of this data is collected by specialists and by formal processes that are based on annual cycles, with the goal of challenging and updating current assumptions, anticipating unforeseen disruptors, and re-balancing research and development funding. The process is known by different names in different businesses, but is generally aligned with functions for corporate strategic planning, scenario planning, business intelligence, consumer insights, or a major trends analysis. Reference materials, such as Peter Schwartz's *The Art of the Long View* (1991) or the *MegaTrends* series by John Naisbitt (1988, 2005) are well-known and have been absorbed by corporate cultures as part of their annual renewal cycle. Care is usually taken so that the team assembling the environment data is from a diverse background and from people who are internal and external to the company.

Technology Trend Forecasts

Technology trend forecasts need to look not only at the straight line extrapolation of technologies that will come available during the development and lifecycle of a product, but also at the "step function" opportunities that may arise due to significant technological break-throughs. These step function changes, if ignored, could hasten a product's obsolescence, or if embraced, could dramatically increase a product line's competitive dominance. Gordon Moore's "Law" (Moore, 1965) is probably among the most well-known and sustained extrapolated predictions in the computer industry. It is famous for accurately predicting that semiconductor technology would double the ratio of circuit complexity to surface area every eighteen months. Examples of step function improvements are also well known, but rarely expressed with such certainty over a long duration. For example, the transistor circuit suddenly afforded manufacturers the ability to create portable radios with reasonable battery life and weight factors. The innovation of portable radios would have been quite unpredictable (if not inconceivable) by looking only at existing radio tube technology and making a straight-line extrapolation. As well, digital cellular communication methods enabled wireless carrier companies the possibility to offer significantly greater capacity than analog cellular systems. Just analyzing bandwidth reduction techniques for analog signals did not help forecasters anticipate the impact of digital compression techniques in dramatically increasing cellular system capacities. For further reading, see Clayton Christenson's *The Innovators Dilemma* (1997) as it provides many examples of step function innovations that opened up new markets, created new products, and caused incumbent companies significant competitive pressures.

Technology trend forecasting requires more that just looking at the technology supply side prediction issues. It requires an understanding of many non-technology areas as well, including: customer demand, consumer demand, regulatory inhibitors, and social dynamics. All of these elements are connected by some method of product or service distribution that often includes a high level of technological and business interdependence. It is important to understand the distribution channel and the business models that support the different members of the channel. In traditional television media, we have seen that several products must be linked for an effective service delivery for the end consumer of the product. For example, the television industry depends on content creators, network broadcasters, and product providers to create an overall experience of "watching TV" to end consumers. The introduction of a higher resolution display has highlighted those interdependent relationships quite clearly for the consumer market. With the introduction of HDTV receivers, the consumer experience has been gated by various technology and business elements in the total distribution chain. The inventing companies of HDTV have had to seek answers to a series of difficult questions.

- Will users accept higher-priced TV sets to get higher-resolution pictures?

- Will network broadcasters upgrade their equipment so that higher-quality HDTV programs can be transmitted?

- Will content creators upgrade their equipment so that higher-quality images can be captured?

If each element in the distribution chain demands improved capability from their provider, then HDTV may happen. However, as users of a regulated commodity (radio spectrum), none of the HDTV components can succeed unless there is adequate radio spectrum allocated or an alternative delivery medium, such as cable, is selected.

Once a trend has been spotted and forecasts are made, the technologists must attempt to predict if there will be sustainable improvements in the technology that will improve performance or cost barriers. Having committed to HDTV and cable is there a sufficient technology platform created so that innovation will continue? For example, a reflective lifestyle community communications product would likely fail if it required HDTV technology that, once deployed, was soon outperformed by an entirely different display technology that offered the same resolution at a ten times lower cost.

Understanding the environment involves understanding the context surrounding an innovation. This context may be grounded in history, hardware, software, physical environment, and myriad other aspects that can be reasonably predicted, albeit

Figure 6.2
Professional perspectives for new product development

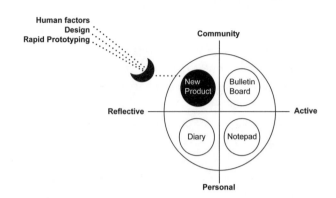

with significant variations of accuracy. For example, consider the ubiquitous email applications that have become inseparable from modern white-collar jobs. If a foundation hadn't been prepared by the acceptance and use of microprocessors, modems, local area networks, the internet, display terminals, operating systems with file managers, and text editors, would email have happened? All the environments' contributing elements matured at their own pace, had different rates of acceptance by users, and evolved under different business models. Yet, all the environmental elements were essential and converged for the successful commercial launch of email. Understanding the environment also involves understanding the proposed innovation from many other perspectives. Figure 6.2 suggests that each concept needs to be evaluated through the lens of a professional perspective. In our sample case, we need to look at the hypothetical "community/reflective" information device through the eyes of human factors, designers, and various members of the product implementation professions. In order to facilitate this, a method of iterative prototyping is most often used, as described below.

Prototypes

Once the environment of use has been analyzed, one proven method for identifying new concepts is to create prototypes that allow product creators to evaluate the user's experience and to test if, and how, different technology elements can be combined for an effective solution. This task should be performed by an "experience design" team that is focused solely on creating and understanding the user's experience with the product or service and is committed to rapid iterative prototypes so that they maintain conceptual flexibility. These teams are comprised of human factors specialists, graphic designers, and rapid prototyping practitioners and are supported by a cadre of business and technology specialists who provide expert guidance on the feasibility of creating the proposed products. This team strives to create experience prototypes that are used to create product concepts and interactions that are implemented with varying degrees of fidelity. The simplest and quickest methods often return the quickest reward, because they allow the user and the product designer to communicate most efficiently, with minimal expense, and with flexibility so that each of the iterations can adapt to new information. For example, a simple drawing of a product concept and key elements of its user interfaces can be used to validate if an intended product is close to satisfying a user need. If more fidelity is required, tools for quickly rendering a high fidelity interface can be used to create a "paper prototype," or a more animated and interactive visualization using rapid prototyping tools such as Macromedia's Dreamweaver or Flash. If even more fidelity is required, an appearance model can be designed and used for validation with a select user community. Once there is agreement on the physical design attributes and the user interface elements, the next level of fidelity involves building a working model using rapid prototyping techniques to keep the initial costs low, maintaining flexibility, and keeping iteration cycles as short as possible.

Technology

At the same time the experience design team is discovering and validating the user experience, a technology team needs to focus on identifying and testing the acceptability of various technology components needed to create the product. The goal of this team is to determine if the technology can deliver the functionality requested at a profitable cost point, and in a reproducible form, that is acceptable to the business and deployment plans. The solution development effort is a separate step from this sourcing of materials; it is performed by a procurement department with professional buyers and is supported by manufacturing engineers who can evaluate the acceptability of competitive offers by different component suppliers.

System Feasibility

Feasibility demonstrations prove whether or not the basic technology works as predicted, force resolution of system integration issues, and reveal the effects of the environment of use. For example, feasibility demonstrations have been quite common in the Application Specific Integrated Circuit (ASIC) industry because of the high cost penalty associated with implementing logic in large-scale wafers. Consider that an entire ASIC industry segment was spawned in the 1980s to address the problem by creating Field Programmable Gate Arrays that allowed chip designers the ability to demonstrate the feasibility of their logic before committing to large wafer production runs. This same concept of proving critical system components with flexible methods has been applied to other aspects of system development, so that user interface software developers now begin with "paper prototypes" that model both graphical user interface appearance and interaction, and then create progressively more complete functions and sub-systems after usability is confirmed. At the same time, special emphasis is placed on stressing each of the software components prior to integration of the total system. Another important trend in feasibility determination has been a general increase in the use of system emulators and simulators to help demonstrate the feasibility of systems before committing to production. For example, in the design of consumer goods, where simple, intuitive user interaction is a premium value, it is common practice to create user interaction emulators that represent a proposed product with high visual and interaction fidelity so that experience design teams can fully explore the user experience including the graphical user interface, audio interaction, and system response times before initiating any concrete product development steps.

Risk Assessments

As product concepts are formulated, methods are needed for formally evaluating the risks that may be introduced. Approaches such as "Failure Modes and Effects Analysis" (FMEA) are well known to the hardware and software product development community and they have helped engineers introduce higher levels of quality and reliability into product development cycles. Encouraging the design community, the development community, and the business community to participate fully and collaboratively in FMEA methods will help remove design-related defects while they are on the drawing board. From a business perspective, guidelines such as the Malcolm Baldrige National Quality Program, "Criteria for Performance Excellence," provide a well-known process description and check list for companies to assess their ability to deliver strategically aligned, customer-focused outcomes (products and services) with consistent quality. Encouraging full team understanding of a company's parent process as described, for example, by the Baldrige process will help ensure more successful product creation.

Figure 6.3
Evaluation factors for new product development

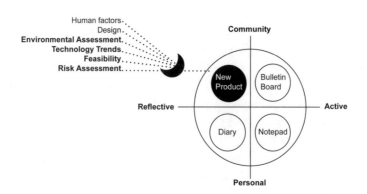

The assessment, selection, and implementation of technology to create novel products requires that many perspectives be considered, as shown in Figure 6.3 and discussed in this section. For our simple hypothetical "community/reflective" information device, many professionals, with many perspectives, need to examine the individual components, the context of their intended use, and their inter-relationship with many other factors. When we add business concerns to the list of product concept evaluations, the assessment complexity continues to grow.

Business Concerns

The business evaluation of new technology and concepts revolves around pragmatic descriptions of the problem being solved by the offering, the value of the solution, and the attendant revenue and profit that can be harvested from the offering. Over the past two decades, the venture capital community has focused on the clear and concise articulation of these principles with the creation of the "elevator speech," which is the statement of a business plan's essence that can be delivered during a relatively short elevator ride. A strong elevator speech memorably addresses the topics listed below.

Problem description: A successful problem description represents the problem in terms that provide sufficient context so that a solution can be conceived within reasonable parameters and with implied acceptance criteria. For our hypothetical "community/ reflective" information device, statements such as, "active people love to communicate publicly with their community of friends," does not help identify a business investment opportunity. However, a statement of, "public information of community interest has ten times more value when posted and consumed within eight hours of inception," starts to approach the community communication problem from a more tractable perspective by providing a clearer problem/value statement. The problem/value statement could lead to the development of proposed solution alternatives as shown below:

Problem: Public information decreases 10X in value after 8 hours.

Alternative Solutions:

1) Post information on public, electronic displays in populated areas.

2) Post information on a community TV channel.

3) Broadcast information to all cell phone users via text messaging systems.

Credible problem statements are based on a sound understanding of user issues and are documented by formal analysis methods. For example, if I could prove through ethnographic derived observations that my problem statement above was true and that there was a tangible financial benefit to communities that posted their public information more efficiently, then a good business analyst would have a sound basis for creating and promoting a focused business case with confidence. What if our ethnographer discovered, for example, that community members were willing, and even inspired, to contribute to the common good just by being informed of recommended local actions that would have the most financially beneficial results for the village budget? And, because of the value of information in the community, what if they discovered that every household owned a cell phone and used text messaging for efficient information exchange? This orientation of valuing community and information could be useful in exploring solutions to various problems.

Solution description: Suppose in the case of our hypothetical "community/reflective" information device, a business analyst identified that the community could immediately resolve public water shortfalls by controlling water usage habits (through mechanisms such as outside watering bans) at certain critical locations and times within the community? And what if, in so doing, the community could avoid the capital expenses for new water treatment and pumping stations? This insight, in combination with the ethnographers insights on their high valuation of community cooperation and information dissemination, could lead to a solution description that communities would entertain seriously, because they could see the direct mapping from their community members' motivations to the conservation of budget dollars and to a system that may require little on-going business expense (assuming that the information needed to drive the solution can be implemented and operated for reasonable costs) since the main engine for savings is information derived from the community's water management IT department. In this case, proposed solution alternative #3 mentioned above, "Broadcast information to all cell phone users via text messaging systems," could allow a village to easily broadcast water usage directions to a caring community for their collective action. Of course, this kind of solution can only occur when there is communication between very separate functions such as an ethnographer, a business analyst, and an IT department.

Business opportunity: In our sample case, given that we have identified one village that might benefit from a proposed solution, the next step would be to evaluate the business opportunity economics. Is there a market? Do many communities experience the same problem and have the same behaviors? Is there a large enough market to warrant our investment and provide a reasonable return? Does the problem manifest itself in a way that communities recognize that they experience the problem, suffer tangible losses from the problem, and can address the problem with a reasonable solution? Are there sufficient elements in place to form a business opportunity? If, for example, our solution alternative #3 depended on existing cell phone infrastructures and high community usage rates, would the roll-out rate of our text message water usage instructions be stifled because too few communities are equipped and educated about cell phone usage? And what price would people be willing to pay to address the problem?

These are all difficult questions, but they can be addressed with some certainty depending on the novelty of the problem and proposed solution. If a new product is targeted toward existing market segments that are addressed by established industries, then there will be reasonable data available to describe the market size, predominating prices, and the potential return. We could know in an existing market, for example, the prevailing price rates for text messages needed for alternative #3. However, if the new product is targeted toward new markets and there are no competitors, the business analysis will depend heavily on early feedback from knowledge about users that is gained from ethnographic studies, scenarios, and early understanding of users' goals. If a community had never used text messages before, introducing the text messaging service and establishing an acceptable price would require iterative exploration between end consumers and the service-offering product managers. If the solution was not based on text messaging, but instead on some new and different technology, then significant ground-breaking work would be required with qualitative and quantitative exploration techniques, and it may require the engagement of experience design teams as described earlier.

Intellectual property: As new concepts are developed, one key consideration for business planners will be to include the degree to which the concept can be protected against unlicensed duplication. Can the concept be protected as either a patent or trade secret? If not, can a change be made in the implementation to create a unique advantage that is protectable?

Figure 6.4
Business factors considered in new product development

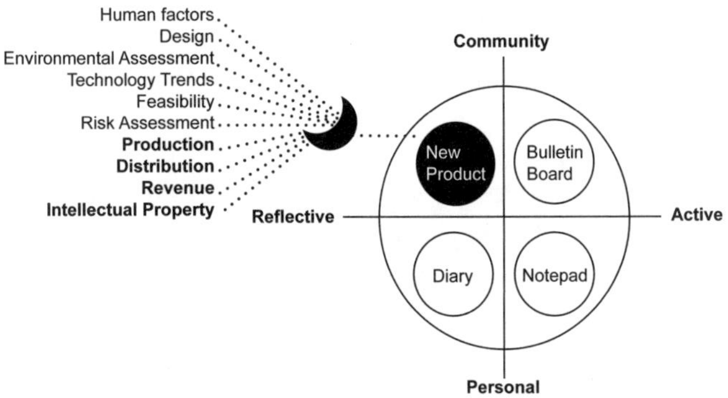

Creating an Integrated View

Now that we have explored some of the major perspectives needed to evaluate and create a new product concept, we can see that, even in assessing a single, simple opportunity such as our hypothetical "community/reflective" information device, there needs to be a capability to support the development, capture, and sharing of in-depth information among the various disciplines. If we increase the functional complexity for our hypothetical product (which might issue one command such as "turn off your water now") by the functionality of a real product with hundreds of features, then multiply by the functions represented by the many products in a commercial product line, and then multiply by the number of work teams that are normally engaged in modern globally developed products, the resulting large number of contributors and perspectives shows the need for a structured approach. We need methods for storing data in universally understandable ways, including file formats and semantics, so that the work done by practitioners in completely different fields, such as ethnography, IT, business analysis, and reliability engineering, can communicate and understand the genesis of requirements and their interplay. For example, if a reliability engineer discovers that by changing an acceptance threshold on a component, they can achieve an overall gain in system reliability at lower cost, how can they follow the root requirement back to a specific user need? How can they determine how the change and its consequences will be interpreted by all the contributing functional specialists who worked on the project? How can they determine if the business analyst or the IT department will be affected by the change?

During the past two decades, we have seen various engineering disciplines recognize and address the need for tools to accurately plan and track project data for individual and team efforts. The Computer Aided Design (CAD) community aggressively addressed electronic capture and evaluation of ASIC chip designs, and this led to major product offerings from companies such as Apollo and SUN. And, at about the same time, general purpose project planning tools such as Microsoft Project were introduced to capture task descriptions, task duration, and associated manpower assignments. In the case of requirements management systems, capturing and correlating requirements has occurred to some degree by automating Quality Function Deployment (QFD) and integrating aspects of it with project planning tools. However, the problem of enabling cross-discipline perspectives, linking back to original requirements information stored in variant media formats, and enabling information sharing across large distributed workforces, remains an unsolved problem. At a minimum, we need a language for allowing different disciplines such as ethnography and engineering to capture their data in semantically base forms so that they can communicate efficiently without loss of meaning as data is translated between them. Better still, we need data definitions and databases that support the detailed, discrete storage, retrieval, and relationship linkage of data in all possible forms including text, audio, and video. For example, at the end of our user investigations for our hypothetical reflective information device mentioned earlier, why can't our various product research team members just query a database to assemble all the references made by a user stating their needs or requirements? Imagine being able to query your research notes, videos and interviews with the phrase (or its semantic equivalents), "Show me all information related to users who declared, 'If only I had information about that event, I would have attended!'" Imagine the great products and solutions we could develop if we could easily and immediately search volumes of disparate data, and alert our colleagues to our findings, who would in turn look at the same data from a perspective that is enhanced to support their knowledge domain. These are the kinds of tools needed by the knowledge-based economy to create products for global markets.

References

Christensen, Clayton. 1997. *The Innovators Dilemma*. Cambridge, MA: Harvard Business School Press.

Gladwell, Malcom. 2005. *Blink*. London, United Kingdom: Penguin Group.

Moore, Gordon. 1965. "Cramming more components into integrated circuits," *Electronics* Magazine, Volume 38, Number 8, April 19.

Naisbitt, John. 1988. *Megatrends: Ten New Directions Transforming Our Lives*. Clayton, VIC, Australia: Warner Books.

Naisbitt, John. 2005. *MegaTrends 2010: The Rise of Conscious Capitalism*. Charlottesville, VA: Hampton Roads.

Schwartz, Peter. 1991. *The Art of the Long View*. New York, NY: Currency Doubleday.

DESIGN
COLLABORATION

7

PRACTICING COLLABORATIVE ACTION IN DESIGN

Sharon Helmer Poggenpohl

Occurring more frequently and with greater diversity among participants, collaboration is an activity without substantial general theory (John-Steiner et al., 1998). No doubt participants reflect on their past collaborative experiences and try to improve current situations, but they lack a framework within which to locate problems and possibilities. Disciplines such as business, science, and education have done extensive research and reflection on collaboration from management (Brown and Druid, 1991; Argyrus and Schön, 1978) and learning perspectives (Lave and Wenger, 1991), but with no resulting general theory. Compounding this lack of structure is recognition that innovation is often the result of collaborative work, so the development of more reliable ways to think about and foster collaboration becomes a priority in many situations.

Business and social science have different viewpoints on collaborative action; business, in large part, attends to product and procedure, as well as to performance and output, while social science focuses on individual and group insight that lead to social process. These are complementary perspectives. Interestingly, learning may provide the collaborative bridge between business and social science approaches as it explores the importance of its social dimension—its relationship to cognitive and behavioral change—while it simultaneously demonstrates outcome-based performance in terms of achieving learning objectives. Design is similar in that it is tied to a performance that is often the outcome of interdisciplinary creative and social process. Along these same lines, others have observed that high performance teams are high performance learners (Leifer, 1996) and that learning is the only competitive advantage (Senge, 2006). Design has no particular collaborative process—collaboration is *ad hoc*. This lack of understanding and structure is detrimental to design collaboration. The following discussion seeks a remedy.

Knowledge and action in the world are most often social constructions among people with different values, agendas, institutional support, disciplines, interaction styles, social sensitivity, humor, timeliness—virtually all aspects of being human underpin this work we call collaboration. It takes many forms: inter- or multidisciplinary, inter-institutional, cross-cultural; it coalesces around stable teams and those that are assembled more fluidly; it involves working with people known or unknown to participants; the work may be on-site or remote or some combination of both; work may happen live or be highly mediated by technology. The variables that define a collaborative action are extensive and often change from one context to the next.

Here, the focus is on design action in collaborative settings. Designers do collaborate, but for the most part, exploration and understanding of its underlying issues remain unexplored. Individuals are increasingly aware of the limitations to their knowledge and skill in a complex technological and increasingly interactive world. Disciplines that structure knowledge and maintain boundaries are seeking interdisciplinary perspectives in the search for new knowledge and solutions to persistent problems. These well-defined disciplines are exploring their edges, looking for new perspectives beyond their boundaries, and seeking out complementary partnerships with individuals from other disciplines. With their established knowledge base, they look for more fluid and productive relationships. In contrast, design lacks a well-defined knowledge base and drifts opportunistically among other disciplines. This is the core problem for design in relation to collaborative action. Design is unsure of what knowledge it has to offer, how to position itself relative to others, and how to present and argue its position.

The difference between interdisciplinary and multidisciplinary is worth noting. Interdisciplinary refers to activities that fall between two disciplines. Multidisciplinary refers to activities in which several disciplines share perspectives (Rogers, 1994, 404). In addition, collaboration may involve inter-institutional work, which joins strengths not found in a single organization, and international work with its border-crossing cultural complexity. These are some of the factors that stimulate interest in collaboration in contemporary society; they range from interpersonal to interdisciplinary to multidisciplinary to inter-institutional to international.

The perspectives developed in this chapter are reflective and only somewhat theoretical. Design collaboration has only a small, recorded history. The current investigation brings us to a definition of collaboration, while knowledge management, decision-making, and presence reveal the importance of communication. Interdisciplinary collaboration reveals the inherent problems in such settings with particular attention to design. The problem of formalizing or theorizing about the practice of collaboration is discussed, along with a suggested practical way forward that trades on experiential perspectives and tentatively identifies variables found in collaborative work. The chapter ends with the introduction to the following chapters that encompass case studies and fieldwork.

Learning about Collaboration: the Early Years in Design

Collaboration has an interesting, if largely unwritten, history in design. It is not a new idea at all. Even in design sources discussing the history of large design offices (the Henry Dreyfuss office, for example [Poggenpohl, 2007]), conscious collaborative association of various kinds dates to the 1930s. Other associations are discussed in *Group Practice in Design*, a mid-twentieth-century book that explores collaborative variations in design practice in the United States and Britain (Middleton, 1967). The book focuses on a simple approach: people within one professional umbrella—doctors, lawyers, designers, etc.—work together for efficiency and scale to achieve an increase in service to the client and to enhance creativity and quality. Case studies of architecture, interior design, product design, communication design, and entertainment (broadcasting) complement the general discussion. Well-known architectural firms, for example, Skidmore Owings and Merrill in Chicago and The Architects Collaborative in Boston, as well as the Industrial Design Partnership (later called the Design Research Unit in Britain), ground the discussion in a practical way.

Group practice was an ideal some aimed toward, as expressed in the following statement (Middleton, 1967, 91):

> ...the idea [is] of [a] group team, composed of talents that are inevitably various and unequal, but which are given the fullest opportunity at every stage to make to the project as a whole such contribution as they may be capable of. In the fullest sense—not easily achieved—the essential purpose of group practice is to link and focus the creative and critical faculties of every member of the team, not just upon one or two facets of the problem but upon every aspect at every stage.

This is directly counter to the romantic notion of the secluded genius whose suffering, determination, and superior creativity bring about excellence. Given the complexity of contemporary life, one can be a "genius" in only a small way, i.e., time is too short to process and master all the knowledge and skill one might want to bring to bear on a project. Consequently, if one aspires to do large or complex work, collaboration provides the only reasonable context for development.

The ideal as expressed in *Group Practice* is seldom realized even today, as many perspectives and expert knowledge from different disciplines are needed on complex problems. Interaction among experts and the synthesis of perspectives can be problematic itself. Design has an additional problem in this context, also described by Middleton (1967, 63), as he explores what design is and what design can contribute. It resonates even more today than it did then [emphasis added]:

> It is the perpetual frustration of the designer, be he landscape architect or typographer or product designer, that he is called in too late, when all major decisions have been taken and the project has already assumed such a form that little can be done to it save clean up some of its superficial ugliness. *This is not design*. The elegant design solution is that which meets maximum requirements with the minimum means. This postulates that *all* relevant factors must be embraced by the creative act of synthesis which we call design.

Today, design repositions itself at both ends of, as well as throughout, the design process spectrum. Well-known as a finisher of work to resolve aesthetic issues and smooth the way through production, design also provides analytical perspectives on what constitutes the problem to be solved at the earliest stage, and also engages intermediate steps toward its solution. The integration of design into a multidisciplinary action allows it to make its most complete contribution to problem, process, and solution, but this integration can be difficult.

In a section titled, "Patterns of Collaboration," in Middleton's book, two primary patterns are identified by their preposition: working *for* and working *with*. In the former, a director tightly controls and designs a project, drawing in others as consultants and workers as needed. In the latter, a group of people share knowledge, work together responsibly, and together make critical decisions facilitated by a leader. Transforming this idealistic vision of the possibilities of collaboration into reality is not easily achieved.

Defining the Collaborative Activity

Collaboration is poorly defined in the literature in which it appears; this is not surprising given its multiple domains of exploration and the particularities of its execution. Fourteen individuals offered definitions of collaboration based on their experience in design, two of them working "collaboratively." Table 7.1 (Poggenpohl, 2004) shows the

Table 7.1
Collaboration definitions

Dietmar Winkler: A supportive, to an extent selfless process, sharing one's expertise and conceptual, interpersonal planning or implementation skills for maximizing the positive result of an activity.	**Gosta Knudson:** Develop your own knowledge by solving a problem together with other professions in a way that makes the world a better place in which to live.
Arlene Gould: The coming together of designers from various disciplines along with other professionals to share knowledge and achieve common aesthetic, business and social goals.	**Jill Dacey:** Two or more people working together on a project or problem. Best case scenario: when each individual is working in his/her own best interests, that interest contributes to the greater good (solution) to the project or problem. Each participant is self-satisfied.
Chris Barlow: Adjustment and combination of disjoint knowledge by diverse individuals.	**Ruth Lozner:** An interactive, cooperative conversation among members who can both contribute and benefit by the outcome and final action.
Alain Rochon: To put in common, actors whose expertise, knowledge, way of working, personality, etc. are different, but complementary. This action is meant to: solve a particular problem or task, or build or disseminate knowledge within a specific time frame.	**Sharon Poggenpohl:** Collaboration is based on a recognition of individual limitation along with the ability to trust others and allow them actionable entry into a situation.
Dirk Knemeyer: Multiple systems with complementary skills and interests engaged in active, respectful, productive activities to achieve more success.	**Jay Rutherford:** A group of people with different capabilities that perceive a task or problem to be solved and use their expertise in a symbiotic way to solve it. At the end — ideally — everyone has learned something new — either directly practical or social that they can use in future problem-solving situations.
Keith Russell: Collaborate = work together Elaborate = work it out Cooperate = do the work together Collaboration is that form of working together where the working together (is the work); it produces an understanding of an outcome (and the outcome) that could not otherwise be produced.	**Roger Remington & Judith Gregory** Collaboration involves negotiating scope, mediating, arguing, participating, interacting, acting, reacting and valuing within various constraints.

thirteen definitions.[1] Analysis of these definitions reveals the following characteristics: "who" participates in collaborative work includes design professionals, individuals with different capabilities, and other stakeholders; "what" they are doing is quite diverse—negotiating the scope and constraints of their work, sharing knowledge and expertise, combining and negotiating disjointed knowledge, performing productive activities, working together, developing their own knowledge, and working in their own best interests as well as allowing actionable entry to others; "why" they are doing this is also diverse—maximizing positive results of their activity, achieving common aesthetic, business, and social goals, solving problems, achieving success, producing something not otherwise possible, and making a better world; "how" they are doing this is also diverse—they mediate, argue, participate, act, react, and value in ways that are supportive, selfless, different but complementary, respectful, cooperative, self-satisfied, symbiotic, and most importantly, in a spirit of trust.

A critical thread in these definitions is the contrast between self-direction and other-direction coexisting in some kind of dynamic balance. The participants are engaged with their own learning and contribution and are equally engaged with the learning and contribution of other participants with whom they interact and for whom they provide support. The variety of purposes and actions reveals a fluid situation in which improvisation and critical reframing are welcome.

Definitions from non-design sources support the definitions above. Fauske (1999) states a definition from the perspective of education: "Collaboration is the interaction of stakeholders with shared language and values taking action toward collective goals. The term 'stakeholders' includes anyone who has an interest in or who would be affected by collaborative action." From business, Schrage (1991, 36) states: "Collaboration is a purposive relationship. At the heart of collaboration is a desire or need to solve a problem, create, or discover something within a set of constraints, including expertise, time, money, competition, and conventional wisdom." Extending these definitions to elaborate critical factors in collaboration, even though not all factors are present in every possible situation, yields the following (Minnis et al., 1994, C-2):

> The principals in a true collaboration represent complementary domains of expertise. As collaborators, they not only plan, decide, and act jointly, they also think together, combining independent conceptual schemes to create original frameworks. Also, in a true collaboration, there is a commitment to shared resources, power, and talent; no individual's point of view dominates, authority for decisions and actions resides in the group, and work products reflect a blending of all participants' contributions.

Further, the distinction between contribution and collaboration is worth noting. One can contribute to a project without collaborating. In a contribution, one's role is narrowly defined—it may happen in a specific sequence, in a special way, or with a particular skill. A contributor may also be part of a marginal group who offers aid or support but does no direct work on and is not essential to the project. In contrast, collaborative work requires more than one person, but all so-called teamwork is not collaborative. Collaboration is marked in its interactive working together and working out performance, such as through shared decision-making, the give and take of ideas exchanged and explored, the integration of multiple perspectives, of course the arguments and conflicting viewpoints, and a synthesis that integrates hitherto isolated or incompatible ideas.

Setting the Context for Discussion: Three Brief Cases

There is extensive literature on crossover collaborations between families and schools or healthcare workers and families; in a sense, the idea of collaboration has been professionalized in these areas. Stepping aside from this, I propose that collaboration is first learned within the family through simple collaborative tasks, some fun and some tedious. Picking up toys with a sibling, making cookies with a parent, or helping a younger child learn to tie shoelaces are shared activities that prepare the groundwork for more sophisticated forms of collaboration.

It is instructive to examine three very different collaborative actions to observe some of the extremes. The first is an extended family collaboration to commemorate a family reunion in rural Nebraska. The activity, the creation of Carhenge, used heavy equipment to upend old cars and stack them according to the pattern of Stonehenge.[2] This was an ambitious family goal involving skills, time constraints, networking needs, and trial and error. The plan for Stonehenge existed (see figures 7.1-7.2) and was well documented in diagrammatic and photographic form, thereby providing a clear conceptual goal for everyone. With a physical plan in place, the collaborative focus was on the logistics of gathering material (old cars), obtaining heavy equipment, and task allocation within time constraints. The work had a knowledgeable and respected leader in Jim Reinders, an engineer and the family patriarch. Save for his wife, all family members were enthusiastic about the plan.

Time to execute the plan was limited and family members entered and exited work as their personal schedules allowed. The work needed to be *fun* as this was a family celebration. Evening meals and even the children's theatrical spoof on the people present gave everyone a chance to contribute to the overall goal. Creating Carhenge through collaborative action marked the family's cohesion and mutual support. The apparent side issue of the children's skit was essential to engage everyone and realize a challenging goal in a spirit of fun. Translating Stonehenge into Carhenge was an ironic act that respected the scale and structure of the original, but used old cars (the wheeled stones of contemporary culture) as replacement tokens. While a substantial undertaking, it was also light-hearted. Its risk was time and cooperative family action.

Figure 7.1
Stonehenge on Salisbury plain in Wiltshire County, England has an estimated completion date of 1500 BC.

Figure 7.2
Carhenge on the plains of western Nebraska was constructed in the late 1980s.

The second example is Linux, or open source software development.[3] This is an idea on a vast scale that needed to appeal to hacker ego and coordinate the contributions of essentially unknown collaborators. Linus Torvalds, the force behind Linux, had a knack for letting people into the development action; he was reported to have an eye for good code and was a master of communication exchange. "Linus was keeping his hackers/users constantly stimulated and rewarded—stimulated by the prospect of having an ego-satisfying piece of the action, rewarded by the sight of constant (even daily) improvement in their work" (Raymond, 1999, 6). Building Linux depended on making a reasonable promise to the community—one that could be kept. Self-selecting participants provided fast development in the open, and some would say anarchic, context of the internet.

Linux was the first project to make a conscious and successful effort to use the entire world as its talent pool. It is not a surprise that the gestation period for Linux coincided with the birth of the world wide web and that Linux left its infancy during the same period (1993–1994) that saw the explosion of mainstream interest in the internet. Linus was the first person who learned how to play by the new rules that pervasive internet access made possible (Raymond, 1999, 14).

This example is completely different than the previous one in that the risk was establishing a collaborative incentive for unknown participants. Torvald considered his collaborators co-developers—he let them into the action, releasing versions frequently, sending chatty messages of encouragement to participants, and taking their suggestions and feedback seriously.

"Human beings generally take pleasure in a task when it falls in a sort of optimal-challenge zone; not so easy as to be boring, not too hard to achieve" (Raymond, 1999, 19). This observation is similar to the "zone of proximal development," which is important to successful learning (Vygotsky, 1978). Another related concept contributed by Mihaly Czsiksentmihalyi (1990) is "flow," or achieving optimal experience and concentration in work. Joy, playfulness, pleasure, and recognition in work are real assets that both Reinders and Torvald appreciated.

Torvald's appeal was domain-specific with shared rules, norms, and structures that smoothed the way to shared understanding and action. From this unified context, together with the reach of the internet and the psychology of egocentric hackers, he created a community of practice. Open source development is a good example of a knowledge-based economy dependent on the synergy between common knowledge and openness (Foray, 2004, 178–179).

The third example is an architectural design competition as reported firsthand by one of the principals, Jeanne Gang of Studio Gang/O'Donnell Architects in Chicago

(2000). Such competitions are voluntary and highly charged with direct competition among peers. Not unlike the ego appeal to Torvald's hackers, participants in these competitions get ego gratification (or not) publicly. Gang identifies six essential ideas for such competitions, including seduction, timing, brevity, clarity, competitiveness, and encouragement.

The case she develops, a solar wall on the south face of the Washington, DC-based Department of Energy, uses the subject matter, a solar wall (what), a highly visible building in the capitol (where), and energy savings and ecology (why) as the hook for participants. Team selection extended beyond the immediate office to a virtual team located on different continents. Creativity, humor, past history, and rapport among the individuals were important to team selection. Gang observes that all collaborators need a sense of ownership in the project; no one can be the "star." Once the team was assembled, live visits kicked off the work. Open communication and trust were essential. Time zone differences were used to advantage, allowing for problems to be shared, reflected on, and addressed as promptly as possible via telephone, fax, and email. Who had what information needs? What had changed, and who needed to know? What decisions were pending? Who needed to be consulted? In a fast-paced competition, information exchange was the glue that held the work together and advanced it. Orchestrating the flow of information was a critical aspect of collaboration. A log that was kept of communication revealed the choice of medium and the frequency of use by various participants. This was useful to change communication strategy, change from telephone to email for example, based on feedback of actual use and success to keep the information flow active.

There are interesting similarities and differences among these brief cases. The logistics of Carhenge and the architectural competition became important as the time frame was limited; in contrast Linux was an ever-evolving, long-term project. The three teams were completely different: a family that happens organically, self-selected and anonymous hackers, and carefully selected multidisciplinary professionals. Motivation and reward in various guises was key to the success of all three. The first was physical, the second was intellectual in a domain-specific realm, and the third was a multidisciplinary creative conceptualization. Equality in collaborative participation sustains authentic communication. Where substantial power differences are apparent, communication is distorted. Within a close family structure and within an anonymous peer-oriented community of practice, power can disappear; both Reinders and Torvald were sensitive to this. Gang may have had more difficulty equalizing power (reputation) differences among her team. Collaborations contain gifts and problematic givens in their many variables.

Managing Information and Communication

As shown in the last brief case, knowledge management is a critical aspect of collaborative work, particularly when the team is dispersed over time and space. Someone needs to control and distribute information in a timely way so all participants are informed about decisions, changes, needs, and opportunities. Such a person is in the catbird seat and must be tuned in totally to the flow of development and its many details; further, they need the ability to anticipate collaborator needs.

Capturing Information

Much has been made in recent years about knowledge management from both corporate and design consultancy perspectives. Knowledge management is about recording, storing, retrieving, and synthesizing information so that the experiences and lessons of the past remain vital guides to future work, giving people the ability to work from an advanced platform of understanding rather than beginning each project from ground zero. Software systems exist and help manage design projects, transfer information, and support decision-making (see Chang and Hsu, 2005, for example).

Information is no longer scarce, but time to accumulate and process meaningful information is costly. Knowledge management tools transform specific project experience into a reusable form, whether as a reference, resource, or case on which to build. In a way, it takes tacit information, knowledge residing in individuals and their experience, and makes it more explicit and sharable through its form. It is obvious that collaborative teams need shared information resources; structuring these resources to be accessible and efficient for various stakeholders and their needs is important.

Modeling Information and Communication

Group model building is an idea that goes further and is an advanced form of information use and collaboration. Pettit et al. (2002) report on a biodiversity project in Australia in which a vast amount of environmental data is combined with expert knowledge, along with weightings and ratings of importance from urban planners to create different urban green system scenarios. The authors anticipate adding other stakeholders, such as interested individuals and community groups in the future, to this mix of data and experts. Their approach is to plan *with* the community rather than *for* the community. They describe "how linked views between descriptive information, mapping and statistical plots are used to decide upon representative regions that satisfy a number of criteria for biodiversity and conservation."

The ability to model various scenarios based on hard data, expert opinion, and manipulation of weightings depends on a Bayesian approach to the accumulated data.

The data include much diversity: rules of thumb, expert advice, scientific reports—all of which are interpreted as quantitative data in a rigorous statistical model in balance with hard data. For example, qualitative information that characterizes a geographical region with a unique biotic or landscape quality is balanced by measurable environmental data regarding climate, terrain, and soil type. The Bayesian modeling computes definitions for eco-regions and produces specific maps.

The collaborative process is inclusive and transparent for participants as changing weights visibly reorder regions. Such ordered, understandable, and transparent processes offer new opportunities for participatory design and the development of more inclusive decision-making processes within collaborative settings. Sharing information is one thing; sharing decision-making is something else. The integration of qualitative and quantitative information from multiple sources, together with its visualization and clear manipulation, offers improved opportunities for group consideration and decision.

Making Decisions Together

Good information alone, even among participants with good intentions and full commitment, cannot carry the day in collaborative work. For this reason, the just mentioned Bayesian decision theory deserves a deeper look as it maps well to design's context. Situations marked by uncertainty and risk, with imprecise, incomplete, and inconsistent information, with necessarily uncertain outcomes, and a wide variety of decision-making perspectives lend themselves to a Bayesian approach. Donald Schön (1983) describes design in similar terms: design is characterized by value conflict, ambiguity, and uncertainty. These three characteristics alone signal a problem for collaborative decisions. Interactive computer-based systems that facilitate working on ill-structured problems and support team-based decision-making (also called Collaborative Decision Support Systems) help to overcome two difficulties present in collaborative design activities: the issue of ill-formed or wicked problems (Rittel & Webber, 1973) that appear to elude solution on fundamental terms, and the issue of equalizing power among decision makers. In the context of design problems, factual knowledge is often insufficient, and qualitative opinions and values are difficult to adequately express and weigh. In this messy context, computer-supported tools often include an array of approaches that: support argumentative discourse, including such reasoning mechanisms as issues, alternatives, positions, and constraints; provide standards of evidence; detect conflicts and inconsistencies; establish appropriate queries based on case-based reasoning; and update participants on the status of a discourse that is necessarily dynamic. The information environment changes with new resources, stakeholder perspectives, and other factors. Tracking and supporting recognition of such changes has been a shortcoming for group work.

While strides are being made regarding support for knowledge management, information transfer, and collaborative decision-making, other more human dimensions of collaborative work continue to present problems.

Exploring the Human Dimensions of Interdisciplinarity and Discourse

Design, a weak discipline as noted in Chapter 1 and restated here, is at a disadvantage in inter- and multidisciplinary work, if considered from a traditional academic perspective. Its body of knowledge is not well established in contrast to other disciplines. But considering design's strengths, its ability to absorb ideas into a working synthesis, and its skill at materially realizing through prototype development an idea that originally was nothing more than a string of words and some hand waving, indicates the significant role it can play in collaborative activities.

Current collaborations in design are diverse, including those with computer scientists, psychologists, business people, sociologists...the list could go on. These collaborations find individuals bringing to the problem (situation, opportunity) diverse perspectives that forge a new vision of possibility. Recent focus on interdisciplinarity (Weingart and Stuhr, 2000, 2) looks to the promise of "cognitive and organizational innovation through evolution by variation, diversity, and combination." Important problems and opportunities today tend to call for multiple perspectives, with shared decision-making. "Interdisciplinarity is a set of dynamic forces for rejuvenation and regeneration, pressures for change, and the capacity for responsiveness. It is the necessary 'churn' in the system. Interdisciplinarity entails knowledge negotiation and new meanings..." (Klein, 2000, 21). Such situations call for different skills in discourse and negotiation coupled with communication, prototyping, and social skills that can anchor the work-in-progress and bring out the best from all participants.

Identifying Cultural Aspects of Interdisciplinarity

To examine discourse and the way process evolves based on framing and ultimately on decisions regarding choice, one can look through a cultural filter. Disciplinary differences contain cultural presumptions with regard to epistemology, for example. Through such presumptions or styles of examining the world, one discipline can feel superior to another; clearly this is not a trivial matter in inter- or multidisciplinary work. Rainier Bromme (2000, 125) comments:

> As a discipline's epistemic style contains a significance guiding both activity and cognition and thus also a normative component, it may well be expected that it contributes to stereotypes of this kind [disdain between

various disciplines]. This again affects how open-minded a researcher will be about data, proofs, and refutations obtained on the basis of other epistemic styles.

This statement reveals what is perhaps the most stressful and disorienting aspect of inter- or multidisciplinary activity, and it is in this context that design is at a disadvantage.

Paradoxically, at the same time we are calling for disciplinary development in design (see Chapter 1), the benefit of interdisciplinary work has emerged. As argued in the first chapter, formal disciplinary knowledge provides a necessary foundation for interdisciplinary work. How can we converse intelligently about epistemological differences with partners from other areas if we are unable to represent our own position? What is "design intelligence"? Disciplines have been criticized as too rigid, even stagnant, with unyielding normative characteristics; they are isolated from each other. However, such grounding provides a position that is understood and from which limitations are acknowledged; it can also be a platform from which to push-off to new territories and investigations.

In contrast to disciplinary isolation, interdisciplinary activity has been identified with a discourse of innovation (Weingart and Stuhr, 2000), providing forces for regeneration and change in disciplinary thinking by strengthening connections between disciplines. "Connections weaken divisions of labor, expose gaps, stimulate cross-fertilization, and fix new fields of focus" (Klein, 2000, 18). Disciplinary understanding precedes inter- or multidisciplinary analysis and collaborative action.

Epistemological difference marks interdisciplinary work—recognizing and working out these differences takes both time and goodwill on the part of various participants. Differences may be subtle or extreme, but if individuals are to not only work together and appreciate each other's contributions, but to creatively collaborate, an understanding of each other's disciplinary presumptions is necessary. There is a paradox with regard to sharing perspective. A shared point of view can eliminate difference—the very point of working collaboratively, yet a common ground is essential if communication and meaningful work is to occur. The harmony/difference paradox is plausible and inescapable. Diversity can give rise to conflict, reduce cohesion, and limit communication and coordination within the group. It can also stimulate new ideas and possibilities.

Disciplines create their own micro-world of knowledge. Taking a lead from philosopher Nelson Goodman's *Ways of Worldmaking* (1978), a direct entry into these differences at a level of abstraction that is useful emerges. Worldmaking is not necessarily a technical activity; we all do it in various ways as we absorb information, rearrange it, and puzzle over its significance. Goodman identifies five elements to worldmaking: composition and decomposition, weighting, ordering, deletion and supplementation, and deformation. They deserve a closer look.

Composition and decomposition: The ways in which we divide wholes and partition the resulting pieces according to some classification varies according to discipline. Features that are noteworthy and signal a need for analysis are also different. Methods for drawing distinctions and recombining sub-components and features while making connections are essential to our disciplinary epistemology. We are assisted by names and labels that may be special to our discipline, but these same names and labels, present in another discipline, may carry different meaning. Essentially, our attention is drawn to what we consider relevant. Goodman (1978, 9) observes, "...worlds differ in response to theoretical rather than practical needs."

Weighting: This provides differences of emphasis or accent through identification of relevance, importance, utility, or value. Their relative importance or value may be subject to negotiation.

Ordering: Establishing a frame of reference—deciding what is in or out of consideration—provides orientation for work. Systems of measurement may vary from formal and precise to informal and approximate. Ordering and weighting are ways to set precedence and coordinate attention to sequences in process.

Deletion and supplementation: "Our capacity for overlooking is virtually unlimited, and what we do take in usually consists of significant fragments and clues that need massive supplementation" (Goodman, 1978, 14). This is best understood through examples in a system and different perceptual approaches. Using Goodman's examples, from a system perspective, the mathematician with sparse data may fill in points to create a smooth curve; or conversely, a musician may understand there is no pitch between C and C$^{\#}$ in a typical scale. We also fill in perceptually, when we see two spots of light flashed a short distance apart but in rapid succession (phi phenomenon), the spot appears to be moving. What is or can be deleted or supplemented is often part of a larger system of understanding.

Deformation: This is similar to deletion and supplementation, but implies less logic and the possibility of going against existing norms.

These elements of worldmaking are not comprehensive or even mandatory; they may appear in various combinations, suggesting processes in use. Even criteria for success in making a world vary; the criteria could be observation, theory validation, truth, fitness to purpose, or something else. There are strong world versions and weak ones as selected by consistency, creativity, utility, etc. All of the above bears on how we acquire knowledge, "…until we see or hear or grasp features and structures we could not discern before. Such growth in knowledge is not by formation or fixation or belief but by the advancement of understanding" (Goodman, 1978, 22).

Goodman's notion of worldbuilding shows at a practical level how disciplines might diverge in their understanding, and how disclosure of certain kinds of information might help participants come to a shared understanding. Taking a more pragmatic perspective on trying to understand another discipline, we need to know what is their work, how do they argue, what form does evidence take, what methods predominate, what is a typical working process, what requires justification, what is given (presupposed or understood), and how has the discipline changed in recent years. Such understanding, while requiring interest and time to process, combats the stereotypes that distort legitimate inter- or multidisciplinary communication. To combat normative assumptions and calcified notions of disciplinary style or interest, open-mindedness is necessary.

The search for common ground involves resolving problems of terminology, expectation, and process. This is a collaborative act of communication in which competing disciplinary discourses are examined, symbolic values are shared, and a hybrid process that appreciates multiple ways of examining a problem or question is employed. It is about communication; the participants need a willingness to embrace new knowledge and perspective, and the resulting new meanings. It is a critical negotiation that sets the platform on which work is done. Such communication and decision-making has multidimensional scholarly, social, and administrative implications. But as mentioned earlier, the goal is not complete agreement or harmony. Difference is an essential reason for collaboration.

Five patterns of interdisciplinary relations have been identified among the sciences (Bechtel, 1986). They provide a means for considering how design as an opportunistic emerging discipline borrows and appropriates ideas and processes from others. The following patterns found in science are elaborated by examples from design with regard to their use.

Conceptual links: Developing conceptual links involves using a perspective in one discipline to modify a perspective in another. For example, design has integrated a practical interest in human factors from the social sciences to better meet people's needs, expectations, and pleasures as it designs objects, information, and services. Physical human factors have historically had a place in design development. Now human factors extend to cognitive factors (how people process information), social factors (how people control shared facilities), cultural factors (how people form and maintain communities of practice), and emotional factors (how people realize pleasure from form, color, or unexpectedness). Conceptual links between ergonomics, cognitive science, sociology, anthropology, and psychology are considerations in design.

Organization and process: This involves recognizing a new level of organization with its own processes in order to solve unsolved problems in existing fields. For example, a design team may go beyond what is reported in marketing studies or focus groups by naturalistically observing how people actually interact with a product, thereby getting specific information regarding their intuitive use and its pleasures and frustration.

Research technique: It may be important to use research techniques developed in one discipline to elaborate a theoretical model in another. For example, grounded theory, a research technique developed in social science (Corbin and Strauss, 1998), is used as an analytical tool to make sense of qualitative design research by coding data from observation or interview. Design borrows many research methods and analytical strategies from other disciplines.

Theoretical frames: Modifying and extending a theoretical framework from one domain to apply in another is another pattern. For example, Gestalt principles, a theoretical framework from psychology, are extended in design to account for principles of human understanding of apparent motion on screen (Kim and Poggenpohl, 2004). In this example, the original theory, addressing two-dimensional form, is extended to include time and motion in a two-dimensional space to better understand motion cues and patterns on screen.

New frameworks: Another pattern involves developing a new theoretical framework that may re-conceptualize research in separate domains as it attempts to integrate them. For example, Design Information Framework (Lim and Sato, 2006) accommodates multiple viewpoints and represents them for effective management of information from different disciplines.

The nature of collaborative action can be understood in terms of the character of its discourse. Donald Schön (1994, 31), following Thomas Kuhn (1992), discriminates between normal and abnormal discourse in science as well as in other fields of inquiry. According to Schön, normal discourse:

> ...proceeds under a shared set of rules, assumptions, conventions, criteria, and beliefs, all of which tell us how disagreements can be settled, in principle, over time.... Abnormal discourse occurs, by contrast, when agreed-upon criteria for reaching agreement are not present as a basis

for communication among the contending actors. These situations are not defined by the participants in terms of an objective framework within which disagreements can be arbitrated or managed.

Comfort is attached to normal discourse. As mentioned previously, in inter- or multidisciplinary work, a hybrid discourse must be invented in which all participants can communicate and operate with respect and understanding if they are to get on with an inquiry that engages their various thoughts and actions. Perhaps two of the largest issues in developing common ground are sorting out and agreeing on the meaning of terms with different reference in various disciplines and negotiating a shared process. The terminology problem is the lesser one as such confusion is usually obvious and can be easily resolved. Negotiating process, however, can be a minefield. Here, both an understanding of disciplinary roles and contributions come into play, to say nothing of epistemological differences and perceived power difference.

Exploring Presence and Its Degrees of Absence

In the past, one was simply present or absent—it was a simple binary situation. Our first technical presence projection was the voice via the telephone. While this is a commonplace today, one might even say ubiquitous, this must have seemed like a miracle at its inception. Even so, presence projection has come a long way from that early instrument. Now there are choices of mediated presence, and we select what we choose to disclose and how through media and content. These choices affect the nature of communication and the recipient's understanding of the message. Presence is modulated, but remains short of Star Trek's "Holodeck" or teleportation.

Isaac Asimov, in his book *The Naked Sun*, describes the subtle differences between "seeing" and "viewing," a distinction that reveals differences in presence, its perceptual qualities and interpreted meanings. Written nearly fifty years ago, the story takes place on Solaria, where physical meetings are rare. Meetings are typically mediated or "viewed" through three-dimensional imaging. In the story, detective Baley from Earth investigates a murder on Solaria and "tunes in" on the wife of the murder victim, emerging from the shower.[4]

> "I hope you don't think I'd ever do anything like that, I mean, just step out of the drier, if anyone were seeing me. It was just viewing."

> "Same thing, isn't it?" asked Baley.

> "Not at all the same thing. You're viewing me right now. You can't touch me, can you, or smell me, or anything like that. You could if you were

seeing me. Right now, I'm two hundred miles away from you at least. So how can it be the same thing?"

Baley grew interested. "But I see you with my eyes."

"No, you don't see me. You see my image. You're viewing me."

"And that makes a difference?"

"All the difference there is." (Asimov, 1991, 6)

In some not too distant future, will we more often replace physical meetings with live video-mediated ones?[5] Telecommunication technology has allowed people to overcome the need for proximity by supplying the ability to communicate easily over great distances. Presuming all participants have the same technological choices: What might be the strategy for representing oneself? Is it relative to the importance of the meeting and its nature? Does it depend on who will attend the meeting? How much does one choose to disclose of one's self? And how will we read the presence of the representations that others choose? Are the representations authentic or some clever substitute keyed to the situation? Is it a carefully crafted persona, an avatar, or an abstraction that changes color in agreement or disagreement?

The following chart is constructed from a sender/receiver perspective and details how sensory message information is filtered and constrained by media choice. At issue is the sender's or author's control of their presence. Also at issue is what the receiver can read from the sender's choice (see Table 7.2).

Clearly, presence is an issue requiring some thought. The richness of presence as delivered through various media depends on how well the recipient of the communication knows the individual sending a message. If the individual is unknown, the mediated presence is all they have to go on. If the individual is known, memories and previous information not only fill in gaps, they deepen and enrich what is presented; the recipient performs a kind of gestalt closure with the limited information.

An example of extended presence that is as close to naturalistic as possible at this time is the Swisshouse in Boston. It is a new type of consulate for science and technology, originally designed to facilitate knowledge exchange between Switzerland and the United States and to keep expatriate Swiss culturally connected to their homeland. Jeffrey Huang, a design professor at Harvard, and Muriel Waldvogel, an architect, conceived a building that houses display technologies to connect people live and life-size in Zurich and Boston.[6] Business meetings and family get-togethers are

Table 7.2
Presence through media choice and media dimensions of presence representation

		Text	Photo	Video Clip	Live Voice	Live Video	Physical Presence
Human dimensions of reception	**Mutually known** sender/receiver	Deeper interpretation	Appearance & memory	Appearance this time & memory of previous	Identity confirmation & emotional state clues	Appearance in current moment & memory	All sense modalities & memory
	Mutually unknown sender/receiver	Surface interpretation of what is present	Appearance only	Appearance this time only	Identity clues: emphasis, rhythm, pitch, intonation	Appearance in current moment and immediate past	All sense modalities
Message characteristics	**Information**						
	Identity as revealed	Name & writing style	Appearance only	Synthesized image, voice, movement	Name & voice qualities	Synthesis of image, voice, movement	All sense modalities, communication patterns, unintended information
	Technical						
	Qualities	Static, asynchronous, disconnected	Static asynchronous disconnected	Dynamic asynchronous disconnected	Dynamic synchronous co-constructed	Dynamic synchronous co-constructed	Dynamic synchronous co-constructed
Communication	**Intention**						
	Sender qualities	Edited reflective	Edited reflective	Edited reflective	Spontaneous adjustable interactive	Spontaneous adjustable interactive	Spontaneous adjustable interactive
	Reception						
	Receiver subtleties	Read literally or between the lines	Background location, style formal, informal, body language	Background location, style formal, informal, body language, action	Background noise, breathing, phatic utterance, pitch, intonation	Background environment, body language, intonation, action	Background environment, body language, action, all sensory cues
	Feedback						
	Receiver feedback	Discontinuous, slow	Discontinuous, slow	Discontinuous, slow	Continuous, immediate	Continuous, immediate	Continuous, immediate

facilitated by the Swisshouse. Except for the difference in time, a party could take place simultaneously in both locations with people seeing and interacting with each other via an interactive media wall (Huang and Waldvogel, 2004). Such an informal setting might support a naturalness that is hard to achieve in more formal, camera-aware circumstances.[7]

Relating presence to collaborative action, the trust issue re-emerges. Can we work effectively with people we've never met? With people we've only "viewed"? Will mediated presence become so commonplace that it becomes natural? We are embodied creatures who take each other's measure in ways that go beyond a visual image or auditory voice. The subtle changes in body temperature, pupil dilation, or odor are all signals inadvertently sent and received, preparing us for action—nothing beats being there.

Exploring Theoretical Limitations and Collaborative Patterns

Information work, taken in the broadest sense—whether design research or design practice—often crosses boundaries; such boundaries can be extensive, as we have seen. Each requires particular sensitivity and offers particular collaborative opportunity. Given the increasing interest in collaborative work, the question of whether a pattern or theory of collaborative practice can be identified is an interesting one. Without such a theory or pattern, what remains are case-by-case exemplars.

Theoretical Limitations

As mentioned at the beginning of this chapter, collaboration is a social practice without substantial theory. The difficulties of establishing theory are explored by the sociologist Pierre Bourdieu, whose presentation of a deeper, more philosophical discussion of social science (networks, associations, reputations) and symbolic space (educational perspectives on form and content of knowledge) and its meaning puts a frame to this problem. According to him, practice does not yield to scientific explanation or modeling for two primary reasons: the difference in time and logic. Bourdieu notes (1998, 81) that the time dimension of science and that of practice are incommensurable.

> The shift from the practical scheme to the theoretical scheme, constructed after the event, from practical sense to the theoretical model, which can be read either as a project, plan or method, or as a mechanical program, a mysterious ordering mysteriously reconstructed by the analyst, lets slip everything that makes the temporal reality of practice in process... Its temporal structure, that is, its rhythm, its tempo, and above all its directionality, is constitutive of its meaning.

This phenomenon is seen in many abstract diagrams that purport to show design process. What appears to be simple and logical on paper is often a messy practice in reality, full of recursions, feedback loops, simultaneous happenings, attention shifts, new ideas, and unforeseen difficulties. The formal logic of a diagram can be only a primitive guide. Recall Schön's (1983) description of design as a process full of uncertainty, ambiguity, and value conflict. To this we add, in this chapter, the emergent purposes of collaboration. These are certainly not characteristics that make for a predictable process; thus we find a situation that is dynamic, causing participants to think and work fluidly, and to encounter conflicting ideas, processes, concepts, criteria, and even sometimes difficult personalities—all within a collaborative situation.

Following Bourdieu further, the logic of practice and theory is also incompatible. He states (1998, 81), "A player who is involved and caught up in the game adjusts not to what he sees but to what he fore-sees, sees in advance in the directly perceived present...anticipating the anticipation of others..." Bourdieu concludes that there is no possibility of giving a scientific explanation of practice (1998, 92).

> This paradoxical logic is that of all practice, or rather of all practical sense. Caught up in the "matter at hand," totally present in the present and in the practical functions that it finds there in the form of objective potentialities, practice excludes attention to itself (that is, to the past). It is unaware of the principles that govern it and the possibilities they contain; it can only discover them by enacting them, unfolding them in time.

The logic of practice is "things to be done," while the objectified logic of science is representation in a homogeneous (abstract) space. Collaboration may be the quintessential practice, as it is unpredictable in its many dimensions. Like attempts to characterize design process neatly in a diagram, the dynamic nature of collaboration, to say nothing of human variability, always eludes our grasp. Together, collaboration and design provide formidable variation and complexity. Does this describe an impossible situation within which patterns cannot be found? Must collaboration be case-by-case in design? Turning away from theory, we look to what can be drawn from experience in the practice of collaboration.

Characterizing Collaborative Variables and Patterns

Keeping in mind Bourdieu's cautionary statements about essential time and logic differences between science and practice, the expanding collaborative situation in which we work stimulates a need for some kind of comparison, tentative order, and understanding. This is not from a particular disciplinary perspective, but in a pattern-finding manner, close to practice, and at a meta-level that could provide some guidance.

Table 7.3
Collaboration variables for a case study database

Category	Variables	Example 1	Example 2	Category	Variables	Example 1	Example 2
Context	Project	Project		Discipline(s)	Same		
	Research		Research		Dual	Dual	
	Teaching				Multiple		Multiple
Goal	Apply knowledge	Apply		Process	Established		Established
	Create knowledge		Create		Negotiated	Negotiated	
	Transfer knowledge	Transfer			Evolutionary		
Scale	Small	Small	Small	Leadership	Formal		Formal
	Medium				Informal	Informal	
	Large				Preset control	Preset	
Speed	Fast				Adaptable control		Adaptable
	Moderate		Moderate	Risk	Low	Low	Low
	Slow	Slow			Medium		
Longevity	Defined end		Defined end		High		
	Sustained	Sustained		Assessment	Internal	Internal	Internal
Funding	Funded	Funded	Funded		External	External	
	Unfunded			Documentation	Detailed		Detailed
Location	Local				General	General	
	Regional	Regional			Process		
	National				Result	Result	Result
	International		International		Formal	Formal	Formal
Culture	Single	Single			Informal		
	Double				External	External	External
	Multiple		Multiple		Internal		Internal
Institution	Industry				Public	Public	Public
	University	University			Proprietary		
	Foundation		Foundation		Archived	Archived	Archived
	Government						

Example 1 is drawn from Chapter 10, the National Graphic Design Archive and
Example 2 is an educational survey for a professional organization.

What can we learn from assembled cases, examined comparatively? While tentative, a table of distinguishing features of collaborative projects is drawn (see Table 7.3).

Against these variables that characterize collaboration, two known projects were mapped as examples to see if the variables made sense. It was easy to pull from the example projects their positions relative to the variables. It may be that these variables are too simplistic, but rich combinations can result from their permutations. They might practically serve as an opening with which to gather modest patterns of collaboration and learn from individual and accumulated cases about their similarities and differences, their tactics and strategies. Perhaps a database could be constructed using these variables as classificatory tags and over time patterns would emerge, identifying a typology of collaboration. Destined never to be a science, collaborative performance nevertheless could be enhanced if we better understood it through its patterns of action. It is with this in mind that the following chapters are introduced; they focus on collaborative *practice*.

Introducing Design Collaboration Cases

The chapters that follow examine many of the issues identified here, but they expand on and contextualize the ideas through reflection or research. Three chapters (8, 9, and 10 respectively) present case studies that reveal various collaborative issues from a corporate, consultative, and institutional perspective.

In Chapter 8, Toby Bottorf takes us inside an organization with deep history and success (WGBH, Boston) to examine the problems and possibilities relating to collaboration in a content and media-based company. What emerges from his telling is collaborative practice that is largely tacit and culturally embedded, but flexible and sensitive to change.

In Chapter 9, Aaron Marcus, with long experience in running a technology-based consultancy in design, shares the transition from live, in-person collaborative work to establishing and running a virtual office with needs for explicit capture of project knowledge and consultancy standards and systems that underpin a fluidly assembling and dispersing team. While technology has smoothed the way for this event, the human dimensions of trust and shared experience remain keys to success.

In Chapter 10, Roger Remington, a design historian and educator, describes problems associated with inter-institutional collaboration—problems that result even though the participants desired and were committed to long-term development. His case is the National Graphic Design Archive, looking back on their mandate, performance, and problems in sustaining the project. The technological platform on which the project was built was too new and unstable, yet part of the energy needed to create such a collaborative project rests on its innovative opportunities.

Two chapters (11 and 12) in this section focus on fieldwork.

In Chapter 11, Nicole Schadewitz draws insight from field studies in which she observed cross-cultural teams in the unique settings of three international interaction summer schools in Europe. The importance of context and communication come to the fore in this fieldwork, along with remedies for the inevitable communication breakdowns that participants experience.

In Chapter 12, Judith Gregory describes a complex international and intercultural collaboration between developed and developing countries with a shared concern: healthcare. From this rich intercultural experience, she proposes principles for design collaboration and a concept of design for negotiation of logics.

Each case study reveals some dimensions of collaboration in general, but more strongly illustrates a constellation of collaborative practices fitting to its context and subject to reflective adjustment based on experience and situational change. These chapters deepen understanding of process and the vital role communication plays in collaborative practice.

Notes

1. Participants in 2byTwo, a symposium held at the Institute of Design, Illinois Institute of Technology in May 2002, explored four contemporary design themes, one of which was collaboration. Participants in this symposium generated the information for Table 7.1.

2. Telephone conversation with Jim Reinders, December 27, 2005.

3. For a good overview of people, projects, tools, and pointers to external links regarding open source, see, http://en.wikipedia.org/wiki/Open_Source (accessed August 2, 2005).

4. I am indebted to Naomi Baron, who cited this Asimov segment in her book *Alphabet to Email: How Written English Evolved and Where It's Heading.* (London, United Kingdom: Routledge, 2000).

5. The failed 1964 AT&T Picturephone comes to mind. Its technical problems with analog phone lines and transmission quality, its expense, the lack of others with whom to visually communicate, and the general tendency at that time to question the social intrusiveness of technology all contributed to its lack of adoption.

6. I discussed this with Jeffrey Huang at a conference in Las Vegas where he presented the communication concept behind the architecture and its technology, July 2002. Swisshouse's success as an architectural and technological space that supports distance communication has brought about similar Swisshouse constructions in San Francisco, Singapore, and most recently, Shanghai.

7. The author, while living in Hong Kong, and her husband, still in Chicago, kept in contact using Apple's "isight" on a nightly/daily basis. The major difficulty was the time difference, which was 14 hours or 10 time zones.

References

Argyrus, Chris and Donald Schön. 1978. *Organizational Learning: A Theory of Action Perspective.* Reading, MA: Addison Wesley.

Asimov, Issac. 1991. *The Naked Sun.* New York, NY: Doubleday.

Bechtel, T. 1986. The Nature of Scientific Investigation. In Bechtel, W. (ed.), *Integrating Scientific Disciplines,* 3–52. Dordrecht, Netherlands: Martinus Nijhoof.

Bourdieu, Pierre. 1990. *The Logic of Practice.* Palo Alto, CA: Stanford University Press.

Bourdieu, Pierre. 1998. *Practical Reason: On the Theory of Action.* Stanford, CA: Stanford University Press.

Bromme, Rainier. 2000. Beyond One's Own Perspective: The Psychology of Interdisciplinarity. In Weingart, Peter and Nico Stehr (eds.), *Practising Interdisciplinarity.* Toronto, ON, Canada: University of Toronto Press.

Brown, John Seeley and Paul Druid. 1991. Organizational Learning and Communities-of-Practice: Toward a Unified View of Working, Learning, and Innovation. *Organizational Science,* 2.1, 40–56.

Chang, Wen-Chih and Yen Hsu. 2005. Electronic Knowledge Management in Design Consultancies. *Design Management Review,* Spring 2005, 51–56.

Csikszentmihalyi, Mihaly, 1990. *Flow: The Psychology of Optimal Experience*. New York, NY: Harper & Row.

Corbin, Juliet and Anselm Strauss. 1998. *The Basics of Qualitative Research: Techniques and Procedures for Developing Grounded Theory*. Thousand Oaks, CA: Sage Publications.

D'Ambrosio, Bruce. N.D. Bayesian Methods for Collaborative Decision-Making. http://www.robustdecision.com/bayesianmethoddecisions.pdf (accessed October 7, 2008).

Fauske, Janice. 1999. Comparison of Interagency Community Based Collaboratives for Improving Education. *Proceedings of the American Education Research Association Conference*. Montreal, QC, Canada, April. A thorough search yielded NO dates. Even though I search Fauske papers and found one that cited this conference – it gave NO dates!

Foray, Dominique. 2004. *The Economics of Knowledge*. Cambridge, MA: MIT Press.

Gang, Jeanne. 2000. Interdisciplinary Collaboration on Design Competitions. *Proceedings of Collaborating Across Professional Boundaries: "From Education to Practice."* Illinois Institute of Technology, Chicago, IL, November 2–3.

Goodman, Nelson. 1978. *Ways of Worldmaking*. Indianapolis, IN: Hackett Publishing, Co.

Huang, Jeffrey. 2001. Future Space: A Blueprint for a New Business Architecture. *Harvard Business Review*, April, 149-161

Huang, Jeffrey and M. Waldvogel. 2004. The Swisshouse: Inhabitable Interfaces for Connecting Nations. *Proceedings of DIS 2004: Conference on Designing Interactive Systems: Processes, Methods, and Techniques*. Cambridge, MA, August 1–4. ACM 2004, 195–204.

John-Steiner, Vera, Robert J. Weber, and Michele Minnis. 1998. The Challenge of Studying Collaboration. *American Educational Research Journal*, 35.4, 773–783.

Karacapilidis, Nikos and Dimitrius Papadias. 2001. Computer Supported Argumentation and Collaborative Decision Making: The Hermes System. *Information Systems*, 26.4, 259–277.

Kim, Jinsook and Sharon Poggenpohl. 2004. Translating and Extending Gestalt Grouping Principles to Include Time to Establish a Research Framework in which to Study Motion. *Proceedings of FutureGround Conference*. Melbourne, VIC, Australia, November, 17-21

Klein, Julie Thompson. 2000. A Conceptual Vocabulary of Interdisciplinary Science. In Weingart, Peter and Nico Stehr (eds.), *Practising Interdisciplinarity*. Toronto, ON, Canada: University of Toronto Press.

Kuhn, Thomas. 1996. *The Structure of Scientific Revolutions*. Chicago, IL: University of Chicago Press.

Lave, Jen and Etienne Wenger. 1991. *Situated Learning: Legitimate Peripheral Participation*. Cambridge, United Kingdom: Cambridge University Press.

Leifer, Larry. 1999. Presentation from July 13, 1999. http://sll.stanford.edu/pubs/preindex.html (accessed March 7, 2005).

Lim, Youn-Kyung and Keiichi Sato. 2006. Describing Multiple Aspects of the Use Situation: Application of Design Information Framework (DIF) to Scenario Development. *Design Studies*, 27.1, 57–76.

Middleton, Michael. 1967. *Group Practice in Design*. New York, NY: George Braziller.

Minnis, Michele, Vera John-Steiner, and Robert Weber. 1994. Collaborations: Values, roles and working methods (Research Proposal). Albuquerque, NM: National Science Foundation, Ethics and Values Studies Program.

Pettit, Chris, D. Pullar, and D. Stimson. 2002. An Integrated Multi-scaled Decision Support Framework and Evaluation of Land-use Planning Scenarios. *Proceedings of the 1ˢᵗ International Environmental Modeling and Software Society Conference*, 34-41 Lugano, Switzerland, June 24–27.

Poggenpohl, Sharon. 2004. Practicing Collaboration in Design. *Visible Language*, 38.2,138–157.

Poggenpohl, Sharon. 2006. Crossing Boundaries in Collaborative Action. *Proceedings of the Design History Society Conference*. Delft, August 31- September 2.

Raymond, Eric S. 1999. *The Cathedral and the Bazaar*. Cambridge, MA: O'Reilly.

Rittel, Horst and Melvin Webber. 1973. Dilemmas in a General Theory of Planning. *Policy Science*, 4, 155–169.

Rogers, Everett M. 1994. *A History of Communication Study*. New York, NY: The Free Press.

Schön, Donald A. 1983. *The Reflective Practitioner*. New York, NY: Basic Books.

Schön, Donald A. 1994. *Frame Reflection: Toward the Resolution of Intractable Policy Controversies*. New York, NY: Basic Books.

Schrage, Michael. 1991. *Shared Minds: The New Technologies of Collaboration*. New York, NY: Random House.

Senge, Peter. 2006. *The Fifth Discipline Fieldbook: Strategies and Tools for Building a Learning Organization*. New York, NY: Currency Books.

Vygotsky, Lev. 1978. *Mind in Society: The Development of Higher Psychological Processes*. Cambridge, MA: Harvard University Press.

Weingart, Peter and Nico Stuhr (eds.). 2000. *Practising Interdisciplinarity*. Toronto, ON, Canada: University of Toronto Press.

8

COLLABORATIVE INFILTRATION IN A MEDIA ORGANIZATION: WGBH

Toby Bottorf

It is not easy to accurately say what kind of a company the WGBH Educational Foundation is. A superficial answer is very easy, and will have to do to start: many in and around Boston refer to WGBH simply as Channel 2. Nationally, television viewers probably recognize our visual and aural signature: an animated, neon-lit version of our logo, the element that closes the programs we produce. These programs, such as *Masterpiece Theatre*, *NOVA*, *Frontline*, *Antiques Roadshow*, and *American Experience*, make up about one third of the public television prime-time schedule. We produce and broadcast television and radio programs, but we also develop courses, media, and libraries for formal education, produce websites and other I.P. (Internet Protocol) media, and invent technologies that make media more accessible, such as closed captioning.

Clearly, to think of us as mainly a TV broadcaster or producer is not quite right, and it misrepresents the kinds of collaboration we need to engage in to thrive at our work. Yet it is a mistake we ourselves make. The only enduring definition of what we are comes from our mission: WGBH is a non-profit foundation, with a broad mandate to "inform, educate, and entertain."

The ways in which we generate ideas and exploit opportunities in the shifting media landscape depend increasingly, and at this point, quite dramatically, on how well we collaborate. At our worst, we are a collection of independent media companies sharing infrastructure. At our best, we are figuring out how to be an integrated content company. And the difference between these two scenarios is how well we are able to collaborate, and especially to break down functional silos and work across business units. If we are a collection of media companies, our strategy begins with a whole lot of air-time and bandwidth that we seek to profitably fill. Only as a content company does our reason for being bring our mission statement to practice, because it lets us begin with ideas—the stories we're passionate about, and our goals for what public, noncommercial media can uniquely achieve.

To understand what it might mean for us to be a content company as opposed to a diversified media company, a little history is helpful. We were founded in 1836 as the Lowell Institute, with a bequest to create "free public lectures for the benefit of the citizens of Boston" on topics such as philosophy, natural history, arts, and sciences. More than a century later, a partnership was struck between higher education and commercial radio. As reported (with curious prejudice toward Boston) by *Time Magazine* on November 25, 1946:

> Last week [the Lowell Institute] joined with six local colleges and universities to form the Lowell Institute Cooperative Broadcasting Council. The purpose: to broadcast learned lectures as a typically Boston bluestocking scheme of adult education. All seven Boston radio stations accepted the plan, which would be financed by stations and colleges, share & share alike. To the Lowell Institute it was one more opportunity to advance the cause of learning which had been the Institute's job for more than a century. ("Old School Tie-Up")

Four years later, this cooperative council was granted an FCC license to operate its own radio station, WGBH, which debuted with a concert of the Boston Symphony Orchestra. By 1955, WGBH entered the medium of television with the launch of Channel 2. We were operating in multiple media, but only as local producers and broadcasters. In the late 1960s, the Corporation for Public Broadcasting was incorporated, paving the way for PBS and NPR.

With an established national model for public broadcasting, our scope as producers grew. *Masterpiece Theatre, Zoom,* and *NOVA* were all launched in the early 1970s. Programs (and now also websites) produced for PBS have always been developed with their input, though we strenuously and contractually defend our editorial authority. With this increasing complexity of stakeholders and contributors came larger audiences, higher visibility, and a greater need for careful design management of the brands.

The foundation has a long tradition of valuing design. 1973 was a pivotal year in that regard, when the architecture firm Cambridge Seven Associates was enlisted to help elevate design as a process and performance at WGBH. There had at this time been significant turnover at the senior level of design, signaling a potential structural problem. Station Manager Michael Rice and President David O. Ives endorsed the fundamental recommendation that design, though it must prove its value, cannot do so from a second-class position. A number of significant steps followed. Chermayeff & Geismar was commissioned to develop an identity program which resulted in the distinct and durable "double shadow" station numerals which was married to the existing synthesized aural signature, and subsequently revised into the animated mark still in use today. The identity program also laid out a design approach based on flexibility and dynamism, rather than one based on rigid standards that were endemic for corporations at the time. A subsequent report from Cambridge Seven called for the hiring of a Design Manager, and laid out their appropriate stature and responsibilities. Chris Pullman, currently our Vice President for Branding and Visual Communications, was hired in that position.

The need for flexibility and versatility in design comes from a historical understanding of the nature of the television medium. It is inherently eclectic and varied, even more so in public broadcasting. We pioneered diverse programming genres—like Julia Child's cooking program, the first of its kind—that now show up on the cable dial as entire channels. We actively cultivated diversity in our programming and in our staff.

In this protean domain, the qualities that define our design cannot be formal prescriptions about how things look. Instead, design is governed by more fundamental criteria. As Chris Pullman puts it:

> If you and your client could answer "yes" to the following questions about a solution, then it probably is a good piece of design:
>
> Is it clear? Can I understand what it is, can I read it, can I sense its purpose?
>
> Is it accessible? Does it engage me, does it invite me in, is it easy and intuitive to use?
>
> Is it appropriate? (to its budget, to the amount of time available to make it, to the language style and level of the audience, to the medium, to the objectives of the project, and to the family of materials it will join, etc.) (Pullman, 2008)

These criteria help collaboration happen because they can be shared values. They do not impose on the designer any esoteric constraints or require that she defend her work with exclusionary designer-speak. More importantly, they do not require that our collaborators deal in any jargon to understand the efficacy of a solution.

Figure 8.1
Elements of a media-based content company.

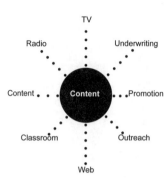

Design and Connective Tissue

While WGBH actively cultivates shared values, the structure of the organization requires many kinds of specialization, which poses problems of isolation. Our programming genres include units that are focused on science, on history, on current affairs reporting, on lifestyle programs, and on children's programming. Any of these kinds of content can take form in an array of media and contexts. In drafting proposals and planning projects, all these ways of reaching different audiences are considered.

The word "Content" in the diagram above can be replaced by "Design" or "Budget" or "Legal": any of the disciplines that that must communicate with many of our more focused, specialized departments. The generalists that work across varied production units function informally as connective tissue in the corporate body.

Perhaps the greatest challenge to our effective collaboration is simply the first hurdle: that of awareness. There would be false security in seeking to make the ways we share information more formal. Just as design standards here are not codified in a manual of standards, and should not be, so our processes for sharing information are perhaps best left informal and somewhat *ad hoc*. I remember that, when I was new at WGBH, I was deeply anxious about unknown unknowns, or the things I didn't know I didn't know. I was reassured by a remarkably welcoming sense that anyone can talk to anyone, which indicates that our approach—purposefully—is not to have protocols for communication, but rather to cultivate channels. This is tacit understanding, embodied mainly in culture. It is supported, at least in the case of the design function, by a welcome peculiarity of our organizational chart. Designers in the Interactive group do not work for the same people they report to. The scope and nature of our work is defined in the department, but we report to (and our performance evaluations are completed by) our VP of design. As Director of Design for Interactive, when I have concerns about the role of design in our work with regard to other disciplines, I have the best possible reference point in seeing the role of design at the highest levels of the foundation.

This balanced allegiance to our discipline (design) and our department (interactive) gives us two differently useful forums for communication. It also makes a useful home for, and thereby abates, the common tension in designers between their expressive aims as designers and the given needs of the communications or interaction problem. Design is used remarkably well at WGBH because it is given a voice at the VP level, but that would not be so true if it were isolated up there, removed from the day-to-day design work. Designers benefit immeasurably from having access to that executive perspective, and the foundation benefits in having design that is well-aligned with the long view.

Collaboration across Units

The "stuff" we develop takes many forms, including broadcast media for radio and television, websites, formal courses, and outreach activities for more personal engagement. In each of these, projects are developed with different goals and values in mind, using different processes and metrics for assessing performance. Coordination among these different cultures is not left entirely to the generalists that work across units. The fundamental work of mutual awareness and shared understanding is supported institutionally through forums for sharing information and teamwork. Some of these are a part of the culture while others are convened only in the service of specific projects.

As an example of the former, the foundation sponsors occasional seminars or "Insiders' Guide" presentations to areas of work that would otherwise be opaque to others. These are open to all, and they offer a general introduction to a specific kind of work and how it relates to the broader enterprise. Recent topics have explained program sponsorship, foundation fundraising, and design. The value of attending these is obvious, but the work of preparing a presentation is harder and more constructive. It requires an engagement with what colleagues don't know, or misconstrue, and it also requires framing the work of a given group in terms meaningful to others.

A more topical and intensive presentation is held at the beginning of large interdisciplinary projects. In effect, we set up an in-house school, inviting world-leading experts to come in and teach us, in all-day sessions over a few days or a week. We did this recently for a *Frontline* project on AIDS and previously, for a limited series on evolution. AIDS school was not strictly collaborative; we mostly sat and listened. But it was crucial that we did it together. School is not merely an efficient way of sharing information with a large, divergent group of people who need to work in concert even though they may not in fact work together. These schools also serve an important ritual and social function by gathering people together (who may not even know one another) for an exciting and challenging immersion in the deep end of a content area. As the broader team returns to their departments to work on the project, often for well over a year, the shared beginning offers both common knowledge and collective purpose. Even the learning has a personal dimension: often what is most memorable is the inspiring passion our teachers have for their work. In developing our content, then, we aim not only to share what the experts know, but also to convey, contagiously, their engagement with their work. I would suspect that for our teachers, who may be project partners or advisors, their sense of fellowship with us is also strengthened.

Projects that are going to be given form in multiple media have the greatest need of these shared beginnings and scheduled check-in points.

At a more basic level, the ability to communicate across these units is greatly fostered by well-cultivated cultural values. There are active efforts to recruit staff from diverse backgrounds, but in fundamental ways, we are all kindred spirits. Nobody comes to WGBH for the money. Non-profit organizations appeal to prospective staff, as they do to those who fund, on the merits of the mission. We're here because we want to give back to the community, because we want to use media to educate, because we believe in the uniquely valuable role of public media and civic institutions, or because we don't want to contribute to the central truth of commercial television and radio: that programming is created in order to deliver large audiences to advertisers. These are good reasons. They attract a specific kind of person, and when you put close to a thousand of these people together, you get a distinctive culture.

The group in which I work, Interactive, works most closely with two other groups in the foundation: the Television Productions team and our Outreach department, responsible for developing materials and programs that extend the reach of our work into classrooms and community settings. This is especially true of children's projects, due to a greater amount of shared resources.

With the Outreach team, we share the same explicit educational goals and curricular standards. Games development is often undertaken with consultation from that group. With the Television Productions department, we share many visual assets between websites and programs. On these, we often work closely with the Print Design group to develop brand identity for the larger project, such as with *Time Warp Trio* and *Fetch* (figure 8.2). Our web work is often made much richer by sharing production tools. Both *Time Warp Trio* and *Peep and the Big Wide World* were animated using Flash. Sharing tools spares us the production work (and cost) of collectively determining what still frames we might need and processing these images for use on websites. Even more valuably, working from Flash animations allows us to build much more seamless and immersive sites because we can blur the distinctions between static art, animations, and interactive elements.

In addition to working together and sharing resources, we also support one another's work. For example, many of the millions of audience submissions to the *Zoom* website become ideas that air on the program. Using the web as a feedback loop with the audience is particularly apt for a show that is proudly, "By kids, for kids!" Similarly, updating websites helps keep shows current while they are in reruns.

Figure 8.2
Three logos developed by interactive and print designers for use across broadcast, interactive media, and print.

Interactive Media Development

The Interactive group at WGBH produces a remarkably broad range of work. Projects can differ in scale by two orders of magnitude or more. They can vary dramatically in audience, in subject matter, and tone. We produce:

- Companion websites for ongoing and limited public television series we produce, such as *NOVA*, *Evolution*, and *Arthur*
- Companion websites for other non-PBS television series, such as *Time Warp Trio* and *Peep and the Big Wide World*
- Libraries of formal education resources, such as interactives and video clips, aligned with curricular standards
- Web- and video-based formal education courses for teachers and professionals
- Websites for outside mission-aligned organizations, usually non-profit and educational
- Additional media for any of the above, such as podcasts, DVDs, CDs

The range of our work is illustrated in this pair of sites below. These sites have something in common: both are built to support science learning, but they look, read, and behave very differently because their audiences are so different (see figure 8.3).

Through our project work, we continue to gain expertise in technical and functional areas, but also in the refinement or correction of processes for working in the kinds of teams that are typical for us. In the area of skills, we have to be comfortable always "living in Beta" and looking to past similar work as the baseline for things we are beginning. Among many evergreen priorities for us are: optimizing for search engines, developing accessible media, increasing data richness, and meaningfully integrating linear media such as video with other modes of presentation and interaction. In terms of improving our work processes, we seek to continually improve the ways in which we learn, not only from each other, but also from both our content experts and our users. This is important because we realize that our work is essentially about translating and interpreting specialized content for general audiences.

We perennially struggle to make the extra effort to include user-centered methods like front-end evaluation and paper-prototyping in our budgets and timelines. There is no disagreement about whether it would be better to include them, but they are not built in to the way we work. If we were as good at designing with our audiences as we are with our experts, this would have benefits beyond improving the effectiveness of the projects. It would require and reward a greater attitude of openness, which would allow us to be more surprised in the things we learn. As it is, we learn rather purposefully, by finding answers to our questions. A more user-centered approach might challenge our assumptions more, and increase our curiosity for different questions, for different ways of framing the purpose and uses of our work. We know, because we monitor it, that our work is uncommonly rigorous yet accessible, but we don't often question how it could or should be more emotionally persuasive.

Figure 8.3
NOVA and PEEP are two sites with similar goals, but they have very different audiences in mind. For PEEP, we don't even assume the audience is old enough to read.

A recurring tension in our workflow is between more autocratic and (hopefully) decisive decision-making and a process of defining and evaluating our work that is based more on discussion and consensus. The latter approach may seem slower, but it is particularly useful at the beginning of a project, and so it is worth the trouble. When we are working at our best, these two approaches represent a false dichotomy. The best-run projects create clearly defined domains for exploration, in which the give-and-take can be quite liberal. A crucial limit on the amount of collective work is, simply, the available time. A producer will sometimes need to say, "Time's up," and make an executive decision to choose a specific direction, to leave certain options open to later phases of work (which must then be addressed under tighter constraints and at a smaller scale) or to resolve uncertainty with informal user testing.

The Core Interactive Team

Our Interactive group is proud of a team model that we apply to all projects, called sometimes the Triumvirate, or more modestly, the three-legged-stool. What this means is that all projects stand on three legs, or disciplines. A team on any project always contains at least one person in each of the following functional roles.

Producers, focused on the content: Producers are the editorial voice of the project. Producers ensure that our projects have unique value by evaluating existing media that deal with the content area. They keep us from repeating others' work or building commonplace features. When they find excellent assets that would work for us, they often build partnerships that allow us to use and build on existing media, data, or code. Because producers are typically the channel of communication with outside partners, they often share with the core team a synthesis of the values and needs of other partners and stakeholders. There is an element of shielding in this, especially as our far-flung constituents may disagree with each other or with us. Producers also play the role of project managers, which is not always for the best. We want our producers to be visionary, which is a personality trait that doesn't typically coexist with a passion for the minutiae of process—like consensus-building, scheduling, and budgeting—that make work flow smoothly and efficiently.

Developers, focused on the medium, and stretching what it is capable of: Developers are our technical experts and masters of the possible. They define the realm of feasible options, often ambitiously. Because our budgets all but preclude speculative research or skunkworks, we must be very opportunistic in how we exploit emerging technology. We do this by something like matchmaking: developers are vigilant in monitoring innovations in platforms and media, with an eye specifically toward how they map to things we do, or reveal things we might do.

In the play of collaborative work, they often (by personality or necessity) assume a skeptical posture. When developers say, "That can't be done," they mean, "That can't be done that way," and often come up with alternatives that sometimes involve only minor changes, but sometimes effect a fundamental change in the nature of the thing we're making. All this might make developers the most disruptive members of a team, but because we involve all disciplines from the start, we almost never confront the two potential gaps between plans and reality: between what we wish for and what we can actually do; and between what we're doing and what we should have done, if we only knew we could.

Designers, focused on the user experience of our brands: Designers are responsible for the user experience of the site and for the effortless-seeming synthesis of editorial and technical strategies into an elegant and appropriate experience. They lead architectural decisions about site structure and navigation, formal decisions about graphic and information design, and behavioral decisions about user interface of custom or rich-media features. The designer informally takes the role of user-advocate in collaborative work, drafting personas and use scenarios, and leading the testing of paper prototypes. Designers also must ensure that a project remains appropriately in its family of branded materials, either in terms of historical continuity or the simultaneous development of brand identity across many media for large projects.

To understand how these disciplines work well together, it's illuminating to consider what can happen when any one is underrepresented, or not contributing fully to the collective development process.

Without enough of the producer role, we might make something that already exists or that isn't compellingly unique. It might also be factually incorrect or lack the necessary credibility that well-marshaled partnerships can bring. More than likely, the project would not come in on time and on budget. Producers ensure that a project has a clear and compelling vision, and that the whole is greater than the sum of parts.

Without enough of the developer role, we might not make anything at all. Our work would lack functional elegance and stability, as well as the kind of graceful innovation that seems like stage magic in the way it escapes conscious detection. Developers help ensure that we are not behind or ahead of what we can ambitiously achieve.

Without enough of the designer role, we might make something that speaks to its creators or contributing experts, but not its intended audience. All audiences might be put-off or disengaged from the content. The thing might be comprehensive and powerful, but rendered dry from the lack of a visual, visceral engagement.

For all of these situations, the more meaningful definition of "not enough" of a given role is its under-representation in the earliest, grandest and most significant decisions about scope and intent. In breaking down the roles like this, there is all the inaccuracy you would expect in generalizations. In fact, these roles are blurry. We are curious about each other's work and learn from each other. Furthermore, if the nature of the work lies mainly in their area of expertise, there are instances when a project might best be produced by a developer or a designer.

On all teams, there are different kinds of tension. Some are commonplace and difficult, like the balancing of quality and scope against time and budget. Another source of tension is constructive if just as difficult, and it deals specifically with the tension among role definitions. There are, on any team, skills and aptitudes that are unique to one person, and others that are shared or duplicated among different people. In terms of a personal engagement, these represent two different ways of asserting a valuable contribution to and ownership over the project, stated respectively as, "How can my unique skills be best used here?" and, "How can I have more say in how this project is defined and comes together?"

Negotiating the balance among roles happens in the daily work of developing a project. Misunderstandings rise to the level of conflict most frequently in the work of setting timetables for projects, which is speculative work at best. A poorly scheduled project can misuse design in two ways. First, designers might complain of being brought into projects too early, before the needs are defined, and feeling stuck with too many options. Alternatively, designers may become involved too late, after all meaningful decisions have been made, and their work consists of little more than presentation. To frustrated producers, this can present a narrow window.

Games Development: a Case Study

An interactive game we recently developed is a good case study, on a small scale, of how such dynamic collaboration can result in excellent work. The game is called *3 Puck Chuck*, and it can be found at http://pbskids.org/zoom/games/3puckchuck/index.html.

The work we develop is almost always constrained in some way or other by specific, formal educational goals. This is particularly true of work intended for kids. In this case, funding provided to the project by the National Science Foundation stipulated that our work should help kids learn about Newtonian physics. It's important to note that while funders may set objectives for us, they are by no means collaborative partners. In fact, we have strict firewalls between funding sources and editorial decision-making. Our credibility requires it.

This project, in proposals, speculated about how this game might be designed. The solution was proposed as a miniature golf game, which would allow users to engage with the science goals through direct action and observation. This seemed like an age-appropriate and pedagogically interesting direction to take. We always assume that a proposal's solution (which is largely an informed guess) can change, so long as we are meeting the goals. In fact, the nature of this game did change a good deal, due to the way we included other voices from other disciplines.

As we began work in earnest on this game, our early brainstorming meetings included not only the core team, but our science advisors, who kept us mindful of the classroom and its culture and audiences in very immediate ways. They also helped us develop scientifically sound and interesting ideas we might not otherwise have thought of, and then later evaluated our work and recommended any needed changes as we entered our Beta phase of production.

Present at this brainstorm were writers, designers, developers, producers, colleagues from Outreach and Television Production, and science advisors. Including a variety of disciplines early in the process helps ensure that the qualities of the game are well-integrated: we avoid creating a poorly-assembled version of a game if the features and requirements of the game are arrived at together with input from all who will be involved in the game's development. In particular, the inclusion of science advisors (or the relevant content experts) makes the learning in the game and the fun in the game more likely to be one and the same thing. By contrast, a badly-designed game is like a bitter medicine in a sugar shell: a surface of distraction and liveliness attempting to cover up for an educational experience that even the creators doubt is interesting. If it's not fun to make, we can hardly expect it to be fun to use.

The brainstorm began along rather typical lines, with the free and playful gathering of ideas. Two things became apparent quickly. We realized that we were off-target with golf, and we noticed that we could very easily model some of the physical issues with tabletop objects. There were two main problems with golf as the idea for this game. First, the impact—the striking of the ball—is instantaneous and therefore illustrates very poorly the transmission of energy to the ball. Second, the opportunity to illustrate "equal and opposite reactions" is absent in a game where there are no collisions. So we used objects of different mass, like coins of different denominations, to literally play with ideas. Before long we were setting up tabletop obstacles and targets, using caroms and combination shots to play the game.

With a game concept that was clear, engaging, and scientifically valid, we proceeded to writing specifications and developing early prototypes. The specification referred to the project as a Newtonian Science Gizmo. It included a conceptual outline of goals, user experience, and game play. Here is a brief excerpt of it:

Summary
This is a Flash-based multi-player, multi-level game in which players earn points by knocking the game puck into a target and opponent's game pieces into traps.

Educational goals
Players can explore Newton's Laws of Motion as they change variables within the game.

User goals
Sink the game puck(s) to earn the value of your game pieces in the arena and get to the next level. Sink opponent's pieces to remove them from play and earn points.

The spec was reviewed by the entire team, and after any necessary clarification or revision, it became the blueprint for prototype development. Our work process

Figure 8.4
The first prototype of this game received almost no attention to the interface design. It was purely functional. The second image shows the final game design, which was directed by our testing of the first version with users.

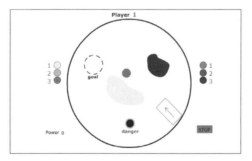

was markedly more fluid and collaborative than is typical for the field, and indeed sometimes for us. Typically, things get made according to a recipe Henry Ford would recognize, with the executive producer developing the game specs, the designer then articulating the interface and look-and-feel, and then the developer building functionality into the static but finished screens. Admittedly, this is an efficient and uncomplicated (if less rewarding) way to work, and we have to work at not falling into this pattern. On this project, however, the essence of game play was so concrete and physical that our first prototype was an experimental Flash file of the behavioral interactions of play. In this game, the direct actions upon objects, and the immediate feedback of effects, or reactions, needed to be the way users learn to play.

So the developer began in parallel with the designer, building the functional model at the same time as the look-and-feel of the objects and arena took form. Our objective was for the game play to be self-evident and instructive, so we tested fully functional but undersigned prototypes with users to see where the gaps in understanding lay. There were places where the user had gaps in understanding what to do next, or what had just happened. Noting these moments, we designed messages and feedback into the game so that it would explain itself at the points where that was needed. Out of this process, we were able to get as little interface as possible between the user and the game, and also to develop engaging variations that scale the difficulty of the game at successive levels. The resulting game is scientifically instructive, playfully accessible, and quite addictive. It is that way largely because of the way it was made.

Challenges and Opportunities

This chapter has examined WGBH's practices in progressively smaller groups, beginning with the foundation, looking at work across units, focusing within the Interactive group, and finally looking at the project work of a given team. I will close by backing out from teams to the foundation, looking at how our collaborative practices must respond to the increasing rate of change in our business environment.

In the Interactive group, our roles on a team are mostly well-defined. Our lumping together of the roles of "producer" and "project manager" is a problem, however. It asks one individual to hold the vision for the project, to manage the project's efficient and timely workflow, and to manage the team's development and contributions. That's probably a superhuman request. As it is, team dynamics are more collectively and tacitly managed, with roles being negotiated rather than dictated. Overlaps in skills are more often a source of mutual understanding than competition. There is a cultural norm in our department of respect for the roles played by others. As a result, we feel entitled to high esteem and meaningful engagement. Of course, the wild card in this is that people have personalities, and sometimes the chemistry on teams can be volatile. We look for no-fault solutions in having the flexibility to staff people to different projects. The same person might be deemed difficult on one project and ideally suited to another.

The ways we share information up and out of a team are informal, through functional meetings (designer or developer) or at staff meetings. The former are good forums for sharing work in progress, while the latter are commonly used to present a completed project. These informal means of keeping aware of each other's work are effective enough for a group of about fifty people, but do not scale up to the challenge of communicating across groups. There may be electronic tools we could use that would make more visible the knowledge and assets that other groups might need, or need to know about. Our endemic problem of "unknown unknowns" would benefit from some means of confidently discriminating between information one can't find and information that doesn't exist.

When we know we have a need to share information broadly, we do an excellent job. The approach of a kickoff school for large projects, such as AIDS school, is immensely valuable. It's supportive of distributed teamwork at its best. These multifaceted projects take good advantage of large check-in meetings for the team. In addition to offering relatively formal progress updates, the "chatter" in these meetings often reveals issues— misunderstandings or divergent assumptions—before they become problems.

At the highest level, strategy and culture are twin expressions of our mission. The greatest challenge for our collaborative practice is a manifestation of both strategy and culture: how well we think strategically across disciplines.

This question arises at the earliest stages of proposal development, because proposals are almost never written by multidisciplinary teams, yet they define the full breadth of a project's scope. Proposals result from solitary work done by visionary producers. In defining a project, they also imbue the whole enterprise with the assumptions and values under which they get made. These values and unstated truths in an organization are what I call "cultural myths," because they function like mythology to frame our experience. One of WGBH's cultural myths is the appealing romantic notion that "Genius Works Alone." When we subscribe to it, it results in opportunities that are too broadcast-centered (or so says a guy who works in interactive media). An alternative cultural myth more common to interactive media and software development is that "The User Can Teach Us." These two views of the world have no overlap, and may indeed be antithetical to each other. Our culture favors the former, and a valid concern about increasing user-centeredness is that it cedes control in ways that clash with our mission. We have an explicit educational purpose, which implies that we know better. If we let audiences tell us what they want, the critique goes, we'll end up no different from commercial media.

This critique, I believe, fails to grasp that we can decide what to say, and work with our audience to resolve how to say it, and how they use it. I think it misunderstands the difference between open practices and passive practices. Openness in how we work is an ancillary benefit of adopting more user-centered and collaborative methods. Put another way, deciding to learn more from our audiences would invariably help us learn more from each other. It would breed different practices and habits of mind.

I'm not advocating a revolution or the overthrow of one cultural idea by another. Rather, I believe our best hopes lie in ensuring that the viewpoints can coexist, perhaps even to mutual benefit. That seems likely to happen if we are indeed thinking across disciplines, or across media. A good use of user-centered methods may be to recast the role of research to focus it more on understanding audiences before we begin projects, since they will increasingly control what they watch and listen to. We may need to assess the value (and cost) of appointing executive producers that are agnostic about media and platforms. We may need better tools for analyzing the landscape of audiences, messages, and media.

The simplest indicator that WGBH does a pretty good job of being a collaborative organization is that we purposefully try to be one, and assess how we're doing. It's a priority. There is a general and growing sense that we need to be better at working flexibly and together to take advantage of the massive changes in our business. At root, the changes are technological, springing from massively cheaper storage and broader bandwidth. As a result, though, we work in a context where our assumptions about legal rights, distribution channels, and business models are all called into question. For design, there are also dramatic user-experience transformations that result from the inversion of our relationship from producer-controlled to audience-controlled. It's clear that audiences expect to determine when and how they consume our media. We need to expect that this could change what audiences want, too, in ways we can only understand by experimentation. Content may change as mass audiences fragment into more passionate but smaller groups, but media platforms are indisputably changing, and chaotically.

In this environment, the greater challenge is not to make conscious changes, but to be ready for unpredictability. What we do consciously, we do well. What we do unconsciously, informally, and culturally will become more important, though. The ways in which we share information determine how well small departmental successes can become entire businesses for the foundation. The openness with which we compare strategic models and allow different cultural myths to coexist determines how easily we can simultaneously develop ideas for radically different possible futures.

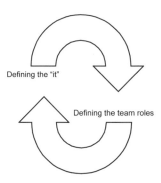

Figure 8.5
Basic issue for defining an unknown, yet to be developed, "it."

Defining the "it"

Defining the team roles

We are in an ongoing iterative and negotiated inquiry into two things: the evolving nature of the "it" we are building (see figure 8.5), and the definition of the set of roles that make up the team.

For us to continue to get better at doing both these tasks involves an increase in flexibility rather than any methodical transformation of our methods. We have historically chosen tacit and informal means of sharing information over programmatic and explicit means, and we have valued open channels over standardized protocols. That has generally worked well for us. There may be a general sense that, "Hey, we collaborate as much as we need to," but there is almost certainly going to be greater need and more ambiguity about how much is right. The only challenges we can prepare for are the ones we create for ourselves. Our focus needs to be on the opportunities that will surprise us.

References

Anderson, Chris. 2006. *The Long Tail*, New York, NY: Hyperion.

Friedman, Mildred, Ed. WGBH, Boston: A Design Anatomy. *Design Quarterly 116*. (1981) Published by Walker Art Center.

Pullman, Chris. *What I've Learned*. December 3, 2008. Design Observer. Available from http://designobserver.com/archives/entry.html?id=38855

"Old School Tie Up." *Time Magazine*, November 25, 1946, p.85

Schrage, Michael. 1999. *Serious Play*. Cambridge, MA: Harvard Business School Press.

9

LIGHT AND LIVELY: RUNNING A VIRTUAL DESIGN STUDIO

Aaron Marcus

What is a "virtual" office? More specifically, what is a virtual design studio? How does one run a virtual design studio? How does it differ from a "real" office or design studio? I will explore in this chapter the similarities and differences by describing the ongoing experiment of running my own firm over the past quarter-century. My firm has been a meeting ground for professionals from many different disciplines, such as the following: branding, culture studies, ethnographic analysis, graphic design, human factors and ergonomics, illustration, information design, localization/translation, music, software engineering, sound engineering, technical editing, technical illustration, usability analysis, video editing, visual design, and design. As Rachel Abrams (2005) has written about collaboration, "These days, [every] one who is anyone has to be working with someone." My own education in science (physics) and graphic design perhaps set the stage for such a collaborative effort. Much writing and research discusses the issues of collaboration in the office (see list of references).

However, first we have to back up a little into the history of Aaron Marcus and Associates, Inc. (AM+A), which in 2007 celebrated its 25th anniversary as a pioneering user-centered, user-interface development firm.

I had already made a career leap by becoming a graphic designer after completing an undergraduate degree in physics at Princeton University. Then I became the first graphic designer in the world to work full-time with computer graphics in 1967 as a summer intern at AT&T Bell Telephone Labs in Murray Hill, NJ, while also a graduate student at the Yale School of Art and Architecture's Graphic Design Department in New Haven, CT. Two years later, as a consultant at Bell Labs while teaching at Princeton University's School of Architecture and Urban Planning, I programmed a page layout system for the AT&T Picturephone®. I had to puzzle out the user-interface for one of the earliest raster-scan displays connected to a computer. This challenge started me along a path that led to my teaching at the University of California at Berkeley's (UCB's) College of Environmental Design and eventually becoming a Staff Scientist at the UCB Lawrence Berkeley Laboratory's Computer Science and Mathematics Department, where I wrote one of the earliest user-interface design guidelines for a device-independent, multiple-database-management system developed for the US Department of Energy. At this point, in August of 1982, I took a deep breath and decided to start one of the world's first computer-based design firms.

The firm began in my house, not in my garage, where some entrepreneurs initiated their businesses in nearby Silicon Valley. Starting with just two other employees, and taking a risky step to start a computer-based visual design firm targeting high-technology firms, our first operations were simple. We started with both modest and extravagant equipment.

Our first computer was an ordinary Atari 600 game machine, coupled with an NTSC-cabled color television monitor and a primitive word-processing program in the Atari computer that drove a small line printer. The Atari Institute had donated the equipment to us for educational research purposes. Thanks to another grant, this one a significant three-year US Defense Department Advanced Research Projects Agency (DARPA) grant for research into program visualization (Prof. Ronald Baecker, University of Toronto, and I were co-principal investigators), we had a Perq high-performance workstation connected to a 300 dot-per-inch black-and-white display and a Xerox laser printer. We used this equipment to make countless experiments in the typography of program visualization, eventually designing new conventions for typographic layout that improved reader comprehension by twenty percent among novice programmers. We published the results of our research in a book, *Human Factors and Typography for More Readable Programs* (1990), published by Addison Wesley.

When the Apple Macintosh appeared, I decided that this device was the wave of the future, and I converted the entire firm to eight networked (via AppleTalk) Macintoshes, each with 528K RAM and a laser printer. Relatively inexpensive, networked technology and effective communication media (facsimile and electronic mail) have been important to our firm's staff communicating with each other and with clients from the earliest years. By this time, we had five to ten staff members, including contractors and interns. When we started the company, the Perq workstation, display, and software cost $85,000, and the laser printer cost $25,000, far beyond any typical small graphic design firm's equipment budgets. When we first bought our Apples at $5,000 per Macintosh, a 20-megabyte external hard drive cost $5,000. Such is life in the fast lane of advancing technology, where prices plummet while technical capabilities soar. The firm continued in this home location until October 1990.

Within a few years of starting the business, the dining room had become the administrative assistant's office, the living room became a combination conference room and reception area, a small side-room connected to the main bedroom became my office and was sometimes used by an assistant, and my children's bedrooms became staff office rooms. The house was restrung with network and intercom cabling that it never had before, in addition to an extra parallel electrical system, in order to facilitate communication among people with high-technology equipment. A house built in 1927 became a somewhat advanced-technology home-office for its time.

Collaboration and Cooperation/Design Philosophy

In the small space of a private home office, perhaps three-quarters of 1700 square feet total among all the rooms involved, it was easy to collaborate. It was easy to move from room to room, to gather in one space for discussions, and to bump into people. It was also hard to hide. Everyone's personal and professional life was quite exposed, especially mine. In the quirky 1980s, this seemed appropriate and natural. I knew of many other small high-technology firms that were starting in people's homes in and around Silicon Valley. I had based my idea of work areas and collaboration on my experience in corporate and institutional graphic design offices of the late 1960s and 1970s, when most work was paper-, print-, and photography-based.

AM+A worked differently than other design firms of which I was aware. Some small firms about our size were ruled autocratically by very strong-handed and firm patriarchs; this individual determined the look and feel of every project that left the office. In contrast, our projects by their nature were often quite complex and evolved over long periods of time, making it impossible for me personally to control every detail or activity. Involved with all aspects of the firm, I could not micromanage everything, even though I tried. Eventually, I came to review proposals, contracts, interim reports, and final reports, as well as prepare documents that served as standards/templates for the designers/analysts. Individually, and in groups, the designers/analysts had a fair amount of independence to proceed as they felt best.

This approach worked reasonably well, and staff members seemed to enjoy the relative autonomy of their individual and work-group efforts. Especially in later years (in the larger office described below), turnover was relatively slow in comparison to many high-technology companies. Even today, some members of our team have been associated with the firm for ten and fourteen years. This perspective enabled them, over the years, to propose new tools (e.g., with emergence of Director, Quark, InDesign, Dreamweaver, and other software applications), new methods (more brainstorming, more group critiques, or horizontal versus vertical documentation formats), and even office arrangements (a common space for group critiques) that eventually were added to the collaborative or individual repertoire.

Even in the earliest years, I relied on the staff's knowledge of best practices, their skill sets, a shared vocabulary and general design process within the firm, and their referral to canonical designs, reports, and other documents as a basis for work. Early on, we spent considerable effort and time to develop a vocabulary, an articulated development process, and an understanding of the philosophy and principles of our kind of work. Some of the terminology came from my own formative publications in the early 1980s and from the research work we completed in 1982–1985 for DARPA. Some of this content was embodied in the book Ron Baecker and I co-wrote that resulted from that research. In later years, a fully developed intranet made archives of best practice documents available to all staff members. Much of this intranet work is directly attributable to the efforts of Joe Dobrowolski, who has served the firm as system administrator, project manager, and technical specialist for more than fourteen years. He gathered content, designed and built the intranet, and maintained it for several years.

Moving to Larger Offices

Beginning in October 1990, as we contemplated further growth, we moved into 3,000 square feet of open office space on two levels in Emeryville, California, a high-technology-oriented location between Berkeley and Emeryville. We now felt like we were swimming in a vast ocean of office space. The designers/analysts, for the most part, worked in the loft area, at first in semi-closed off cubicles, then more and more in what was left of cubicles adjoining an open central space. Meanwhile, the administrative staff moved into more closed and cloistered offices. There was now a clear distinction between the administration/management and the designers/analysts, for better and for worse. The office manager, marketing person, or I could carry on sensitive conversations in the privacy of a closed-door office. The designers/analysts could carry on group project discussions in an open area accessible to all without disturbing those who needed to carry on private conversations with vendors, prospects, and clients. However, the designers/analysts felt strongly the separation of their team from "the others," which fostered an "us versus them" mentality. Having company in-house lunches, picnics, birthday parties, restaurant nights out, in-house retreats, and off-site retreats helped to counter the inevitable distance that grows between groups. It seemed necessary approximately every three years to gather together in retreats to re-define our mission, objectives, and goals.

Our network connections, telephone system, and other equipment continued to improve, helping us to communicate amongst ourselves, with our clients and vendors, and with the world at large. Still, we generated much paper: reports, guidelines, analyses, sketches, etc. In 1992, CD-ROM-based multimedia arrived. In 1994, a Lawrence Berkeley Laboratory (LBL) colleague advised me that the web was coming, and that we should prepare for that revolution. At AT&T, decades earlier, around the corner from my own cubicle, Unix was invented at Bell Labs by Brian Kernigan and Dennis Ritchie. I had been using the internet in a Unix environment at LBL in 1979. In the mid-1990s, the web and the internet leaped into the public's awareness. By 1997, we were already consulting, analyzing, and designing web-based applications and websites. Our staff, which had typically remained at five to ten people, began to grow larger.

By 1999, I decided to open a New York City office within the offices of one of our main clients, Cogito Learning Media, for which we eventually designed the user-interfaces of more than thirty products in three lines of computer-based training and educational products. By 2002, our New York office had grown, requiring its own space, and we moved into an open single-room office space about fifteen blocks north of the World Trade Center. That office grew to about ten staff members with occasional assistance from several part-time contractors. The New York office had its own networked computers, local vendors, local clients, office culture (more informal, being something of a satellite office), and local methods, which were not always consistent with the California headquarters.

Meanwhile, the California office had grown to its largest size in 2002, with about twenty employees and occasional assistance from its own fleet of part-time contractors. The primary systems administration, corporate standards, and company management was in the California location.

Challenges of Collaboration/Cooperation and Designer/Analyst Philosophy

While I was pleased that AM+A had successfully grown a second, "cloned" office, the company now faced collaboration challenges more formidable than any it faced earlier. Some of them are described below.

While for years we had accommodated clients in four USA time zones, in the UK, Finland, Israel, and Japan, now we were faced with our own designers/analysts living simultaneously in time zones separated by three hours. Phone call scheduling, including their cost, became more demanding in terms of planning. We tried to overcome the physical separation by encouraging frequent phone contact. Together with email connection (not so much instant messaging or web-cams yet in the early years), we managed to stay reasonably in touch. However, inevitably, the people and culture of the two offices grew to be distinctly different based on the individuals involved, the long versus short history of the two locations, and their geographic milieu. People and things could become hidden or forgotten simply by being 3,000 miles away.

Life was much more complex. Eventually, we used web-cams and monitors at each location for weekly staff meetings. We debated the best method for reviewing projects, issues, and other matters in the agenda of these meetings. Although we began with a recital by each person of the project on which she or he was working, we later adopted a somewhat less rigid, more freeform review to keep the meetings interesting and engaging.

The cultures of the two locations grew separately and were distinctive, because most of the staff at each location had never met the other staff and because the local urban environments, weather, and culture differed dramatically. We attempted to solve the challenge of keeping people close and in-sync by occasionally sending some of the California staff for a week to work on a project in New York, and vice-versa. Needless to say, the travelers enjoyed the experience, even though the trips added significantly to overhead.

On particular projects, we tried to involve at least one person from each office in a major project in the other office, even without travel. Being involved in email exchanges, telephone conference calls, and document exchanges enabled a given individual to collaborate with team members 3,000 miles away. However, distance and time-zone differences still worked against team cohesion. For example, when a team in California felt they really needed to take a lunch break, it might be the middle of the afternoon work session in New York. Discussion meeting times had to be carefully coordinated to maximize uncomplicated times of discussion and "bonding."

Having two physical offices did have some distinct benefits. One was that we could offer a local-facing office to prospective clients. Some companies we interviewed with would simply not want a contractor who was not local. Now we had two local offices. I know for certain that at least one New York City prospective client would not work with anyone who was not substantially already in New York City. We lost a number of projects in which, all things being equal, the prospective client decided in favor of the local firm that could be counted on to run quickly over to attend unexpected meetings or to fix a problem. Sometimes we were in that fortunate circumstance, being both near Silicon Valley as well as New York-area companies.

For myself, the challenge was being able to foster independent decision-making while at the same time adhering to AM+A's best practices in each office. I appointed a Director of each office, concerned with project efficiency and effectiveness, with a third Director of Design to encourage best practices across both offices. The results were good in that each Director fostered individual efforts of corporate culture and best practices that reflected their orientation, and at the same time the Director of Design published cross-office documents to help establish a consistent base of typical documents for task analysis, user profiles, use scenarios, and heuristic evaluation check lists. However, there were also inevitable weaknesses dependent upon the individuals involved and the challenges posed by the local teams, clients, and local circumstances. For example, the founding office, the one I was located in most of the time and which housed the primary accounting, marketing, and office management resources, inevitably was seen as the base office and the other as a satellite.

AM+A also made impressive efforts to collaborate locally and across offices on projects. We exchanged staff between the two offices on projects at an unprecedented rate, and regular meetings kept people in-sync on projects. AM+A also made efforts to develop a set of archival templates on its primary and secondary servers that would enable all designers/analysts to use a standard set of documents for letters, proposals, reports, heuristic analyses, guidelines, past project deliverables, etc. We kept standard template forms for such items as reports, which showed all of the components of contact data, introductions, standard titling and headers/footers, conclusions and appendices, so that staff members would be less inclined to forget to include one or more of these. We were gradually working towards a "database" of documents, which was somewhat informal, but whose location and availability was made known to all.

As it had been throughout the years, the media and terminology of the firm continued to evolve (see Figure 9.1). We continued to rely on our basic premises that we developed user interfaces and focused on information-intensive projects that required information design and information visualization. We had begun working on many paper-oriented projects, from designing laser-printed forms, books, and documentation to calendars. We had migrated to CD-ROMs after 1992, designing more than thirty computer-based training products for Cogito Learning Media in 1995–2000. These last projects in particular required extensive and careful management of digital assets (photography, video, music, text, illustration, animations, etc.) and the coordination of teams of many people (writers, illustrators, editors, user-interface

Figure 9.1
AM+A Specific heuristics

• **Aesthetic integrity and minimalist design**
Dialogues should not contain information which is irrelevant or rarely needed. Every extra unit of information in a dialogue competes with the relevant units of information and diminishes their relative visibility. Information should be well organized and consistent with principles of visual design.

• **Consistency and standards**
Users should not have to wonder whether different words, situations, or actions mean the same thing. Follow platform conventions.

• **Direct manipulation/See and point**
Users should be able to see on the screen what they're doing and should be able to point at what they see. This forms a paradigm of noun (object) then verb (action). When the user performs operations on the object, the impact of those operations on the object is immediately visible.

• **Error prevention**
Even better than good error messages is a careful design which prevents a problem from occurring in the first place.

• **Feedback / Visible system status**
The system should always keep users informed about what is going on, through appropriate feedback within reasonable time.

• **Fitt's Law**
The time to acquire a target is a function of the distance to and size of the target.

• **Flexibility and efficiency of use**
Accelerators—unseen by the novice user—may often speed up the interaction for the expert user such that the system can cater to both inexperienced and experienced users. Allow users to tailor frequent actions.

• **Help and documentation**
Even though it is better if the system can be used without documentation, it may be necessary to provide help and documentation. Any such information should be easy to search, be focused on the user's task, list concrete steps to be carried out, and be concise. Help users recognize, diagnose, and recover from errors Error messages should be expressed in plain language (no codes), precisely indicate the problem, and constructively suggest a solution.

• **Information legibility/Density**
Maximize the amount of data to the amount of ink or pixels used. Eliminate any decorations on charts and graphs that do not actually convey information, such as 3-dimensional embellishments. Less is more is the rule in information design as every pixel used that does not contribute to information dilutes it.

• **Match between system and the real world**
The system should speak the user's language, with words, phrases and concepts familiar to the user, rather than system-oriented terms. Follow real-world conventions, making information appear in a natural and logical order.

• **Modelessness**
For the most part, try to create modeless features that allow people to do whatever they want when they want to in your application. Avoid using modes in your application because a mode typically restricts the operations that the user can perform. Modelessness gives the user more control over what he or she can do and allows the user to maintain context of the work.

• **Perceived stability**
In order to cope with the new level of complexity that computers introduce, people need stable reference points. To give users a conceptual sense of stability, the interface provides a clear, finite set of objects with a clear, finite set of actions. When particular actions are unavailable, they are not eliminated, but dimmed.

• **Recognition rather than recall**
Make objects, actions, and options visible. The user should not have to remember information from one part of the dialogue to another. Instructions for use of the system should be visible or easily retrievable whenever appropriate.

• **User control and freedom**
Allow the user, not the computer, to initiate and control actions. Users often choose system functions by mistake and will need a clearly marked "emergency exit" to leave the unwanted state without having to go through an extended dialogue. Support undo and redo.

• **Visible interfaces/WYSIWYG**
Don't hide features in your application by using abstract commands. People should be able to see what they need when they need it. Most users cannot and will not build elaborate mental maps and will become lost or tired if expected to do so.

Figure 9.2
AM+A's User-interface design heuristics

The following heuristics apply to all of the user-interface components that AM+A describes in its publications:	• Graphic Design for Electronic Documents and User Interfaces (Marcus, 1992).
	• The original list of usability heuristics authored by Jakob
Metaphors	Nielsen, in Usability Inspection Methods (Nielsen, 1994).
Mental models	• The classic Human Interface Guidelines (Apple, 1992). These
Navigation	guidelines deal more with the quality of modern user interfaces in
Interaction	general, rather than specifically with usability concerns.
Appearance	• Principles of clear information visualization and graphic
Information-visualization schema	excellence espoused in The Visual Display of Quantitative
They are adapted from various sources:	Information, Envisioning Information, and Visual Explanations, by
	Edward Tufte, 1983, 1990).
	• Basic principles of user interface design from TOG on Interface
	(Tognazini, 1992).

designers, and scripters). The typical electronic tools of telephone, email, fax, express shipping, and project management software enabled us to manage the content and processes. Then we added the design of websites and web-based applications while continuing our major client-server software applications projects.

Throughout these years, in marketing, sales, publications, and project work, we continued to use these primary verbs in describing our development tasks: plan, research, analyze, design, document, evaluate, train, and maintain. The primary nouns or user-interface components were these: metaphors, mental models, navigation, interaction, and appearance (see Figure 9.2). However, over the decades, other terms became popular among designers, vendors, and clients, e.g., interaction design, information architecture, and user-experience design. Gradually, we have had to add these terms to our professional vocabulary in order to facilitate communication, collaboration, and trust among all the colleagues involved in projects.

The Turning Point: 2003

AM+A survived many economic challenges. These included the recessions of 1982–1985 when the company started, the stock market crash of 1987 (when the value of most stocks shrank by about twenty to twenty-five percent), the recession of 1992–1995, the fantasy boom of 1999–2000, the dot.com bust of 2000–2001, and the aftermath of September 11, 2001.

At the time of 9/11, our New York City office was closed for one week because it was located behind police barriers set up to ensure safety and efficient clean-up in the neighborhoods surrounding the World Trade Center's ground zero. All of these activities challenged us to find ways to communicate and collaborate more effectively. Our phone, network, fax, web-cam, website, intranets, extranets, and email techniques of collaboration were probably quite typical for small, high-tech businesses. Some employees had to use home offices to complete work. Laptops, mobile phones, and email became more indispensable. Gradually, normal operations were restored in New York City.

From about October 2002 through July 2004, sales for AM+A faltered while the company, unfortunately, lost one of its major supporters, the US Federal Reserve Bank, and another major client, Visa, went through a period of indecision because of its own financial, organizational, and political circumstances. In March 2003, due to an insufficient project base (i.e., cash-flow), I had to close the New York City office. With other staff leaving in California, AM+A shrank to about twelve employees. At least we were now back in one place, but we were still facing challenging circumstances. It seemed intriguing that two of our competitors, who also had boutique-sized firms in the San Francisco Bay area, had also shrunk to twelve staff members from even larger sizes of forty-four and sixty-six. We were one to two years late in this shrinkage, with MarchFirst's demise and other larger scale catastrophes occurring one or two years earlier. At one point, sometime in the 2001–2002 period, I was told that half of the graphic design studio telephone numbers in the San Francisco Yellow Pages were no longer working. We had lasted a bit longer, unscathed because of the strength of our major corporate clients.

We thought we were emerging from this challenging time, but it was not to be. After losing some further proposals, I had to recognize that the firm was in danger of closing due to the worst absence of projects that we had faced in two decades. Reluctantly, I closed down the California office and moved the firm back to its original home: my home office.

The Phoenix Rising, Again

At this point, AM+A became a true virtual office; specifically, it became a virtual design firm, attempting to complete its ongoing client work, to present a professional, corporate brand to the world, but conducting business in a much different way. Fortunately, my previous employees and emerging technology permitted this transformation. The previous employee participation was crucial: people shared an established company culture, terminology, familiarity with working together, and trust. What made it possible and efficient were the well-established internet-based access and communication through email servers, document servers, websites for file transfer, instant messaging, and even voice-over-internet telephony. We were now in a position to make these technologies work for us, from necessity, not just convenience.

Approximately eight former employees continued with the firm as contractors, while approximately ten new contractors have been added to AM+A's regular roster since 2003. In addition, approximately ten interns have worked for the firm for three to twelve months at a time. AM+A continued to relate to all of these people as a close "work family," using the contractors repeatedly, as often as possible, and encouraging sharing of information resources, techniques, and AM+A documents, as appropriate.

We strengthened our reach to associates in other locations, as well. For example, Dr. Emilie Gould in New York, with whom I have co-taught tutorials and co-published articles and papers, and who has presented AM+A's tutorial on culture, remains an associate of the firm. In addition, AM+A made informal arrangements with individuals and small firms to be "on-call" to provide specific services (e.g., usability analysis, website design, ethnographic analysis, remote testing, and illustration) in several countries, including Austria, China, Finland, Germany, India, Israel, Japan, South Africa, and South Korea. For the most part, these groups are experienced professionals with whom I have been in contact over the decades through conferences, publications, and project work. These resources are available to be put into action depending upon the needs of specific local or international clients.

Working as a completely virtual firm has had many challenges, costs, but also benefits to AM+A.

Challenges

Challenges include the following. In each case, solutions have emerged that are a work-around or at least partially solve the problem.

How does one present a virtual company to a prospect or client? We never hide the fact that we are a virtual company, but we also do not necessarily present this fact immediately. Rather, we let it emerge in the course of discussions, in case some prospects or clients are nervous about working with a virtual company (see below in the section on costs).

How does one present individual contractors to the client? AM+A has focused on using, for the most part, independent contractors who are usually single-person businesses. They have usually agreed to work as AM+A Associates, carrying AM+A business cards (provided by AM+A) that list AM+A addresses (aliases), but individual phone numbers at which they can be reached. Not everyone agrees to this, especially those with two or more people in their businesses. It is constantly a challenge not to confuse the client with more than one brand being presented.

How does one handle file, folder, and document maintenance? AM+A retains its server with transfer locations, FTP downloading sites, client and contractor extranets, and other commercial document servers, especially Basecamp, by which documents are exchanged among team members and client project team members. AM+A has to manage more carefully the AM+A assets that are made available to independent contractors. AM+A is careful in its maintenance of non-disclosure agreements and in archiving all project files at its main server. AM+A relies on trusted relationships with known contractors as the core of its team, but gradually absorbs new members into the work family after trial periods on projects.

How does one handle email? AM+A retains an outside email server to enable all email to and from AM+A to pass through one server. All of the AM+A team is encouraged to use AM+A aliases in their email to clients.

How are client meetings handled? AM+A uses a home office dining room as a conference room. The room is equipped with a conference phone, ethernet hub, wireless connection, removable large screen display, removable video projector and screen, and seating for eight to ten people. Because of the surrounding gardens and deck in a northern California environment, it is usually an attraction for corporate clients, usability test subjects, focus group subjects, prospects, and AM+A team members. In other cases, meetings occur by phone, using either AM+A's external conference phone number arranged for at www.conferencecall.com, or the client's conference phone number, or occasionally, during web meeting conferences, through Webex.com.

A colleague, Charles Kreitzberg (2006), who also runs a virtual office, Cognetics, Inc., in Princeton, New Jersey, has commented on this issue:

> We started working with more contractors and fewer employees. Today, some of our key players are contractors who work out of their homes. There are a couple whom I have never even met because they live in other parts of the country…. I was concerned that clients might be put off by the fact that we are a virtual organization but that has not happened. Even the largest companies seem to feel that a virtual organization is legitimate and trustworthy. We maintain a high quality phone system

that provides a seamless interface to the outside world and allows us to contact any staff member. We also have a high quality website. These two elements seem to inspire a lot of confidence…. We are careful with all our deliverables to make them elegant and well produced. We have a high speed color copier/printer and use very high quality paper. When we send out hard copies we bind them. The goal is to always look professional…even in a private home one can provide a professional, corporate-quality area reserved exclusively for business purposes, or in some cases shared.

How does one maintain a "corporate team spirit" with a decentralized, more loosely coupled group of people? It is important to pass on client compliments to all team members involved who might not otherwise learn of them. To some extent, instant messaging, email, phone calls, and small group meetings help to build project-group interaction, communication, group spirit, and exchange of information. These are supplemented by informal social gatherings that naturally occur among some of the group members. In order to re-sync the entire corporate team, to introduce new members, to reinforce company policies, and to enjoy each other's company, AM+A schedules quarterly meetings followed by lunch, to which all key designers/analysts especially are invited. At these meetings, project leaders or the key account manager show selected project case studies or summaries to help inform everyone (all attendees have signed non-disclosure agreements). Even with best efforts to be inclusive, there emerge, even in this situation, some central participants and others who are more peripheral. In part, this difference arises from the natural greater familiarity with long-standing members of the AM+A team. It is not clear to me whether there is a maximum size limit to a virtual design firm, where each member operates in physical separation (it is not strictly true for my executive assistant and myself; but although we are in the same building, most of our communication between separate rooms on separate floors consists of telephone, email, and instant messaging). It seems certain, if we were much larger, that we would definitely need more extensive techniques of virtual meetings and document management to keep ourselves in-sync and together in spirit as well as in documents and processes.

How does one maintain ongoing corporate training? With a decentralized group of independent contractors, support for attendance at conferences is reduced or absent. In a few special cases, AM+A has arranged for and paid expenses and partial time for associates to attend portions of conferences, sometimes as a presenter of AM+A materials, at other times as a note-taker and informal marketer. Nevertheless, there is abundant sharing of newly discovered techniques, discussion groups, documents, applications, and URLs available on the internet. In addition, AM+A continues to maintain a well-stocked corporate library of recent conference proceedings, magazines and journals, and books. Associates can borrow these for study or for use on projects, in addition to using their own resources. Most of our virtual team is in the San Francisco Bay area, which makes this library a functional resource. It was always a struggle to get staff to make project summaries and to archive projects properly when closing them down. It is even more so now. Nevertheless, it has been possible to maintain project summary and archiving of materials, in part because the likelihood of loss of "group memory" is even greater. The designers/analysts also carry out greater sharing via email of new resources, whether it is books, URLs, conferences, concepts, etc., in part because they are less likely to see each other daily. As mentioned earlier, we also gather at least once per quarter for a group lunch to re-bond and share project activities. Again, this is seen by all as more crucial than ever because of the asynchronous, physically separated activities. Physical meetings become more precious experiences.

Kreitzberg (2006) comments:

> [There is] software that supports remote work especially well, or especially inexpensively...Our In the Know!® is our core collaboration tool, [which we have developed ourselves]. We also make a lot of use of webcasts and remote desktop sharing. We use a lot of websites: extranets for our clients and places for us to store documents and work product. We started to use video conferencing, e.g., with Macromedia Breeze. Even usability testing became more feasible in a remote environment with the product and service offerings of Techsmith's Morae, Keynote Systems, and UserZoom.

How can one maintain leadership of the team and establish corporate standards? In a small virtual company like AM+A, similar to a working group in larger corporate institutions, or even a small corporate design/analysis company (ten to twenty-five people), it is possible to maintain direct email, phone, and face-to-face contact with all associates. Even at this scale, AM+A requires a project manager who also serves as an account manager, client-relationship manager, and sales closer. This person is a contractor, working on commission for closed sales, but also doubling as project manager for contracted projects. Through his/her and my efforts, we communicate and maintain the key policies and philosophy of the company. This approach is feasible because of the number of projects the person manages (about three to five). When we have had more, we've taken on additional project managers. Beyond an immediate group of eight to ten designers/analysts, it will be necessary to hire

Figure 9.3
AM+A Usability Severity Ratings

The severity of a usability problem is a combination of three factors:

1. **The frequency** with which the problem occurs: Is it common or rare?
2. **The impact** of the problem if it occurs: Will it be easy or difficult for the users to overcome?
3. **The persistence** of the problem: Is it a one-time problem that users can overcome once they know about it or will users repeatedly be bothered by the problem?

Finally, of course, one needs to assess the market impact of the problem since certain usability problems can have a devastating effect on the popularity of a product, even if they are "objectively" quite easy to overcome. Even though severity has several components, it is common to combine all aspects of severity in a single severity rating as an overall assessment of each usability problem in order to facilitate prioritizing and decision-making.

Severity ratings used in heuristic evaluation reports are:

Severity level 1 Cosmetic problem only—need not be fixed unless extra time is available on project.

Severity level 2 Minor usability problem—could impair users' productivity and ability to learn.

Severity level 3 Major usability problem—important to fix, so should be given high priority; impacts users' productivity and increases likelihood of errors.

Severity level 4 Usability Catastrophe—imperative to fix this before product can be released.

---

multiple project managers and client relationship managers, as well as sales closers and account managers. As an additional aid to culture-building, AM+A maintains a two-volume notebook for new contractors and interns, which contains much of AM+A key's terminology, processes, and philosophy. These notebooks derive from AM+A's corporate training services and therefore naturally embody AM+A's knowledge and best practices, including examples of user profiles, use scenarios, user-interface guidelines tables of contents, and heuristic-evaluation checklist contents (see Figure 9.3). Without this basic grounding, conversation among associates and client stakeholders would be difficult. This is particularly true when professionals from different disciplines, different educational backgrounds, or different previous professional practice within one discipline come together. We found this to be true among our clients as well. For example, when we assisted Siemens USA's corporate user-interface design group, they faced a typical challenge of trying to coordinate different conceptions, terminology, and processes among research-oriented and practice-oriented individuals within their team. One of our tasks for them, as it is for us, was to develop a communal, shared vocabulary of "reserved terms" for internal discussion, which may be shared with clients.

Costs

Costs of running a virtual design office include the following.

Some prospects and clients may have rational, or irrational, phobias concerning virtual companies. Only one client has expressed concern and negativity about working with a virtual company. In fact, that is more accurately expressed as one corporate marketing/branding group of a major corporation for which AM+A already had a multi-year corporate contract. That singular group decided that, for philosophical reasons (they were labeled official corporate and practical reasons), the business officials were hesitant to build a long-term relation with companies of the virtual kind. Considering that we had been in existence for twenty-four years, had consulted with this corporation over the past nineteen years, had already recently completed projects as a virtual company for one of its business lines, and had already signed a multi-year contract with the corporation, this unusual behavior was an aberration of more typical client reactions, which are focused on whether we can get the job done effectively, on time, and on budget. Also, considering that AM+A's staff has, in general, remained active with AM+A for three to ten years, while typical corporate job lifetimes are about two years, this seemed to represent a double standard.

Some human resources may not be available because of their commitments to their own separate clients. Planning for scheduling of contractors is considerably more complex. However, this complexity is not much more than the typical challenge of scheduling one's employees when they work on multiple projects with diverse milestones and unexpected client demands or project pressures.

Some designers/analysts have expressed concern about reduced contact time with other associates. This is an unavoidable and natural consequence of a physically dispersed team. Nevertheless, some small groups do tend to socialize and to exchange information in the course of project work, even meeting in each other's home offices for internal meetings. Some people are happier being less interrupted by social and political activities of the typical corporate office setting, and work more productively on their own timetables and in their own environments. Others prefer to socialize more. As mentioned previously and below, some technology changes may assist in helping co-workers to feel less isolated, more part of social groups, less isolated or left out of the company mainstream. Some associates do in fact become somewhat disconnected; they may become involved in long-term projects of their own which prevent them from working on AM+A projects. For the most part, their relations remain friendly and involved. They may still come to quarterly meetings and/or be involved in email discussions as part of the work family. Some may depart for corporate positions, as has happened in several cases, but social/communication connections remain positive and relatively strong among the AM+A staff members who have converted to the virtual team. It may be that the virtual form of the group makes it clear that staying in touch and staying connected are precious aspects of a team. This aspect of our culture also derives from my own personal approach to bonding with staff members as a work family.

Kreitzberg (2006) comments:

> How important is it (or not) to know [our] virtual collaborators and to have some history of working with them? Or, do [we] feel like [we] have become merely a broker for contractors?…Not at all. We are a team and we work together. We communicate frequently. Everyone in the current team has good communication skills and a solid work ethic, and these factors mean a lot.

Benefits

Benefits of the virtual office include the following.

In some ways, there is a better "paper trail" of communication. Much more of a virtual office seems to operate via email and instant messaging, which means there are documents that represent or summarize asynchronous conversations. These can be checked for data, commitments, misunderstanding, etc. Formal project documents and deliverables become part of project archives; emails generally do not, except those that pass through me, and I attempt to have many crucial, but not all, emails copied to me. This means that I have much more email management than before. One solution in the future would be to require that a project email archive persona be created for all project-team email distributions, which would streamline records and access. In many projects (but not all), there is a post-project discussion to assess what went right and what went wrong. In some cases, discussion notes are made.

Kreitzberg (2006) corroborates these observations on the formality/informality of project development in a virtual office:

> There is definitely a shift. I would say that we maintain tighter control than in the face-to-face environment. Because we don't see people all the time, we take their emails and interim deliverables very seriously. On the other hand we are not particularly formal. We want results, not reports. There is little room for "spin" and honesty is important. To manage in a virtual organization we need to know what is going on.

In some ways, taking notes and participating in discussions is enhanced. With a headset, it is easier for me to take real-time detailed notes without having to make eye contact or being distracted in a physical meeting, as opposed to a virtual meeting.

In addition, instant messaging services, e.g., Skype or AOL or Yahoo, can be used to tie in individual team members to query them about what is being said, or to carry on back-door conversations on multiple threads and topics, to say nothing of checking websites or doing web searches to corroborate statements or to check on assertions, uncertain data, or other facts. In fact, this kind of multi-tasking is really essential to carrying out projects and resolving project issues. One can check for documents, search the web, or even contact other people to resolve unknowns or ambiguities. On more than one occasion, I have had to ask an associate, or even a client, to pause for a moment to check something that enables us to make progress. This happens more than it might in face-to-face meetings, and most people involved seem to accept this practice as normal business practice. I certainly respect similar occasions when others on the phone need to take an important call or to check for documents. In fact, it gives me a few more seconds to deal with incoming email, resolve some other document or process issue, etc. It seems to me that technology supports multi-tasking more than ever before, and it enables us to learn, communicate, analyze, decide, and act in a multi-threaded, multi-layered, non-linear way, one which is more like our normal thinking, at least for some of us. It is not unheard of for me to be looking at my computer screen while another high-definition screen above it is showing the latest satellite video channel feed, as I balanced two simultaneous conversations from two different headsets in my left and right ears, carefully orchestrating mute moments as I cross-check among two different discussions and my latest email. For those occasions where it is not appropriate, or disruptive rather than constructive, we can always take steps to return to more linear norms, which I do myself if I have to write, edit, or undertake other focused activities.

Conference calls with clients and team members enable one to cope with email, checking documents, and messaging without distracting colleagues or client representatives. Of course, this can also lead to inattentiveness and non-participation. Each participant must judge carefully how much one can effectively multi-process.

The virtual office, as many commentators have pointed out, lets one work almost any time, wearing almost any clothing (or, as some have reported, almost none at all). This flexibility and freedom of work environment can lead to enhanced focus, greater satisfaction and pleasure, and actual increased productivity and effectiveness. This way of working can enhance one's being in "the zone" or the "flow" of intense, concentrated work. It is also possible that it can be overdone, leading to detriments in one's physical condition and social life. It is for exactly this reason that I make it a practice to get up from my desk to undertake some physical activity, almost any physical activity, to change my environment and to seek social connections with an executive assistant, family members, or even the postal delivery person. If this necessary change of pace can't be accomplished voluntarily, it might be recommended to set up timer triggers to help encourage the practice.

The virtual office, for better or worse, has distributed the challenges of systems maintenance to individual contractors. Consequently, although the cost of human resources has increased to pay for individual contractors, AM+A operates with about one third of the administrative and systems maintenance costs that it required previously for approximately the same number of designers/analysts and with a much reduced office rental space cost. The financial result is approximately the same corporate profit as before despite the changes of operation.

Conclusion

Rachel Abrams (2005), writing for Adobe.com, commented. "Contemporary work demands collaboration, communication, speed, interaction, teamwork, and creativity...The old office was based on a Taylorist notion of dedicated tasks, standards, and hierarchy. The new office demands the networking of intelligent, autonomous individuals as a prerequisite to problem solving." This approach certainly describes the functioning of AM+A as a virtual firm, with contracted, independent professionals who are linked by the specific requirements of projects and clients.

Some technology innovations are at work to make dispersed people and/or teams feel more in contact with each other. AM+A was privileged to work on the initial user-interface design of the Hewlett-Packard Halo virtual meeting (telepresence) product (see Yi, 2005 in the references for this chapter, or www.hp.com/halo). This product features three large, high-definition screens in special rooms connected by very fast broadband communication links. I know from direct observation that the experience is so "real" that within a few minutes, participants often forget that the person(s) they see in front of them behind a "window frame" are not really there. The images at HP's website give a reasonable impression of the set-up. In these rooms, personal communication, emotion, nuance, in short "face-time" experiences, are made possible for people who may, in fact, be thousands of miles and multiple time zones apart. Currently, such systems are costly, but presumably this kind of powerful communication experience will eventually be available at a fraction of that cost. The system already has helped disparate work groups within Dreamworks to act together as a virtual team.

AM+A now operates with much reduced paperwork, much reduced administrative overhead, with increased reliance on high-technology telecommunications, but with continued effectiveness and teamwork. We have made a successful transition from physical to virtual office.

One of the lessons I learned from this experience is to be careful of what you wish for. I had been lamenting that I was never able to stay home one or two days per week in order to work on strategic planning, marketing, writing, or research. I seemed to be caught in the trap of going in every day to fight sales, email, or other demanding circumstances. I longed for the days of working at home. Now, I am always working at home.

Acknowledgments

The author acknowledges the assistance of the following persons in providing feedback and suggestions from AM+A colleagues: Sam Ackerman, Key Accounts Manager; Eugene Chen, Senior Designer/Analyst; Joe Dobrowolski, Systems Manager; Jennifer Dumpert, Senior Designer/Analyst; Jim Gasperini, Senior Designer/Analyst; Yingzhao Liu, Designer/Analyst; and Charles Kreitzberg, President, Cognetics, Inc., Princeton, NJ.

References

Abrams, Rachel. 2005. All Together Now: Communication Networks and Collaborative Spaces. http://www.adobe.com/motiondesign/MDC_Think_Tank.html?u_sSection=Think_Tank&u_sContent=All_Together_Now (accessed January 2, 2005).

Apple Computer, I. 1992. Macintosh Human Interface Guidelines. Reading, MA: Addison-Wesley Publishing Co.

Baba, M., J.C. Gluesing, H. Ratner, and K. Wagner. 2004. The Contexts of Knowing: Natural History of a Globally Distributed Team. *Journal of Organizational Behavior*, 25, 547–587.

Baecker, Ronald M. and Aaron Marcus. 1990. *Human Factors and Typography for More Readable Programs*. Reading, MA: Addison-Wesley.

Bellotti, V. and S. Bly. 1996. Walking away from the desktop computer: distributed collaboration and mobility in a product design team. *Proceedings of the 1996 ACM Conference on Computer Supported Cooperative Work*. Boston, MA: ACM Press, 209–218.

Butler, B., L. Sproull, S. Kiesler, and R. Kraut. 2008. Community effort in online groups: Who does the work and why? In Weisband, S. and L. Atwater (eds.), *Leadership at a Distance*. Mahwah, NJ: Lawrence Erlbaum.

Conklin, Michelle. 2005. The Easiest Commute of All. *Business Week*. December 12, 78–80.

Duarte, D.L. and N.T. Snyder. 2001. Mastering Virtual Teams. Chicago, IL: Society for Information Management Advanced Practices Council. http://www.emerald-library.com/Insight/ViewContentServlet?Filename=/published/emeraldfulltextarticle/pdf/2300080406_ref.html (accessed February 28, 2006). [Contains an extensive bibliography of virtual teams.]

Gluesing, J.C. 1998. Building Connections and Balancing Power in Global Teams: Toward a Reconceptualization of Culture as Composite. Special volume on Anthropology of Business Organizations. Hamada, T. (ed.), *Anthropology of Work Review*, 18.2, 18–30.

Gluesing, J.C. 2004. Teaching Culture "On the Fly" and Promoting "Learning in Working" in Global Teams. In Goodman, L., N. Boyacigiller and M. Phillips (eds.), *Crossing Cultures: Insights from Master Teachers*. London, United Kingdom: Routledge.

Gluesing, J.C. and C. Gibson. 2003. Designing and Forming Effective Global Teams. In Lane, H.W., M.L. Maznevski, M. Mendenhall and J. McNett (eds.), Handbook of Global Management: A Guide to Managing Complexity. Malden, MA: Blackwell, 199–226.

Gluesing, J., T. Alcordo, M. Baba, D. Britt, W. McKether, L. Monplaisir, H. Ratner, K. Riopelle and K. Harris Wagner. 2003. The Development of Global Virtual Teams. In Gibson, C. and S. Cohen (eds.), Virtual Teams That Work: Creating Conditions for Effective Virtual Teams. San Francisco, CA: Jossey-Bass.

Hewlett Packard. 2005. Halo Collaboration Service Press Release. http://www.hp.com/hpinfo/newsroom/ press/2005/051212xa.html (accessed January 2, 2006) and http://www.hp.com/halo (accessed January 21, 2006).

Hinds, Pam and Sara Kiesler (eds.). 2005. Distributed Work. Cambridge, MA: MIT Press.

Hinds, Pam and Sara Kiesler (eds.). 2005. Bibliography on Complex Collaboration. http://hciresearch. hcii.cs.cmu.edu/complexcollab/bibliography/complexcoordBib.pdf (accessed December 25, 2005).

Kreitzberg, Charles. 2006. Private email communication, January 24.

Marcus, A. 1992. Graphic Design for Electronic Documents and User Interfaces. Reading, MA: ACM Press.

Nielsen, J. 1994. Usability Inspection Methods. Conference Companion on Human Factors in Computing Systems. Boston, MA: ACM Press.

Pinelle, D., J. Dyck, and C. Gutwin. 2003. Aligning Work Practices and Mobile Technologies: Groupware Design for Loosely-Coupled Mobile Groups. Proceedings of Mobile Human-Computer Interaction 2003. Udine, Italy. New York, NY: Springer-Verlag, 177–192.

Riopelle, K., J. Gluesing, T. Alcordo, M. Baba, D. Britt, W. McKether, L. Monplaisir, H. Ratner and K. Harris Wagner. 2003. Context, Task and the Evolution of Technology Use in Global Virtual Teams. In Gibson, C. and S. Cohen (eds.), Virtual Teams That Work: Creating Conditions for Effective Virtual Teams. San Francisco, CA: Jossey-Bass.

Scupelli, P., S. Kiesler, S.R. Fussell, and C. Chen. 2005. Project View IM: A tool for juggling multiple projects and teams. In CHI 2005 Late Breaking Results. New York, NY: ACM Press, 1773–1776.

Tognazzini, B. 1992. TOG on Interface. Reading, MA: Addison-Wesley Longman Publishing Co.

Tufte, E. 1990. Envisioning Information. Cheshire, CT: Graphics Press.

Tufte, E. 1983. The Visual Display of Quantitative Information. Cheshire, CT: Graphics Press.

Yi, Matthew. 2005. HP introduces state-of-the-art video conferencing system. San Francisco Chronicle, December 13, D1 ff.

Zeller, Jr., Tom. 2005. For Workers, It's Face Time Over PC Time. New York Times, December 25, 4-1 ff.

10

LOOKING BACK AT THE NATIONAL GRAPHIC DESIGN ARCHIVE COLLABORATION

R. Roger Remington

Today, collaboration in a professional design context is the norm, working as an effective strategy for individuals, groups, companies, and institutions. But these collaborations do not exist without attention and care. What follows relative to the history of the National Graphic Design Archive in the United States is an instructive example of collaboration among three institutions of higher education. This case study will document a vision that led to an experimental national collaboration including determination of its purpose and its history. This chapter concludes with commentary about the successes and shortcomings of the joint venture that will provide interested readers with constructive suggestions for those beginning new collaborative ventures.

The word collaboration has at least two meanings. In the past, collaboration had sinister implications such as collaborating in a crime. During World War II it also had a negative connotation referring to those individuals who identified with the Axis powers. Today, collaboration is generally considered a positive strategy as it stands for two or more people or groups working together cooperatively. In his book *The Planning of Change*, Warren Bennis (1969, 147, 152), a management science guru from the late 1960s, and his colleagues offered a detailed and useful definition of the collaborative relationship. They wrote:

A collaborative relationship is a complex series of expectations and encounters that include:

- joint effort that involves mutual determination of goals;

- spirit of inquiry – a reliance on determinations based on data, publicly shared;

- relationship growing out of a concrete, here-and-now encounter;

- voluntary relationship between change agent and client with either party free to terminate the relationship after joint consultation;

- power distribution in which the client and change agent have equal or almost equal opportunity to influence one another; and

- emphasis on methodological, rather than specific, substantive goals.

The Archiving of Graphic Design History

During the 1980s, interest in the history of the field of graphic design emerged. This manifested itself in important events such as the publishing of *A History of Graphic Design* by Philip B. Meggs in 1983 and the "Coming of Age" symposium on graphic design history at Rochester Institute of Technology. This conference is now viewed as an historic meeting in and of itself in that it was the first major gathering of most, if not all, of the important teachers, archivists, researchers, designers, writers, and students who were part of this new field of academic scholarship in design history.

In tandem with this trend came the need to preserve and document this history. Many Modernist design pioneers were passing on and their professional archives were important historical records needing to be saved. Several universities began developing archive projects. The University of Illinois at Chicago (UIC) collected materials about design in the context of the history of Chicago, including special collections such as design from Container Corporation of America and the International Design Conference at Aspen. Cooper Union had acquired the archive of designer Herb Lubalin and shaped it into a study center for history, interpretive exhibits, and noteworthy publications. Rochester Institute of Technology (RIT) acquired designer Lester Beall's archive, cataloged it, and began developing an interactive image bank utilizing the then state-of-the-art digital and laserdisc technology. A series of National Endowment for the Arts grants supported this documentation as well as other aspects of RIT's archiving initiatives.

Today there is a high degree of interest around the world in preserving designers' archives and using digital media to make them widely accessible. RIT has grown its physical collections from one (Lester Beall) in 1983 to over thirty by 2008, making it the definitive repository for the majority of Modernist American Designers. Its collection scope has expanded from the first generation of Modernists working from 1930 to

1950 (e.g., Dr. M.F. Agha, Walter Allner, Saul Bass, Lester Beall, Alexey Brodovitch, Will Burtin, Louis Danziger, Mary Faulconer, William Golden, George Giusti, E. McKnight Kauffer, Leo Lionni, Alvin Lustig, Cipe Pineles, Paul Rand, Rudolph Ruzicka, Ladislav Sutnar, Bradbury Thompson) to the next generation with designers such as Lella, Massimo Vignelli and Fred Troller. RIT has produced two online modules in its DesignArchiveOnline (http://design.rit.edu/ and http://design.rit.edu/DAO/) that are used to support its history of graphic design courses. These sites are available to others as well. RIT also is the location of the Melbert B. Cary Jr. Graphic Arts Collection, one of the world's premier libraries in the history and practices of printing. In 2008, RIT began work on the Vignelli Center for Design Studies which will house and exhibit the extensive Vignelli archive, as well as develop many program activities related to design studies (history, theory, and criticism).

The American Institute of Graphic Arts (AIGA), the eminent advocacy organization for graphic designers has begun its own online archive. This new initiative is described as a record of annual juried selections of excellence in design. In this way AIGA honors the work of these designers. These archives are interactive and provide broad accessibility to an extensive collection graphic works. They are frequently used for reference and research. The online collections are intended to expand each year with the addition of new award-winning selections.

In addition to making available imagery and information about contemporary designers, the website also has extensive materials on the 116 designers who have been honored with the AIGA Medal. The AIGA Design Archives are especially valuable in their breadth and scope and, while available only in a digital online format, preclude the user from access to original source materials in print form. Other schools and museums are joining the endeavor, namely Stanford University with the Herbert Matter collection, Yale University with the Paul Rand collection, Carnegie Mellon University with its Swiss Poster collection, and the School of Visual Arts with the Milton Glaser collection. Indiana University is also known for its Lilly Library of historic books and manuscripts. Of particular note is the New York Public Library's Digital Gallery that makes available 500,000 images (http://www.digitalgallery.nypl. org). Also in New York, the Cooper Hewitt Museum, America's design museum of the Smithsonian, has a number of important collections including those of architect Donald Deskey and designer Ladislav Sutnar.

In Dessau, Germany, virtually in the shadow of the Walter Gropius Bauhaus building, a massive project called the Digital Design Archive has been initiated by the Dessau Department of Design at the Anhalt University of Applied Sciences (DDA). This digital interface is sophisticated yet functional in design, and it allows student and professional users to access design imagery and information from several categorical perspectives. The project is supported by a number of industrial and institutional sponsors. The DDA is linked with Promethius, a large data/image bank for art history in Germany.

The resources mentioned here are those most familiar to this author; however, there are many other archives of design materials, real and digital, in the United States and around the world, each with its own collection focus, goals, and operational procedures.

The National Graphic Design Archive Consortium, a Vision for Collaboration

In the late 1980s, Professor George Sadek of Cooper Union in New York and his colleague Marilyn Hoffner, from Cooper Union's Alumni Office, conceived a national project to bring together several leading archiving institutions with the intent of creating a national network. Initially, the other participating schools were the University of Illinois at Chicago (led by Gretchen Lagana and Beverly Lynch) and Rochester Institute of Technology (led by the author, R. Roger Remington).

The Participating Institutions

Rochester Institute of Technology (RIT), founded in 1829, has a long history of career orientation in diverse disciplines. Its eight colleges offer programs in Applied Science and Technology, Business, Computing and Information Sciences, Engineering, Imaging Arts and Sciences, Liberal Arts, and Science, as well as the National Technical Institute for the Deaf. RIT offers Associate, Bachelor, Masters, and Doctoral degrees for over 15,000 students. It is located on a 1,300-acre suburban campus five miles from Rochester's city center. Its design archives are located in the Wallace Library's Archives and Special Collections resources. The Cary Library is also located in the Wallace Library.

The University of Illinois at Chicago (UIC), a part of the Illinois University system, is located in an urban setting in Chicago. It offers fifteen professional colleges and programs for its 25,000 students, namely in Applied Health Sciences, Architecture and the Arts, Business Administration, Dentistry, Education, Engineering, Liberal Arts and Sciences, Education, Pre-Professional programs, Medicine, Nursing, Pharmacy, Public Health, Social Work, and Urban Planning. Degree programs include Bachelor, Masters, and Doctoral. Its archives are part of the UIC Library.

The Cooper Union for the Advancement of Science and Art is located in New York City. It was established in 1859 and is among the nation's oldest and most distinguished institutions of higher learning. It is the only private, full scholarship college in the United States dedicated exclusively to preparing students for the professions of art, architecture, and engineering. Student enrollment is 950.

Similarities and Differences

Each institution had its own collection focus, policies, and working organizational structure. The Cooper Union collection, named the Herb Lubalin Study Center, is part of the School of Art. This resource centers on holdings of the work of the American design innovator Herb Lubalin (1918–1981). The Lubalin Center has initiated many extensive exhibitions in its gallery spaces, written and designed quality publications relevant to each exhibit, and served as a focal point in New York for the history of graphic design events. In contrast, at UIC and RIT, the archives are part of university libraries with trained archivists and full library support services. In addition, both schools have faculty and staff advocates who are teaching design history and utilizing the original source materials to support classroom activities. The three schools are different in size and different in the ways in which the archives are organized and utilized. In addition, they were quite different, at the time of the consortium, in terms of the technological capability to support new and innovative interpretive programs based on the collections. RIT was unique in the technological resources it brought to the National Graphic Design Archive (NGDA). Its American Video Institute (AVI) was the first organization in the country whose sole purpose was interactive media design. Members of its staff hold the first U.S. Patent awarded for an interactive videodisc application method and device.

Each school, however, was in agreement about the importance of preserving historical exemplars of the history of graphic design and of the potential for sharing their experience and knowledge with others.

The Consortium Begins

Cooper Union was successful in obtaining a grant from the National Endowment for the Arts to support the formation of a consortium. Implicit in this grant was the fact that each participating school would be required to support the project with matching funds and in-kind resources. The first organizational meeting was held in New York at Cooper Union. This was followed by visitations at each of the three schools and, after extensive discussion, a vision statement was written and adopted:

> The National Graphic Design Archive is a consortium of individuals and organizations that will systematically coordinate the archiving, documentation and interpretation of the artifacts of the history of graphic design in America so that this heritage will be preserved for the future.

There is a national need to identify and facilitate access to the artifacts of the history of graphic design in America to ensure that these materials will be saved and made available for study, reference, and interpretation throughout the country.

The National Graphic Design Archive will be an innovative network of people, projects, and institutions that will provide collecting frameworks, investigate appropriate technology for the documentation, access, and sharing of materials electronically, and become a clearing house for information about this history. NGDA intends to be perceived by its users and others as being a reliable, technologically-oriented, productive, and approachable institution.

Beyond the vision statement, the three schools articulated a set of goals that make the mission more specific:

1. To coordinate the collection and preservation of significant images and data about the history of graphic design

2. To utilize the database for educational and informative interpretive programs as demonstrations

3. To apply appropriate technology for the development of pilot programs, networking, and sharing of information

4. To disseminate information about NGDA, its activities, products, and goals

5. To seek ongoing development resources to sustain the organization and its activities

6. To develop a functional organizational structure that will enhance the project operations and activities

7. To regularly evaluate the organization and modify it as necessary

Formative Evaluation: Accomplishments Relative to Goals

An effective strategy of evaluation is to weigh the accomplishments and shortcomings of NGDA against its stated goals.

1. To coordinate the collection and preservation of significant images and data about the history of graphic design

   ■ Each school maintained its own ongoing archival work and, in addition, contributed to the consortium.

■ Since the UIC archives were well-established and the staff experienced in standard archival practices, they were to contribute descriptive standards and archival protocols for graphic design materials. These standards involve following archival procedures in terms of the terminology, categories, and definitions used in organizing and describing graphic design artifacts.

2. To utilize the database for educational and informative interpretive programs as demonstrations

■ Cooper Union produced a digital module documenting the history of Lou Silverstein's tenure as art director of *The New York Times*.

■ RIT produced an interactive image bank utilizing laserdisc storage in its AVI lab. Much of the Beall Collection was stored in an analog laserdisc format in addition to many other artifacts from graphic design history. In total, the image bank contained over 31,000 images.

■ RIT also produced educational and informative modules on corporate identity, posters, and the work of Bradbury Thompson for Westvaco.

■ Other institutions, on a program basis, participated in the consortium. The Massachusetts Institute of Technology and the Society of Environmental Design contributed to the interactive image bank prototype.

3. To apply appropriate technology for the development of pilot programs, networking, and sharing of information

■ Through RIT's AVI, a prototype program was developed for NGDA. The two-screen workstation brought together archival images, stored on laserdisc, with a Macintosh IIse computer using HyperCard, version 2.1 software. The "home page" for the interface was a diagrammatic map in text form with multiple functions listed under generic titles such as Library (Database, Timelines, Classification Tree, Bibliography, Glossary), Learning Center (18 Designers, Lester Beall Archive, Corporate Identity, Society of Environmental Designers, American Newspaper Design), Theatre (*Fortune* Magazine, Constructivist Typography,

American Design Roots, Dada, Westvaco, Designer Biographies), and Resource Center (Videodisc Index and Controls, Presentation Maker). The Macintosh screen was devoted to navigation, selection, and text information while the accompanying video monitor brought up design images from the laserdisc.

4. To disseminate information about NGDA, its activities, products, and goals

   ■ Since it was located in New York, Cooper Union was in a logical location to generate publicity for the project and, because of a positive ongoing relationship with the National Endowment for the Arts (NEA), to seek continued grant support.

   ■ In response to perceived expressions of need, an international "what's where" directory was produced at RIT. This book provided information on existing archives and special collections of graphic design work in the United States and abroad. This publication data was drawn from research done previously at AIGA. A questionnaire was developed and widely distributed to museums, schools, universities, and archives. The returned questionnaires provided data that was integrated into a 157-page printed directory.

   ■ This textual information also became the basis for a database of archives and special collections.

   ■ RIT also produced, for the duration of the project, *ArchivalUpdate*, a NGDA Consortium newsletter.

   ■ Potential new members were informally sought, primarily through word-of-mouth by founding members.

5. To seek ongoing development resources to sustain the organization and its activities

   ■ Cooper Union administered the NEA grant while continuing to develop interpretive programs at the Lubalin Study Center.

6. To develop a functional organizational structure that will enhance the project operations and activities

   ■ RIT offered planning expertise through its participating members and through an associated consultant.

7. To regularly evaluate the organization and modify it as necessary

   ■ Evaluation was entirely a subjective compilation of who was doing what when it came time to re-apply for the NEA grant.

Formative Evaluation: Shortcomings Related to Stated Goals

1. To coordinate the collection and preservation of significant images and data about the history of graphic design

   ■ There was an uneven degree of interest and ability to collect and catalog original source archival materials.

   ■ A functional set of agreed-upon descriptive standards was not developed.

2. To utilize the database for educational and informative interpretive programs as demonstrations

   ■ The database was developed and facilitated only at one school.

3. To apply appropriate technology for the development of pilot programs, networking, and sharing of information

   ■ A large technical difficulty was that the Macintosh computer and the internet were in early stages of development, so the three schools were wed to different current technologies. One school had state-of-the-art digital capabilities while another had to farm out the work to several alumni who were in business in New York. The third school had minimal on-campus digital resources available for supporting the project. If the consortium had begun in 2006, the technology and standardization issues would have been diminished.

   ■ Disagreements occurred regarding the digital formats and the network upon which the NGDA would operate.

   ■ Networking expertise was not available among the three schools. When RIT brought in a networking, planning, and evaluation consultant, he was not accepted because his proposals and concerns for detail were intimidating to members present.

4. To disseminate information about NGDA, its activities, products, and goals

    ■ This goal, to an extent, was realized largely through RIT's NGDA newsletter and the *Directory of Graphic Design Archives, Collections and Resources*. Dissemination of information was difficult because the majority of the "news" was emerging from only one of the schools and that was localized to New York City.

    ■ Members should have been much more aggressive in getting out the word about the consortium to professional and academic communities that would have helped the cause.

5. To seek ongoing development resources to sustain the organization and its activities

    ■ The only source of funding continued to be the National Endowment for the Arts; alternative granting sources were not pursued.

    ■ There was considerable administrative pressure at one school for accountability for deliverables in relationship to matched funds, which caused tension.

6. To develop a functional organizational structure that will enhance the project operations and activities

    ■ The organizational planning process was incomplete in that the founding group set a mission and goals, but it did not or could not go beyond this level of planning to more detailed objectives, processes, and strategies (see Figure 10.1). For example, a schedule for expansion of the consortium was not developed.

    ■ On a more comprehensive level, the NGDA overview was discussed in its draft form, but it was never accepted by the consortium representatives. It was an attempt to create a whole system view of NGDA program development.

    ■ According to the NGDA goals, a work plan was to be developed with each school involved in developing parts of the project according to its unique strengths and resources. This was loosely accomplished at the beginning but fell far short of the kind of detailed network plan that was necessary for a functioning consortium.

Figure 10.1
National Graphic Design Archive project operations

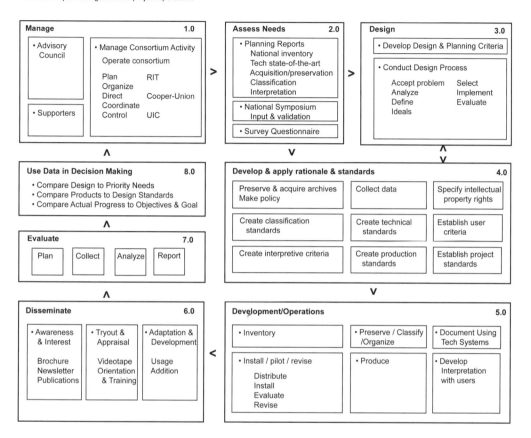

The physical distances between the schools and the lack of a central administrative person meant that, while work was being accomplished on a program basis at each school, there was diffusion as to governing policies and incomplete agreement on the hierarchy of priorities implicit in the mission and goals. It was difficult for the three school representatives to agree on a priority of establishing a tightly knit organizational plan.

Between 1989 and 1994, the span of NGDA's formal existence, changes in personnel occurred at the three original schools which brought in newcomers, who infused new energy into the original vision. But without solid organizational consensus, the three original schools seemed to be "spinning their wheels" as they met to attempt to define policy and operations. The institutional representatives, because of their diverse backgrounds, found it difficult to understand and agree on terminology. There was a reluctance to commit to a given set of operational policies.

- It appeared as though the traditional difficulty in colleges and universities of finding agreement on a shared governance organization also afflicted the consortium. Democracy proved to be an institutional stumbling block.

- The consortium received continuing funding from the NEA through the mid-1990s, but without planning and decisiveness, full participation by representatives of the three schools began to wane. In time, resources became more limited and several of the sponsoring schools felt internal administrative pressure to pull back the effort in order to support internal goals that were, in effect, more controllable. Academic administrators are often skeptical of involvements in "floating centers" such as NGDA, projects that have no clear relationship to one college or department.

- A system was not initiated to ensure continuation of the consortium should representatives change or funding disappear.

- A more disciplined, rigorous process should have been in place to ensure that there were clear agendas for meetings, deliverables to be seen, reviewed, and critiqued, and predictable outcomes evident in relationship to an organizational plan.

7. To regularly evaluate the organization and modify it as necessary

- Because the participants were unable to design and agree on a functional organizational structure, no evaluation plan was established.

- In addition, there were perceived inequities with the project load and deliverables, questions about equitable resource allocation, and resistance to a tighter, more structured organizational plan that was fully understood and agreed upon by the schools. When one member proposed a working structure for the consortium and its program development process, others felt threatened by the implicit discipline involved. Several members expressed concern that having a clear and accountable work plan was alien to their normal way of functioning. This mirrored the fact that different schools have contrasting forms of planning and working. So there was a fundamental difference of preferred organizational style among the participants ranging from a very loose, figure-it-out-as-we-go style to another school that was advocating a systematic form. Fear of a tighter organization meant that costly meetings (travel, lodging, meals in addition to lost time at home base) consistently involved rehashing the same issues. Without leadership, it was impossible to negotiate the differences that became more apparent as time went on. One founding member institution chose to retire from participation and focus on internal program priorities. The two remaining participants continued for several years in the mid-1990s, developing and maintaining a new website/image bank under the NGDA banner at Cooper Union. There were considerable differences among the schools in their digital capabilities and technical support. This created a serious imbalance when it came to delegation of resources as the institution with the greater computer resources felt the need for a larger portion of the grant monies.

Summative Evaluation: Lessons Learned

The National Graphic Design Archive, which had started out with such a utopian potential, foundered in realizing its major goal of collaboration toward a functional national network. A more realistic and manageable scope for NGDA from the beginning might have ensured a more successful outcome. Inter-department and inter-college programs are difficult for many campuses to facilitate because of natural "turf" issues. On a higher level, the NGDA was a victim of the risky challenge of inter-institutional collaboration.

In retrospect, what lessons were learned from this project? What might institutions be aware of as they sense a need and respond to a motivation to work together in addressing a common challenge?

Many possibilities exist in terms of critically reflecting back on the history of the National Graphic Design Archive Consortium. What follows is one participant's look in the rearview mirror, offered as a set of constructive suggestions for future collaborative ventures between institutions:

- When establishing a consortium, there needs to be a conscious equity in every aspect of the project, in the organization, in the mission, in the administration, in the program development plan, and in the expected deliverables.

- The consortium should consider hiring an organizational consultant to bring objectivity to the planning process.

- In the initial planning, the group should emphasize strategies for sustaining the vitality of the organization into the future.

- Participants must realize up front the amount of energy and passion that will be necessary to overcome the lethargy and pressure for maintaining the separate institutional status quo.

- Participants should read the current and classic literature on organizational planning, such as the book *Why Change Doesn't Work* by Robbins and Finley (1996).

- From the outset, participants should devote time, energy, and resources to monitoring the psychodynamics of the organization itself and the means by which participating individuals interrelate.

- Consortia provide excellent opportunities for participants to evaluate their own work in relationship to others.

- Consortia are very appealing organizations for funding agencies because they can maximize every dollar contributed when the funds are spread among several groups.

There were clear and lasting benefits gained from involvement in the NGDA. Each participating institution left the experience with a better sense of what was involved in operating a consortium. Professional and collegial friendships were established that continue to this day. All involved gained a better understanding of how other institutions are structured and operate and how they may or may not interface. Allocated grant monies from the consortium advanced the individual program work at each school in ways that would not have been possible without the consortium. It was clear that each representative was better for learning from the expertise of the others. As an example, this author learned a great deal about descriptive standards and archiving methodology from those at a partnering school with that experience. The needs, potentials, and dreams that prompted the NGDA remain to this day for the graphic design field as well as for all archives and libraries. Technology may now provide a more effective meeting ground.

Sociologist Warren Bennis was realistic in his views in 1969, when he wrote, "Collaboration is always an achievement, not a gift. It is usually attained through open and grueling confrontation of differences, through conflicts faced and resolved, through limited areas of collaboration growing into larger areas of collaboration as fuller trust develops" (Bennis et al., 1969). Finally, when thinking about collaborative relationships, it is useful to remember the wisdom of the Gestalt psychologists when they offered that, "the whole is different from and greater than the sum of its parts."

References

Bennis, W.G., K.D. Benne, and R. Chin. 1969. *The Planning of Change*. New York, NY: Holt, Rinehart and Winston, Inc.

Meggs, Philip. 1983. *A History of Graphic Design*. New York, NY: Reinhold Publishing Corporation.

Remington, R. Roger. Rochester Institute of Technology, Rochester, New York. Lecture, 11 March 2008.

Robins, Harvey and Michael Finley. 1996. *Why Change Doesn't Work, Why Initiatives Go Wrong and How to Try Again and Succeed*. Lawrenceville, NJ: Petersons Guides.

11

INNOVATIVE COLLABORATIVE DESIGN IN INTERNATIONAL INTERACTION DESIGN SUMMER SCHOOLS

Nicole Schadewitz

Introduction

Fostering innovation in early design phases is a topic rarely discussed in research. Theories and studies into innovation usually schematize or classify design innovations, considering, for example, successful products or processes of established businesses. However, there is little knowledge about the early and informal stages in the design process in other contexts leading to innovative design processes and products. Therefore, this chapter describes and analyzes the collaborative design and learning process of three interaction design summer schools as examples of "early design phases." Interaction design summer schools teach interaction design principles through hands-on, user-centered design and learning experiences in an international setting. The analysis of the data supports the proposition that design innovation can be initiated in educational settings when special attention is paid to the context of learning and design. Hence, summer schools do not aim to produce a concrete innovative product, but offer a platform for acquiring knowledge and learning processes that support innovation through contextual, user-centered design.

Contextual learning and innovation are known concepts (Falk and Dierking, 2002 Ghosh and Chavan, 2004). However, international design summer schools utilize user-centered and contextual design in combination with situated and collaborative learning in pioneering ways. Summer schools establish a context for learning and design innovation in a two-week program bringing together a heterogeneous group of participants from various cultural and professional backgrounds with the aim to accomplish a collaborative design project in and for the location where the summer school is held. There are no limitations to the scope of the design proposals despite the encouragement to interact with the local context as often and in as diverse ways as possible. This inclusive setup and intense experience shapes the learning process and outcome of the participants. This chapter will show how cross-cultural and interdisciplinary teamwork, as well as extensive fieldwork and frequent contact with the local population, strongly influence the design proposals and innovations for new markets.

To the author's knowledge, there is no research in the area of contextual and user-centered design innovation that explicitly addresses collaboration and facilitation practices of intercultural teams that seek to innovate for a local market. There is a need to look at the intercultural collaborative design and learning processes in much greater detail. In particular, this chapter explores how a local cultural context and a multicultural team composition influence the collaborative design and learning process. It summarizes the challenges and misunderstandings in the design process and proposes solutions to intercultural collaborative learning and design, leading to innovative design ideas for products and services for a specific local market. In conclusion, it suggests a model and framework to support collaborative learning and design processes in international interaction design summer schools.

Background and Literature

User-centered, Contextual Design Innovation

In the past decades, researchers identified a variety of frameworks, systems, and theories to identify modes and processes of innovation (Walsh, 1996; Edquist, 2001; Heskett 2005). Design innovation can be characterized as a process- or product-oriented activity. While process innovation refers to technological, organizational, or methodological improvements, product innovation includes new or significantly improved ideas, goods, and services (Edquist, 2001). In the early years of research into design innovations, theories described innovation as being fueled by technological advances. However, while theories in this field advanced, user-centered innovation was reported to guide design innovation activities in business and education (Dinçer, 2003). Innovation by user-centered design was discussed in several accounts (Chayutsahakij and Poggenpohl, 2002; Dinçer, 2003; Mutlu and Er, 2003). Questioning the definition, Mutlu and Er (2003) suggest that design innovations contribute to the incremental improvement of the quality and usefulness of a product in order to suit user needs better.

A growing body of research suggests that design innovation is a collaborative, user-centered, and multidisciplinary process that relates to a specific locality (Chayutsahakij and Poggenpohl, 2002; Mutlu and Er, 2003; Ghosh and Chavan, 2004). The process and philosophy of user-centered design innovation is discussed by a variety of scholars (Chayutsahakij and Poggenpohl, 2002; Rogers et al., 2002). They argue that user-centered design innovation largely depends on the context in and for which it is designed. User-centered design usually begins by looking at the activities and interactions of humans in a certain situation. Observing an activity system, which consists of humans, a certain social setting, and a related use of artifacts or technology, allows one to identify design opportunities that might lead to innovative solutions.

Chayutsahakij and Poggenpohl (2002) presented results from expert interviews to determine which user-centered research and design methods are predominantly used in design innovation situations. Ghosh and Chavan (2004) stressed that collaboration and fieldwork are absolutely necessary in bringing up contextually relevant insights to innovate, especially for new markets. They coined the term "contextual innovation" as a user-centered strategy and methodology in design and business innovation intended for local markets. Moreover, many researchers agree that learning and gaining new knowledge through experimental, user-centered and contextual experiences is a fundamental component of successful innovation practices (Ashton, 2004; Edquist, 2001; Dinçer, 2003). Hence, to explore the relation of design innovation, user centered-design, and learning processes in more detail, the next section will discuss various collaborative learning theories.

Situated, Collaborative Learning and Design

Team learning is seen as an important factor in design innovation processes (Ashton, 2004; Evers, 2004; Zhang et al., 2004). However, for a long time, based on the dominant behaviorist approach in education, learning was viewed as a process of acquiring pre-structured knowledge, which was mediated from a more knowledgeable person (a teacher) to the learners. In the 1970s and '80s, education research found that collaborative learning increases the learners' enthusiasm and confidence, promoting the development of learning supportive social skills in a specific situation inspiring creative thinking, and leading to the formation of novel knowledge (Piaget, 1973). The idea of collaborative learning was pioneered by Piaget and named the constructivist approach to learning. This theory maintains that knowledge is socially constructed and learning a social process, based on problem-solving in the real world. The constructivist approach informed the generation of a variety of theories of collaborative learning through social interaction (Wenger, 1998). In an interview, Judee Hamburg stressed the connection between a specific context, learning, creativity, and innovation. She argued that user-centered learning is about making people more creative, intelligent, and innovative (Conner, 2004).

Similar to contextual and collaborative learning, constructivist theories influenced the advancement of contextual and collaborative design (Lewin, 1973). Following this line of thought, interaction design places a premier interest on involving a multiplicity of stakeholders and participants in the collaborative process. A variety of models of the design process are proposed in literature (Rogers et al., 2002; Westerlund, 2005). Generally, interaction design processes focus on a specific context and the user within this environment.

Based on the above-mentioned contextual and user-centered traditions in learning and design, it is not unusual that the setup and implementation of interaction design summer schools include collaborative design and learning practices. User-centered design and situated learning practices are connected to an immediate context in which knowledge is gained and applied. In a contextual model of collaborative learning, Falk and Dierking (2002) itemize that: learning begins with the individual, learning involves others, and learning takes place somewhere. Hence, educators stress that it is important for contextual learning to incorporate as many different forms of experience as possible (social, cultural, physical, and psychological) in working towards the desired learning outcomes.

Applying Falk and Dierking's (2002) contextual learning framework to the interactions in international design summer school suggests that being embedded in a team of culturally diverse members and a foreign cultural context offers rich experiences and enhances learning, but it might also contribute additional challenges to the learning and design process of the participants. The individuals are drawn from varying culturally-influenced approaches towards knowledge acquisition. Learning takes place through intercultural teamwork interacting with co-participants, whose learning and design attitudes, expectations, and motivations are not necessarily shared. Hence interaction and production of a shared understanding is more difficult and time intensive. Last but not least, the summer school participants interact in a very different cultural and physical context, which requires the learners to accomplish a common design project for this local market. Participants need to learn to utilize the benefits and overcome the challenges of cross-cultural collaborative learning and contextual design in these early phases of design innovation.

Cross-cultural Communication and Collaboration

As outlined in the previous section, knowledge is gained interactively in collaborative learning and design. However, research into cross-cultural communication reports that differences in interaction styles across cultures have an enormous impact on intercultural learning and teamwork (Bonk and King, 1998; Gudykunst, 2004; Oritz, 2000; Ostwald, 1995; Scollon and Scollon, 2001).

Figure 11.1
A composite model to address breakdowns and gain common ground
in the inter-cultural collaboration process

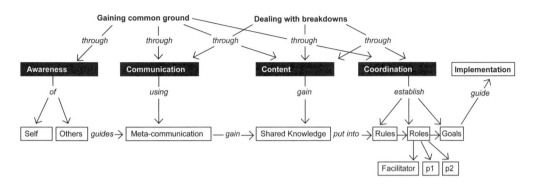

Differences in the interaction and learning styles among culturally diverse people can be described and explained using cultural value dimensions mentioned in cross-cultural communication literature (Hall, 1990; Hofstede, 1997; Marcus and Baumgartner, 2004). It has been stressed in the literature that knowing about the differences in communication and interaction across cultures is necessary to successfully deal with possible breakdowns. Moreover, in order to sufficiently facilitate cross-cultural communication and collaboration, researchers identified that building up a base of shared knowledge helps to overcome misunderstandings in intercultural interactions (Bonk and King, 1998; Ostwald, 1995; Scollon and Scollon, 2001). Therefore, many researchers have taken an interest in differing communication strategies and how to overcome misunderstandings in intercultural communication. A variety of collaboration support frameworks (Ostwald, 1995; Rogers et al., 2002) refer to the areas of awareness, communication, coordination, and content in collaboration as issues that need special attention, support, and facilitation in order to build common ground and deal with breakdowns. Drawing on the resources mentioned, Figure 11.1 synthesizes and expands on these concepts.

The model suggests that breakdowns can be addressed, and shared understanding can be gained through facilitating awareness, communication, coordination, and content in collaborative design and learning. In detail, it suggests that the collaborative learning and design process starts with acquiring self-awareness—it is very important to recognize one's own work style. Self-awareness leads also to an awareness of others, which enables working alongside another. Discussing results and strategies with others through meta-communication enables collaborators to gain a shared understanding about similarities and differences among their work styles and aims. This encourages trust and helps to build a shared team culture, to establish team rules and roles, and to accomplish goals. Finally, this new, shared perspective is incorporated into the collaborative project. Although this model gives a good overview of aspects of intercultural collaborative learning processes, it also shows many limitations and knowledge gaps, especially in relation to user-centered, contextual learning, design, and innovation. These require further research. Therefore, despite the shortcomings of the model, and in order to define a framework for intercultural, contextual learning and design innovation, it guided the analysis of the case studies introduced in the remainder of this paper.

Methodology

Approach

Since there has not been much research conducted in the field of intercultural collaborative design and learning, international summer schools afforded a situated study to gain a first understanding of practices employed in such contexts. Methodologies for studying an entire activity system within a certain context were established in ethnographic research. The major research interest was discovering regularities within interaction design summer schools and discerning patterns in the interactions between the participants. The author chose to conduct a qualitative evaluation of interactions observed within this long-term naturalistic inquiry using a holistic ethnographic approach (Tesch, 1990) and a qualitative content analysis (Mayring, 2000). Qualitative content analysis, which relates more closely to interpretational analysis of ethnographic data, offers two levels of content analysis: a) the main contents of ideas and themes, and b) the latent contents within contextual information of the text as areas of interest (Mayring, 2000).

Data Collection

The author observed three international information and interaction design summer academies between 2003 and 2005 as case studies. Each summer school was held over a period of two weeks. Around 40 postgraduate students and young professionals aged between 22 and 35 came from a variety of design-related professions like fashion, graphic, or product design, but also computer science, social studies, or marketing. Participants were assigned to teams with five to ten members. Team membership focused on bringing together a variety of professions, cultures, and ages among the students, atelier leaders, invited lecturers, and local experts. A typical team was composed of six to seven international participants from Europe, Asia, and the Americas, and two to three local students, who were indispensable for the teams. The scheduling of each day reserved the morning for guest lectures, while the afternoon was for the teams' individual projects. The overall setting of the summer school supported experimental, exploratory, and open-ended design projects, and encouraged the discovery of needs and requirements of an unfamiliar target audience. The school prescribed neither a design goal nor a project framework. Instead, the team facilitators introduced a broad design topic, as well as models and methods to structure the design process on demand. Taking the role of a participant observer, the author examined team communication and coordination practices, made notes of communications, conducted informal interviews, collected documents and made pictures of the use of artifacts and activities. In order to triangulate the data gained from the observations, collaborative design pattern workshops[1] were carried out with some school participants at the end of two of the three observed summer schools.

Coding and Analysis of the Data

In the following step, the data were viewed, sorted, coded, and analyzed using TAMSAnalyzer™ and GraphViz. Two types of codes were used to structure the observations: data codes and context codes (Mayring, 2000). While data codes were applied to a single idea, context codes structured bigger chunks of observations. First, the data codes were categorized into *breakdowns, dealing with breakdowns,* and *gaining common ground*. Those categories were further divided into *awareness, communication, coordination,* and *content*. Second, the context code and concept of cultural value differences framed the analysis of collaborative design and learning activities in this international setting. For this context code, the author used the six most frequent cultural value categories proposed by Hall (1990) and Hofstede (1997): 1) Authority Conceptions, 2) Community Aspects, 3) Activity Orientations, 4) Context in Communication, 5) Time, and 6) Uncertainty Avoidance.

Occurrence of codes was counted; more recurrent codes were interpreted as dominant factors influencing collaborative design innovation. Content codes were correlated to other content codes and context codes to gain a better understanding of the context in which contextual design innovation occurs.

Findings and Discussion

Previously, a lack of knowledge regarding how intercultural collaborative design and learning support contextual innovation was identified. A major question this

Table 11.1
Frequencies of the breakdown data code and sub categories

Code Categories	Breakdowns		Dealing with Breakdowns		Gaining Common Ground	
	Total	%	Total	%	Total	%
Awareness	105	18	0	0	698	39
Communication	218	37	183	34	230	12
Content	63	11	24	4	426	24
Coordination	198	34	334	62	441	25
Total	**584**	**100**	**541**	**100**	**1797**	**100**

section seeks to answer is how intercultural collaborative learning and design can be supported in a specific locality leading to contextual design innovations for a local market. The focus is on how contextual, user-centered innovation (iteration of designs and user involvement) interplays with collaborative learning and design activities in international design summer schools. Hence, the findings are outlined to introduce first the most significant tradeoffs and breakdowns in collaborative learning and design, and subsequently to explore strategies to deal with breakdowns and gain common ground thereafter. Later, a model for intercultural collaborative design and learning processes supporting contextual design innovation is proposed.

Breakdowns

This section identifies the most common challenges and misunderstandings, which sometimes lead to misinterpretation of behavior and breakdowns in the interaction among team members. The numbers in brackets stand for the frequency of occurrence of this observation in the context discussed.

Figure 11.2
Observations and frequency of occurrences in data code
category breakdowns

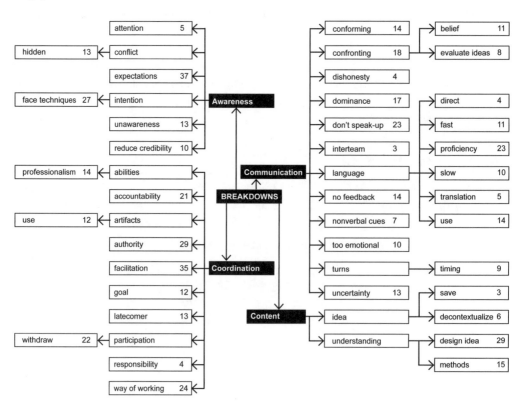

Table 11.2
Breakdown frequencies, dealing with breakdowns, and gaining common
ground correlated to cultural values

Differences in Cultural Values regarding	Breakdowns		Dealing with Breakdowns		Gaining Common Ground		Total	
	Total	%	Total	%	Total	%	Total	%
Activity	41	7	55	10	188	11	284	10
Authority	96	17	89	17	140	8	325	11
Community	151	26	99	19	370	21	620	21
Context	160	28	157	29	697	39	1014	35
Time	38	7	50	9	85	5	173	6
Uncertainty	91	16	83	16	309	17	483	17
Total	577	101*	533	100	1789	101*	2899	100

*Due to rounding, not all percentage totals equal 100.

A total of 584 instances of breakdowns were identified in the data, as displayed in Table 11.1. Figure 11.2 shows a graph of all data codes in the breakdowns category. Communication and coordination accounted for one-third of the most recurrent categories in which breakdowns were coded. Nearly one-fifth of breakdowns were based on awareness issues. In the awareness category, Figure 11.2 indicates that the most frequent cause for miscommunications was found to be a *lack of awareness of the other participant's expectations* [37]. The second most recurrent reason for breakdowns was observed to be *facilitation methods* [35] followed by differences in the team members' understanding of the *function of authority* [29] in the coordination of activities. Often members simply *did not speak up* [23] in an open manner, if they had difficulties accepting *the way another member was accustomed to working* [24]. Rather they *hid their resentment* [13] and accumulated small problems until major breakdowns occurred. In many cases, not daring to speak up could be related to a lack of *English language proficiency* [23] of some members and *culturally varying face-saving techniques* [27] of Asian team members in particular. Varying expectations and communication strategies were an issue that influenced the ability to fully *understand design ideas* [29].

According to the data in Table 11.2, community or contextual communication values that differed among the cultures represented in the teams caused the majority of breakdowns. Team members' mutual *awareness of each other's expectations* [37] relates to the way a group is organized. Breakdowns occurred based on clashing expectations among individualist and collectivist values when setting up a community structure for collaboration.

Another frequent reason for breakdowns in collaboration was the *use of differing face techniques* [27] (see Figure 11.2). Face-saving techniques can hide or expose intentions, separate or integrate individuals, challenge or maintain harmony within the team. Face-saving techniques manifest themselves in the use of *confronting* [14] or *conforming* [18] communication strategies. In addition, context values in communication can further explain misunderstandings in communication caused by differing communication styles. Some members prefer to say directly what they think and intend to do, whereas others prefer to take action and expect the others to interpret those actions rather than reply on words. A member, who uses *face-saving techniques and hides intentions* [13], makes it difficult for members with a more direct and hence low contextual communication style to read the contextual signs of the other team member. This leads to misunderstandings, which often end with weak work morale i.e., *latecomer* [13] or *withdrawal from participation* [13] of the member with a high contextual communication style in order to keep harmony in the community. Hence, differing contextual communication strategies influence the group dynamic and social relations in the team, which has an effect on the *accountability* [21] of team members, and the *acceptance of design ideas* [29] put forward by those members respectively. Some members *conform* [14] to *dominant members* [17], *others confront* [18] *through communication,* especially when the team *evaluates design concepts* [29].

Another breakdown in communication in relation to understanding design concepts and the way work is coordinated is based on *differing use of language* [14] of team members. Language use is not just limited to *proficient use of English language* [23]. A much more subtle communication problem arises from how *fast* [11] or *slow* [10] members develop and communicate ideas. Some members need time to formulate the perfect idea and communicate it only if it exactly expresses the intended meaning (slow); however, other members communicate their ideas at the time they pop-up in their head, without considering how elaborated the idea is as presented to the team (fast). Especially *dominant team members* [17], who push design ideas in their intended direction, do not realize that this causes slower members to *withdraw* [13]. Dominant members often have little patience for the *facilitator's use of authority* [29] to reintroduce withdrawn team members; this causes breakdowns in teamwork.

This was a very brief discussion of reasons for misunderstandings in cross-cultural collaborative design and learning. Knowing the possible reasons for breakdowns is important. However, more important is to know about specific awareness, communication, coordination, and content supporting collaboration strategies to gain common understanding and deal with breakdowns in this particular international design education setting. Therefore, the following section describes how specific collaborative design and learning techniques and cross-cultural team composition prevented breakdowns, approached misunderstandings, and turned them into valuable knowledge for the summer school participants and contextual design innovation.

Figure 11.3
Awareness: Observation and frequency of occurrences
in this data code category

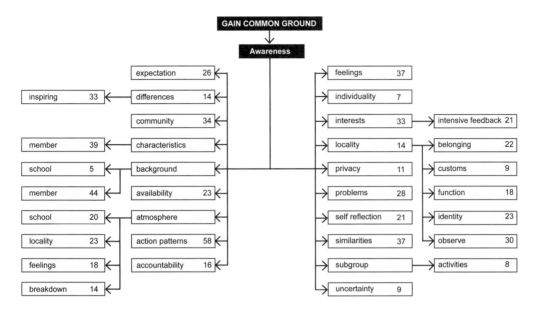

Gaining Common Ground and Dealing with Breakdowns

As mentioned before, intercultural communication literature suggests two strategies: gaining common ground and dealing with breakdowns, and four specific techniques: awareness, communication, content, and coordination to overcome misunderstandings and support collaborative processes leading to implementations and innovations based on the teamwork.

Table 11.3
Co-coding frequencies in dealing with breakdowns and gaining common ground in the awareness category

Gain Common Ground: awareness: action patterns	Co-coding frequency	Total
gain_common_awareness>characteristics>member	16	39
gain_common_ground>awareness>similarities	13	37
gain_common_ground>awareness>community	11	34
gain_common_ground>awareness>background>member	8	44
gain_common_ground>awareness>availability	7	23
gain_common_ground>awareness>feelings	7	37
gain_common_ground>awareness>locality>belonging	6	22
gain_common_ground>awareness>locality>function	6	18
gain_common_ground>awareness>locality>observe	6	30
gain_common_ground>awareness>problems	6	28

A total of 1,797 data codes in the category of gaining common ground were counted as displayed in Table 11.1. The data in Table 11.2 shows that, while the majority (two-fifths) of the observed techniques to gain common ground were coded in the awareness category, one-fourth of all observations used either coordination or content techniques. Moreover, Table 11.1 shows that among 541 data codes in the category of dealing with breakdowns, nearly two-fifth of the techniques to deal with misunderstandings were communication strategies. The most frequent strategies (over three-fifths) were observed in the coordination category. This result supports the idea that the most successful way to learn and design collaboratively is based on gaining common ground through awareness and content, and by dealing with breakdowns through coordination and communication. These findings will now be explained in greater detail and analyzed in the context of cultural values in the following sections.

Awareness

The data code frequencies displayed in Figure 11.3 show that members most frequently gained common ground through the awareness of *action patterns* [58]. The co-coding frequency of this code with other data codes displayed in Table 11.3 suggests that awareness of action patterns was gained predominantly through *awareness of the characteristics of the team members* [39], especially *awareness of similarities* [37]. Awareness of similarities among members was achieved though *intensive feedback* [21] on shared topics of interest. Additionally, an awareness of the *members' differences also inspired* [33] the participants' interactions.

The data show that gaining common ground through making *observations in the locality* [30] not only helped to develop potential design ideas but also helped to get to know about different perspectives among fellow observers and teammates. The main focus of these observations was gaining *awareness of the functionalities in the*

Table 11.4
Comparison of cultural values and collaboration support in the code categories dealing with breakdowns and gaining common ground

Cultural Values	Awareness		Communication		Content		Coordination		Total	
	T	%	T	%	T	%	T	%	T	%
Activity	64	9	18	4	55	13	103	13	240	10
Authority	34	5	47	11	27	6	120	16	228	10
Community	164	24	73	18	54	13	169	22	460	20
Context	285	41	206	50	188	44	171	22	850	37
Time	27	4	27	7	17	4	64	8	135	6
Uncertainty	121	17	41	10	90	21	139	18	391	17
Total	695	100	412	100	431	101*	766	99*	2304	100

*Due to rounding, not all percentage totals equal 100.

Figure 11.4
Communication: Observations and frequency of
occurrences in this data code category

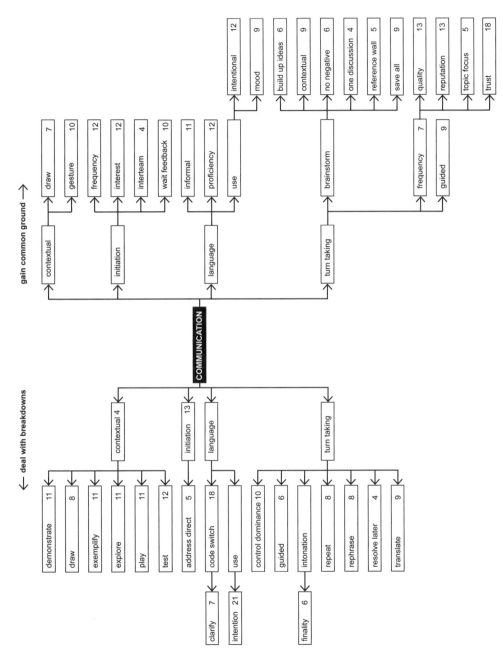

locality [18] and reaching a minimal understanding of the *local identity* [23]. Gaining an understanding for the locality and interacting with the local population generated a *feeling of belonging to this community* [22].

A mix of *community* [24%] and *contextual communication* [41%] of *cultural value orientations* played a dominant role in gaining awareness in collaboration (see Table 11.4). Within collaborative design and learning activities, a collective community value orientation stimulated members to get to know as much as possible about their fellow members, which enhanced specific relationships [*buddies, 17*], and expressive interaction styles [*intensive feedback, 21*]. Engaging in communal activities, e.g., museum visits, leisure and evening activities, or home stay opportunities, reduced uncertainty in social relations and offset the high uncertainty within the teamwork in the beginning of the course. Awareness of others and the context of learning and design seemed to support collaborative learning and design in international design summer schools.

Communication

Several distinct intercultural communication strategies to deal with breakdowns and gain common ground were introduced, as Figure 11.4 illustrates. The findings from the previous section suggest that awareness of different cultural backgrounds and the members' characteristics made them aware of the *level of English language proficiency*

Table 11.5
Cultural values in dealing with breakdowns and gaining common ground in communication code category

Differences in cultural values regarding communication use:	Activity	Authority	Community	Context	Time	Uncertainty	Total
Dealing with Breakdowns:							
Code switching	0	2	2	13	1	0	18
Intentional language use	2	4	2	9	3	1	21
Initiation	0	0	5	6	2	0	13
Contextual testing	1	0	2	4	0	4	12
Contextual play	0	0	1	9	0	1	11
Contextual exploration	0	0	2	5	0	4	11
Contextual exemplification	0	0	0	8	1	2	11
Contextual demonstration	0	1	1	8	0	1	11
Gaining Common Ground:							
Turn taking fequency, trust	1	1	8	5	1	2	18
Turn taking frequency, quality	1	1	7	4	0	0	13
Turn taking frequency, reputation	0	2	5	5	0	1	13
Intentional language use	1	1	2	6	1	1	12
Language proficiency	0	1	2	6	1	2	12
Initiation frequency	1	1	1	7	1	1	12
Initiation by interest	0	1	4	7	0	0	12

[12] of co-participants. This understanding stimulated participants to employ *intentional communication techniques to deal with breakdowns* [21] or *gain common ground* [12]. An initial awareness was gained through *informal communications* [11] prior to work-related discussions. Participants frequently *initiated communication* [13] based on *shared interest in a topic* [19] among the team members and with the local population to learn about the subject and each other. The more similar the interests, the more likely a *high communication frequency* [18] was maintained. High turn-taking frequency led to growing reliance on the *member's permanent engagement* [18]. However, this practice sometimes created a *communication dominance* that needed to be *controlled* [10]. Native English speakers usually exhibited this dominance in conversation since they were more comfortable

Figure 11.5
Contents: Observations and frequency of occurrences in this
data code category

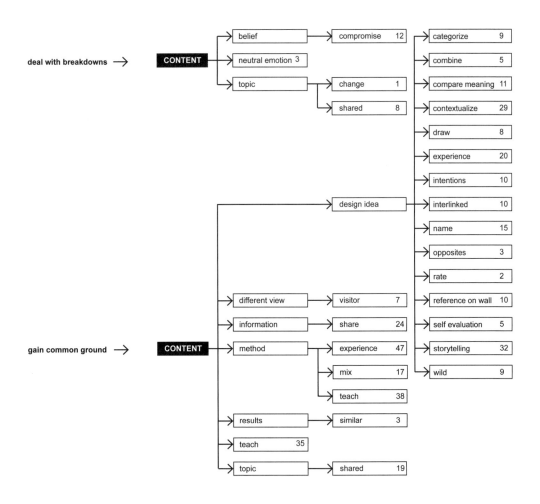

expressing their thoughts and ideas in English. In order to deal with such an apparent breakdown, native speakers were asked to let non-native speakers take the first turn in a discussion. Such an *active mediation* [18] as well as *switching between local and English language* [18] facilitated communication within the team or with the local population. If dominance could be controlled and code switching was employed, brainstorm activities helped overcome breakdowns by *involving all members in the discussion* [22].

In addition, various *contextual communication practices* [9] like *demonstrating* [11], *exemplifying* [11], or *testing* [12] design ideas using *explorative* [11] and *playful communication* [11] could inspire a creative use of design ideas and artifacts. This fostered innovative design solutions, which only arose because team members were forced to go beyond verbal communication in this intercultural setting. In this context, *storytelling* [32] was found to be an often-used technique to contextualize and communicate design ideas to gain common ground. Stories often combine *observations made in a locality* [30] with the *background knowledge* [44] and *interests of a member* [33]. They evolve around *observations of the functions of the surrounding locality* [18], or *the specific use of an artifact* [35], while *experiencing various user-centered design methods* [47]. Stories and design ideas can more efficiently be mediated in international settings using *gestures* [10] or *drawings* [7].

High contextual communication is the most prevalent culturally-influenced strategy to gain common ground and deal with breakdowns through communication in collaborative design and learning (see Tables 11.5 and 11.6). A high contextual communication style enables individuals to communicate using fewer words because they share the same context. Furthermore, contextual communication styles intersect with community values. Particularly, awareness of action patterns leads to the repeated use of high contextual communication strategies to gain common ground. In design activities, this awareness turns into social information that can be used to communicate in multiple modes.

Content

Figure 11.5 shows that the most outstanding way to gain understanding about content in the collaborative design project occurred while *experiencing user-centered methods* [47]. Participants were able to understand and experience methods as a *variety of promising methods in lectures* [38] were taught. Daily *lectures* [35] not only listed possible methods, but also exemplified successful projects using these methods; this contributed to establishing norms and giving direction for possible content in collaborative design activities. Furthermore, the data in Table 11.6 suggest that lectures reduced uncertainty about the processes and expectations of the participants. Lectures and hands-on experiences offered a rich and lively picture of the market

Table 11.6
Selection of correlations of experiencing user-centered design methods with other codes

Gain Common Ground: content: experience method	Co-coding Frequency	Total
Gain Common Ground: content: teach method	19	38
Gain Common Ground: content: mix method	14	17
Gain Common Ground: coordination: facilitation, interest direction	8	28
Gain Common Ground: coordination: facilitation, give a task	7	21
Gain Common Ground: awareness: community	7	34
Gain Common Ground: content: teach	6	35
Gain Common Ground: awareness: differences inspire	6	33
Gain Common Ground: awareness: interests	6	33
Gain Common Ground: content: design idea: contextualize	6	29
Gain Common Ground: content: information: share	6	24
Gain Common Ground: coordination: artifact use	6	35
Deal with Breakdowns: contextual communication: test	5	12
Deal with breakdowns: coordination: define process	5	18
Deal with Breakdowns: coordination: self-organization	5	29
Gain Common Ground: awareness: members' background	5	44
Gain Common Ground: content: shared topic	5	19
Deal with Breakdowns: coordination: subgroups	4	20
Gain Common Ground: awareness: action patterns	4	58
Gain Common Ground: awareness: expectation	4	26
Gain Common Ground: awareness: locality: identity	4	23
Deal with Breakdowns: contextual communication: explore	4	11
Deal with Breakdowns: contextual communication: demonstrate	4	11
Gain Common Ground: coordination: activities	4	30
Gain Common Ground: coordination: facilitate a vision	4	20
Gain Common Ground: coordination: goal	4	18

and users for which the participants would design. They established a *shared topic* [19] for all teams. Based on this, participants from different *teams shared information* [24] about the findings and insights gained by making inquiries in the local context. The teams were encouraged to *mix various methods* [17] in order to learn through tangible experiences and in order to triangulate data. Probes or prototypes supported the exploration and *experience of design ideas* [20] and *methods* [47], and generated innovative *design ideas* [36] for the local market. Collecting contents through design probes, prototypes [*creative artifact use, 35*], or scenarios [*storytelling, 32*] were aids to experience the applicability of design ideas. *Sharing the information* [24] that was found through these experiments with other teams helped gain an awareness of the *design community* [34]. The findings also suggested that the difference between their recent experiences in the local context and the members' previous expectations was very *inspiring* [33] and encouraging.

For the purpose of testing designs in the local environment, participating local team members pay a key role as *local experts* [10], to *coordinate activities* [30] and act as *translators* [9] in interviews and tests. Therefore, *code switching* [18] for *mediation and clarification* [7] purposes among locals and between local and non-local participants

Figure 11.6
Coordination: Observations and frequency of occurrences in
this data code category

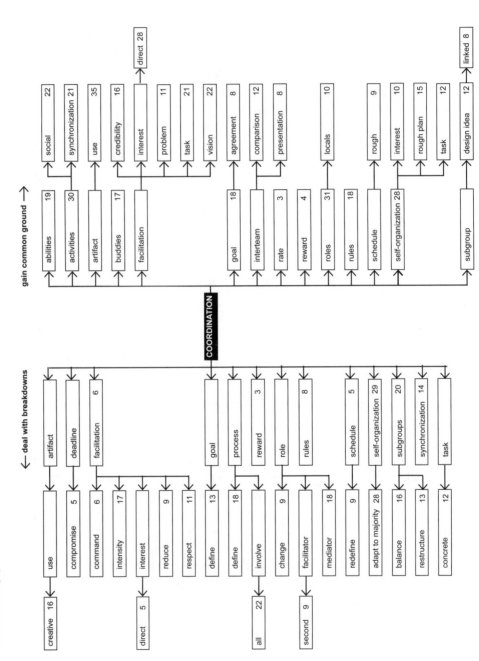

helped gain specific knowledge about *customs* [9], *artifact usage* [35], and other *functions of the locality* [18]. In conclusion, a mix between conveying new knowledge through formal teaching and experience with new methods in a real context provided the best mix of contents for a collaborative design project that led to a successful learning experience.

Coordination

The coordination of the *teams' activities* [30] needed to strike a balance between *facilitation* [17] and *self-organization* [29] of the team. Looking at the results displayed in Figure 11.6, *self-organization* was observed to be one of the most successful coordination strategies to gain both *common ground* [28] and *deal with breakdowns* [29]. In the beginning of the teams' self-organization, basic teamwork *rules* [18] and the awareness of a *shared process* [18] were established, inspired by the *lectures* [35] and by the *facilitator's interests* [28]. Often the process was laid out on the basis of a common interaction design process model (Rogers et al., 2002; Westerlund, 2005).

Looking at the co-coding frequencies displayed in Table 11.7 suggests that while advancing in the process, experiencing, and testing possible design methods and ideas, the team gains confidence and the *facilitation intensity should ideally decrease* [17]. Due to *interest* [10] or *ability* [19], members take up *roles* [31] in the team. Some members' roles are strong and can lead to conflicting situations. Hence, in order to test and explore as many design ideas as possible, but separate potential dominant members, a team splits into *subgroups* [20]. Subgroups cluster around strong members or members with *similar interests* [33]. The less experienced or less language-proficient *members adjust to the majority* [28]. This accommodation strategy is based on culturally varying community and

Table 11.7
Selection of self-organization data code co-coding frequencies

Gain Common Ground: coordination: self-organization	Co-coding Frequency	Total
Gain Common Ground: coordination: roles	7	31
Gain Common Ground: coordination: self-organization: interest	7	10
Gain Common Ground: coordination: self-organization: rough plan	6	15
Gain Common Ground: awareness: action patterns	5	58
Gain Common Ground: content: method: experience	5	47
Deal with Breakdowns: coordination: self-organization		
Deal with Breakdowns: coordination: synchronization	9	14
Deal with Breakdowns: coordination: role: mediator	6	18
Deal with Breakdowns: coordination: subgroups	6	20
Deal with Breakdowns: coordination: subgroups: balance	6	16
Deal with Breakdowns: coordination: role: change	5	9
Deal with Breakdowns: coordination: rules	5	8

communication techniques, which help to *balance subgroups* [16] and to *compromise if a deadline approaches* [5]. Another strategy to involve all members in teamwork is the coupling of only two members as *buddies* [17] rather than forming large subgroups. This gives those members who have difficulties speaking up in front of a big group a chance to have their ideas considered, too. A third method involves finding *concrete tasks for members* [12] who have difficulties speaking up in order to give them a chance to *change their role* [9]. With the satisfactory completion of an explicit task, these members can show their *accountability* [16] and gain attention, *trust* [18], and *acceptance of their ideas* [11] within group discussions. Nevertheless, a problem with grouping around strong members, and accommodation of other members, is the lack of consideration of potentially valuable ideas from members with face hiding communication techniques and strong hierarchical authority perception. They often *don't dare to speak up* [23] to the main facilitator of the team, because she is perceived as higher-ranking. To address this cultural difference, more specific relations and instrumental interaction styles can be employed. A second facilitator, who is perceived on the same hierarchical level, can have the task to look for problems and suggest ways to solve problems among team members.

The significance of self-organization within the team is affirmed looking at the cultural value of contextual communication and uncertainty avoidance. To overcome breakdowns in situations of high uncertainty, collaborative design activities benefit from self-organization within the team. In self-organizing teams, members are more self-conscious about how to use their abilities and find their roles and responsibilities. A low contextual communicating member might be able to summarize ideas or control dominance in a brainstorm session. Such a member might define more concrete goals after high contextual communicating members explore various ideas using experimental, playful, and hands-on design exercises. A possible breakdown, based on the feeling of not being needed or not being understood, is hence avoided.

Implementations: Contextual Design Innovations and Learning

The preceding sections demonstrated that learning occurs through frequent design implementations throughout the entire collaboration process. This section gives two examples of collaborative design and learning processes that utilized the above outlined practices to develop innovative designs for a local market. The design proposals of the teams were presented in the form of low- to high-fidelity prototypes and scenarios, which were captured in drawings or animations, or acted out as moving or still photo images.

A team from the summer school held in Split, Croatia in 2004 introduced several design proposals to support sustainable tourism and foster interaction between different groups of people in the town. This particular case focused on communication between

Figure 11.7
Scenario to demonstrate communication strategies between locals and tourists in Split

locals and their guests, the tourists. By collecting public artifacts, conducting interviews with the residents, observing them within their local environment, and continuously reconciling design constraints, the team was able to generate several conceptual alternatives to address the city's socio-economic needs (see Figure 11.7).

The perceived open-mindedness and hospitality of the local people in Split was used to explore a scenario of sustainable tourism through an exchange of local and personal experiences with interested tourists (see Figure 11.8). An "online-dating" type of service was proposed as a way to match locals and tourists who shared common interests. Travelers often inform themselves about the history, activities, and sights they might visit during their stay. Local people enjoy meeting tourists for cultural and language exchange. A communication and knowledge-sharing area in an online matching service would benefit both sides based on mutual interests. Moreover, a system for identifying and sharing key spots in the city was proposed as a means to introduce tourists to hard-to-find local places. And finally, a concept was

Figure 11.8
Methods used to determine the relation of food mediation in Romania

Figure 11.9
User testing used to determine the acceptance of an alternative food mediation device in Romania

Contextual Interview
Results

❖ Would use it
❖ Want smell
❖ Want taste
❖ No sound
❖ Photos, not drawings

developed to let locals and tourists collaboratively create a continuing story thorough interacting with e-boards placed throughout the city. The aforementioned design suggestions were then united into a single video-photo story to convey the workability and interconnectedness of the communication concepts in the scenarios.

Teams from the summer school that was held in Timisoara, Romania in 2005 dealt with how storytelling can be used to sustain informal communication about the past, present, and future of the city of Timisoara among its townspeople. Participants came up with an experimental and novel recipe communication device called the Umami-E-Card and a supporting service, the Umami-E-Market. The design team used multiple user-centered methods to determine the requirements for communicating recipes from the past into the future. In iterative phases of low-, medium- and high-fidelity

Figure 11.10
Users engaged with prototypes for an innovative food mediation device and service in Romania

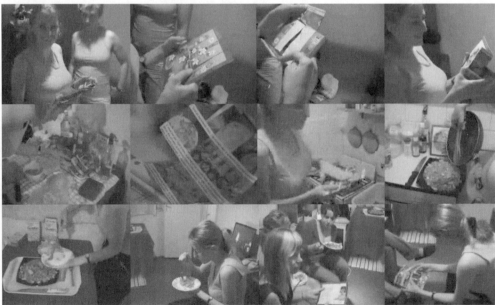

prototypes, a paper foldable card, called Umami-Card, was prototyped and tested (see Figures 11.9 and 11.10).

This card captured different dimensions of recipe-mediation and carried the user through the entire cooking process. When testing the Umami-Card prototype, it quickly became apparent that users were connecting personally with this object. Many expressed interest in annotating the content of the historical context, recipes, and explanatory text with their own stories and experiences. No one could imagine giving the device away as a gift, let alone returning it at the end of the evaluation cycle. However, many users talked about exchanging content with other users or updating the device to include new recipe variations.

To support this changeability, the idea of a tangible interface that is connected to Umami-E-Market, an internet-based peer-to-peer sharing platform, evolved. A photo-scenario described the idea of a recipe database that collected the recipes from all over the world. In this case, people would use a tangible interface, the Umami-E-Card, to up and download data to and from the Umami-E-Market. This presents a way of saving the user's own experiences and allowing communication and sharing of stories with other users, thus prolonging the user's personal enjoyment of this object.

The examples above show that "quick and dirty" implementations and frequent tests of the designs were used to advance knowledge at various stages in the design project. Teams continuously learned and evaluated the designs in order to determine the acceptance of novel design ideas and interaction strategies in specific local environments.

A Model for Cross-cultural Collaborative Learning and Design Fostering Contextual Innovation

The main findings of this study clearly show distinct intercultural collaborative design and learning strategies that allow teams to gain common ground and deal with breakdowns. The model shown in Figure 11.11 synthesizes all the discussed issues and proposes a framework to support cross-cultural collaborative learning and design that fosters contextual innovation. The framework proposes that knowledge about the local context, as well as the characteristics and backgrounds of other team members, make members aware of action patterns within the design community. This initiates a conversation with fellow teammates and the local population, increases consciousness about the use of language, and stimulates high contextual communication practices in collaborative design and learning. Storytelling is an important communication strategy that supports agreement on design ideas in collaboration. These contents are experienced through hands-on design experiences in the local setting and are supported by lectures given by experts in the field. The team activities are coordinated

Figure 11.11
A model of cross-cultural collaborative design and learning for
contextual design innovation

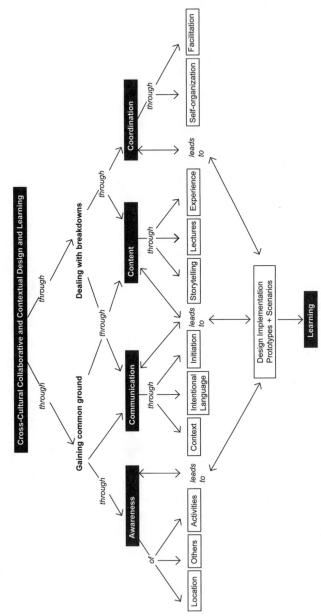

mainly through self-organization, fostered through a growing body of knowledge and confidence, by testing design ideas in a concrete local setting. This allows decreased facilitation intensity and improves contextual learning and the design innovation process. Various implementations in the format of probes, prototypes, or scenarios at different stages of the design workshop increase awareness, inspire conversations, and help participants open up to new content, as well as helping self-organization and coordination of the team's activities (see Figure 11.11).

Conclusions

This chapter argues that cross-cultural collaborative learning and design fosters contextual innovation in early design phases, as found in interaction design summer schools. The results of the observations of three cases of interaction design summer schools were discussed in light of cross-cultural collaboration theories. The findings of this study confirm that misunderstandings and breakdowns in cross-cultural collaboration can be prevented or addressed by raising intercultural awareness, engaging in contextual and multi-modal communication, experiencing the content of collaboration in hands-on activities, and through frequent and quick implementations of designs in a local environment. These experiences enhance confidence and encourage self-organization of the team while facilitation intensity decreases.

The results of this study also confirm the positive role of user-centered design in design innovation. Moreover, user-centered design in and for a local market benefits from culturally and professionally diverse team composition. While a foreign design context inspires international summer school participants, local participants are motivated to go beyond the known design solutions from this alternative design perspective. This might lead to the possibility that intercultural teams designing in and for a local market can trigger design innovations for this market. Furthermore, participants learn contextually about themselves, their culture, and others; they discover how to engage in intercultural communication and collaboration, which can lead to design innovations.

Contextual innovation in early design phases was demonstrated through collaborative work in interaction design summer programs. The findings and model introduced here may also guide summer school organizers, team facilitators, and participants through a successful collaboration process and inspire contextual design innovation. Furthermore, the author believes that the findings have broader implications and might be considered in other educational or business-related contexts where teams collaborate in a search for design innovations.

Note

1. Design Pattern Workshops introduce a certain structure to team discussion. The expert participants are asked to think about good solutions to problems they encounter in their design and learning processes in a particular setting (here, activities in the summer school). The results of the discussions are summarized and compared. Recurrent solutions are considered as "interaction design patterns."

References

Ashton, P. 2004. The Role of Occupational Communities in the Transmission and Embedding of Design Innovation – a conceptual framework. In *Proceedings of Futureground, Design Research Society International Conference*. Melbourne, Australia, November 17–21.

Bonk, C.J. and K.S. King (eds.). 1998. *Electronic Collaborators: Learner-Centered Technologies for Literacy, Apprenticeship, and Discourse*. Mahwah, NJ: Lawrence Erlbaum.

Conner, M. 2004. User-centered Learning: An Interview with Judee Hamburg. http://www.limezine. com/3.1/features/jhmcul.htm (accessed March 2006).

Chayutsahakij, P. and S. Poggenpohl. 2001. Value Framing: Enhances Design Team's Internal and External Affective Performance. In *Proceedings of the International Conference on Affective Human Factors Design*. The Oriental, Singapore, June 26-29, London: Asian Academic Press.

Dinçer, B. 2003. New user-centered methods for design innovation: a study on the role of emerging methods in innovative product design and development. Unpublished M.Sc. Thesis, Istambul Technical University, Institute of Science and Technology, January.

Edquist, C. 2001. The Systems of Innovation Approach and Innovation Policy: An Account of the State of Art. *Proceedings of the DRUID Conference*. Aalborg, Denmark, June 12–15.

Evers, Madelon. 2004. *Facilitating Multidisciplinary Design Teams*. Delft, Netherlands: Eburon Academic Publishers.

Falk, J.H. and L.D. Dierking. 2002. Contextual Model of Learning: Institute for Learning Innovation. http://www.ilinet.org/ contextualmodel.htm (accessed March 2006).

Ghosh, K. and A. Chavan. 2004. Collaborating on Ethnography and Design Research: Centre for Ethnography and Contextual Innovation at HFI. In *Proceedings of CHI2004*. Vienna, Austria, April, 24-29, New York, NY: ACM Press, 1069–1070.

Gudykunst, W.B. 2004. *Bridging Differences: Effective Intergroup Communication*. Thousand Oaks, CA: Sage Publications.

Hall, E.T. 1990. *Understanding Cultural Differences*. Yarmouth, ME: Intercultural Press.

Hofstede, G. 1997. *Cultures and Organizations: Software of the Mind*. New York, NY: McGraw-Hill.

Heskett, J. 2005. Structured Knowledge, Practical Wisdom and Values in Design. *Journal of Designing in China*, 1, Summer, 18–25.

Lewin, K. 1973. *Resolving Social Conflicts: Selected Papers on Group Dynamics*. London, United Kingdom: Souvenir Press.

Marcus, A. and V.J. Baumgartner. 2004. A Practical Set of Culture Dimensions for Global User-Interface Development. In *Proceedings of APCHI 2004*. Rotorua, New Zealand, June 29-July 2, Berlin, Germany: Springer, 252–261.

Mayring, P. 2000. Qualitative Content Analysis. *Forum: Qualitative Social Research*, 1.2. http://www. qualitative-research.net/index.php/fqs/article/viewArticle/1089 (accessed March 2009).

Mutlu, B. and A. Er. 2003. Design Innovation: Historical and Theoretical Perspectives on Product Innovation by Design. In *Proceedings of the 5th European Academy of Design Conference*. Barcelona, Spain,28-30 April.

Ortiz, A.M. 2000. *Expressing Cultural Identity in the Learning Community: Opportunities and Challenges. New directions for teaching and learning*. San Francisco, CA: Jossey-Bass.

Ostwald, J. 1995. Supporting collaborative design with representations for mutual understanding. In *Conference Companion on Human Factors in Computing Systems* (Denver, Colorado, United States, May 07 - 11, 1995). I. Katz, R. Mack, and L. Marks, Eds. CHI '95. ACM, New York, NY, 69-70.

Piaget, J. 1973. *To Understand Is to Invent: The Future of Education*. New York, NY: Grossman.

Rogers, Y., H. Sharp, and J. Preece. 2002. *Interaction Design: Beyond Human-Computer Interaction*. New York, NY: John Wiley and Sons.

Scollon, R. and S.W. Scollon. 2001. *Intercultural Communication: A Discourse Approach*. Oxford, United Kingdom: Blackwell.

Tesch, R. 1990. *Qualitative Research: Analysis Types and Software Tools*. New York, NY: Falmer Press.

Walsh, V. 1996. Design Innovation and the Boundaries of the Firm. *Research Policy*, 25.4., 509–529.

Wenger, E. 1998. *Communities of Practice: Learning, Meaning, and Identity*. Cambridge, United Kingdom: Cambridge University Press.

Westerlund, B. 2005. Design Space Conceptual Tool – Grasping the Design Process. In *Proceedings of the Nordic Design Research Conference*. Copenhagen, Denmark, May 29–31.

Zhang, Q., J.S. Lim, and M. Cao. 2004. Innovation; Team learning; Knowledge Management; Product Development; Organizational Development; Information Management. *Industrial Management & Data Systems*, 104.3, 252–261.

12

A COMPLEX MODEL FOR INTERNATIONAL AND INTERCULTURAL COLLABORATION IN HEALTH INFORMATION SYSTEMS

Judith Gregory

Introduction

Scandinavian participatory design, based on a tradition of respect and collaboration among diverse stakeholders, has a history of more than thirty years. Such a design approach or process is challenged to adapt when used in new contexts that cross cultures, institutions, and continents. As an underpinning philosophy for project development concerned with technology and systems design, Scandinavian participatory design begins from the premise that "the people destined to *use* the system play a critical role in *designing* it" (Schuler and Namioka, 1993, xi). The tradition of Scandinavian participatory design is the foundation for the Health Information Systems Programme in which I had the extraordinary opportunity to work from 2000 to 2005 while I was on the faculty of the Department of Informatics, University of Oslo, Norway.

The Health Information Systems Programme (known as HISP) is a large-scale, ongoing international collaboration in open source health information systems for public health and higher education through the dual International Master Programmes for Master of Science in Information Systems and Master in Public Health of the informatics and medical faculties of the University of Oslo, Norway and the University of Eduardo Mondlane, Mozambique, University of the Western Cape, South Africa, and University of Dar Es Salaam, Tanzania-Zanzibar, as well as universities in Ethiopia, India, and others. This program explicitly strives for democratization of health reforms in health districts in developing countries, where there are frequent shortages of trained health personnel, diagnostic tests, medicines, electricity, and infrastructure (Werner, 1980). Challenges abound—the viewpoint is that it is not enough to blame weaknesses in the infrastructure for persistent problems but to focus on what can be done. The Health Information Systems Programme began in South Africa with the post-apartheid turn towards democratization in 1994.

The people engaged in this ongoing information and communication technology design collaboration have a strongly shared concern in healthcare as fundamental to human development and to capability building of local resources (Nussbaum and Sen, 1993; Sen, 1984, 1999, 2002). The doctoral and master students also serve as teachers and mentors for health sector workers in their own countries and in other participating countries, and doctoral candidates have teaching opportunities at the University of Oslo while pursuing their own doctoral research. During the years of my involvement, 2000–2005, this "South-South-North" collaboration in the HISP and the International Master Programmes in southern Africa were regarded as the flagship projects of the Norwegian development agency NORAD and its counterpart for international higher education fellowships, NUFU, as well as by the University of Oslo as a whole and the Department of Informatics in specific.

Open source software development of the District Health Information Systems (DHIS) software is carried out through the HISP Global Network, a multi-country collaboration by geographically distributed in-person and virtual teams in and between nodes in South Africa, Norway, Mozambique, Ethiopia, Malawi, India, Vietnam, Nigeria, and Finland. By the end of 2008, an estimated 100 University of Oslo master and doctoral

Figure 12.1
An overview of the Health Information Systems Programme (HISP)

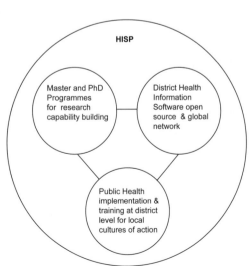

students had been involved in the District Health Information Software design and development. Figure 12.1 presents an overview of the Health Information Systems Programme.

Overview of the Health Information Systems Programme

The HISP is committed to cultivating locally grounded cultures of "information for action" in public health at the district health level, the strategic unit for primary health care. This large-scale multi-level collaboration is driven by constant expansion motivated by the urgency of epidemic health problems and commitment to research, education, and training for capacity building. An ever-expanding network of additional countries chooses to adopt and co-develop the free open source software that supports effective collection and use of health data at the district level. In the four years that I came and went to and from Mozambique, the average life expectancy dropped from 43 to 38 years as a result of the combined devastations of malaria, tuberculosis, and HIV/AIDS (Chilundo, 2004; Mendes, 2004). Given the urgency of addressing the confluence of pandemic illnesses, pervasive poverty and malnutrition, and inadequate means for safe drinking water or essential infrastructure (Epstein, 2001; Farmer, 2005; Garrett, 2000; Sen et al., 2002), the principal designers of the DHIS software adopted the slogan, "If everything's under control, you're moving too slow."

How does such a complicated collaboration in computer systems design (or informatics design), information systems implementation, and master and doctoral education manage to move fast, sustain itself and expand, iteratively develop the software through globally distributed rapid prototyping and localization, and accomplish commitments to the development of the many people who lead participatory action research and participatory design within and across country and community contexts? The answer lies in part in the program's methodology for contextual research, information systems, software research and development, and infrastructure design, which has deep roots in the principles and practices of Scandinavian participatory design and participatory action research, which are being extended and adapted to new contexts (Puri et al., 2004). The community of participating informatics and medical faculty, master students and doctoral candidates also share a commitment to theory building in informatics. Crucially important to the project's success are the spirit of mutual learning and respect, shared understandings of constraints in specific contexts, and shared decision-making that includes frontline health care workers at the grassroots level in decisions about priority problems, informational content, norms, development of tools for continuous learning "where you sit," the need to re-invent standard health indicators to adapt to material conditions, and realistic goal-setting to be implemented in information systems design.

Participatory prototyping is central to the DHIS (software) design and development strategy in the context of modular, distributed development and rapid iterative prototyping cycles. Within the project's approach of *cultivation* of practice and technical standards and information infrastructure building, autonomy of action and local improvisation is valued and encouraged. The embrace of improvisation keeps the design open for innovative local adaptations to become integrated into the software and supports ways of working in different places. "First you have to re-invent the indicators" refers to iterative development of World Health Organization indicators. For example, standard measures of maternal and infant mortality need to be re-invented in the specificities of locally situated practices, means, and contexts. Thus the participatory prototyping approach as it is broadly conceived in relation to both system design and work practices orients towards what Anselm Strauss calls "continual permutations of action" (Strauss, 1993). Health information systems must be reconfigurable for evolving knowledge, infrastructure, practices, and illnesses.

What can designers and design researchers learn from this contextually located yet far-reaching, heterogeneous yet coherent model of sustained and ever-expanding interdisciplinary, intercultural, international information and communication technology design? This chapter offers principles for design collaboration across difference and complexity in intercultural, international and inter-institutional design collaborations that are distilled from my experiences of collaboration in the HISP. I conclude by proposing the concept of *design for negotiation of logics* that can foster the emergence of new kinds of design knowledge in the "spaces in between" and new "meeting grounds" that can arise in cross-cultural and cross-disciplinary collaboration. How may we re-imagine and theorize the realities and possibilities of working with and in actor-networks of institutions, technologies, nature, and the multitude of human and non-human actors to creatively evoke new kinds of collaborative spaces for design concepts and action? The principles of the Health Information Systems are realized and revealed in participatory design practice by presenting case examples and explicating the Health Information Systems Programme's multi-level multi-country collaborative model in practice in Sub-Saharan Africa and India. Challenges, dilemmas, and contradictions for cross-cultural and interdisciplinary design collaboration are critically and constructively discussed.

Developing my own competencies to work across diverse contexts has fundamentally meant reciprocal learning by contributing to the collective development of competencies, participation, and skills of others—doctoral and master students, faculty researchers and health sector colleagues, diverse practitioners, and distributed designers of health information systems, as individuals and in networks.

The HISP received the Artful Integrators Award in Participatory Design in 2006. The Artful Integrators Award highlights the accomplishment of a group of people who, through collaboration with diverse communities and artifacts, create new configurations that incrementally transform practice and action (Suchman, 1994, 2002). The award is given to a collective of designers for their exceptionally creative accomplishments through participatory design process. The award to the HISP commends the program as follows:

> The aim of the HISP country projects is to move fast and expansively but in a sustainable way, to develop software iteratively through globally distributed rapid prototyping and localization, and to enhance the capacities for action of the many people who engage in participatory action research and participatory design within and across the country and community contexts. The program's methodology for contextual research, information systems and software research and development has deep roots in Scandinavian participatory design and participatory action research, which in turn are being extended and adapted to new and very different contexts through HISP's international collaborations.[1]

Convergence: Interdisciplinarity, Interaction, and Open Collaboration

We are in an epochal period of three convergent turns: the turn toward an interdisciplinary generation of knowledge that engages diverse doctrines of science, industry, and publics; the turn toward interactivity enabled by digital technologies and social media by which interaction design has transformative influence for all design domains; and the turn toward open collaboration in which the special position of design as an inherently transdisciplinary practice is highlighted. These three general trends coincide with the momentum of the HISP and what it suggests for design collaboration at large.

In the transformation toward interdisciplinarity and modes of scientific knowledge production, design is especially well-positioned to deliberately develop into a transdisciplinary practice. Interdisciplinary Mode II knowledge is generated through multi-party partnerships between public and private research, policy and civil society organizations and institutions, including participation of interested communities, corporations, civil society organizations, and transnational research projects within Europe and between European countries and developing countries (Kuutti, 2007; Dunin-Woyseth and Nielsen, 2004; Gibbons et al., 1994 Nowotny, 2005; Nowotny and Gibbons, 2001). Because transdisciplinarity is concerned with integrated knowledge in relation to specific problems in the specific context of application, Kari Kuutti (2007) observes that, "a broader social accountability permeates the whole process from the start." He further suggests that, "Mode II knowledge production is native to design" due to design's "balance between theory, practice and production" for relevance to worldly practices (2007, 15).

With the advent of interaction design and the general turn toward interaction, all design specializations are being transformed by new interactive digital media. The interaction turn further expands the responsibility for designers in all specializations. What could be conceived previously as a bounded product or service may now be designed for a personally configurable interface meant to be altered by the persons who use, enjoy, or destroy it. The interactional qualities and affordances of ubiquitous computing and digitally enhanced designed artifacts can also be understood as potentialities for new forms of participatory design and co-creation that are already "out there" among publics and individuals.

The general turn toward open collaboration and reciprocity is not only about projects that are explicitly open source, such as the HISP, but includes many forms of open collaboration and partnerships across disciplines and knowledge domains, public, global, and local boundaries, and through fluid social networks. Designers can also create interfaces and platforms as enabling means and media to foster and enhance open collaboration.

Principles for Design Collaboration across Difference and Complexity in Intercultural, International, and Inter-Institutional Design Collaborations

The principles below are distilled from experience in the HISP to provide some guidance and synthesis for the overall discussion. These are principles on which the HISP is explicitly based. The principles are revealed through the design processes of the project as it enters and progresses in contrasting contexts and through reflective analysis of the program's foundational principles in practice. Case examples are presented to illustrate how the principles were revealed and to illustrate contradictions, paradoxes, and dilemmas in collaboration.

- Smart capability building is required for richer and sustained collaboration; capability building for leadership in design research and local cultures of action requires foresight, planning, resources, and time.

- Participation is essential; the context for participation must first be collaboratively constituted. Without participation, nothing will happen or last.

- Mutual learning and reciprocity among design collaboration partners and between designers and users is key to success in intercultural, interdisciplinary, international, and inter-institutional contexts.

- Participatory design is a culture of principled argument, in the most positive meaning that critique always offers a proposal in which conflict, mistakes, dilemmas, and contradictions become resources in design.

■ Respectful dialogue in which difference is valued is essential to intercultural sensitivity and collaboration; shared ground is co-created, not given.

■ Formal scientific contributions and social commitments in which participatory relations in design are essential, expanding designers' responsibilities, knowledge, and practice; these in turn "change the formal" through articulation of new theory and philosophy for design practice.

The Health Information Systems Programme as a Complex Model

The Health Information Systems Programme began in South Africa in 1994 as a participatory design collaboration between South African and Norwegian physicians and health information systems designers. Figure 12.2 presents a timeline of the beginning years of the HISP. In 1995, a proposal by the South African and Norwegian informatics designers and physicians was funded by the Norwegian Development Agency NORAD for a pilot phase to last until 1998. The software was designed and successfully implemented in three health districts in Cape Town. In contrast to two high profile multi-million dollar projects that did not succeed, the software of the HISP open source South African-Scandinavian collaboration worked and the project survived. In 1999, the District Health Information System was adopted as a national standard for all health districts throughout the country, including the HISP's overall participatory strategies and processes. Rapid implementation was accomplished with varying degrees of use in each district in South Africa between 2000 and 2002.

A chronology of important dates in the Health Information System Programme (HISP)

From 2001 to 2005, the HISP developed rapidly as the multi-country and multi-institutional South-South-North collaboration it is known as at the time of writing. The HISP as a whole represents a complex model for international and intercultural collaboration in higher education in health informatics and public health, capability building through advanced research qualification, participatory institutionalization of health information systems at the local level of health districts, and open source software research development carried out through a global network. The program entails collaboration and capability building at five interrelated levels: *Collaboration 1*: International Master Programme in Informatics and Public Health; *Collaboration 2*: Research Qualification of Master and Doctoral Graduates; *Collaboration 3*: Capability Building in Information Technology, Health and Higher Education Sectors; *Collaboration 4*: Health Information Systems Research and Implementation through Participatory Design; and *Collaboration 5*: Open Source Development of the District Health Information Software.

Figure 12.2
A chronology of important events in the Health Information Systems Programme (HISP)

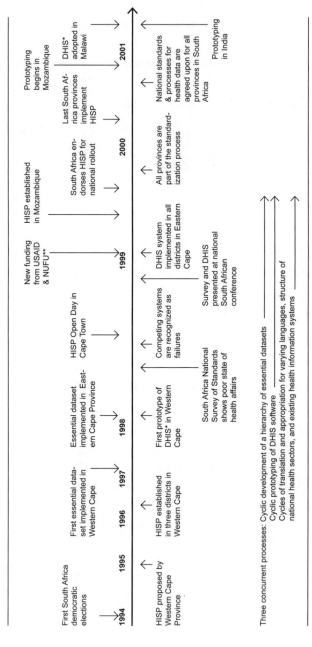

* District Health Information Software Project
** Norwegian International Higher Education Agency (NUFU)

Smart capability building is required for richer and sustained collaboration; capability building for leadership in design research and local cultures of action requires foresight, planning, resources, and time.

Collaboration 1: International Master Programmes in Informatics and Public Health. The dual International Master Programmes of the University of Oslo and University of Eduardo Mondlane offer a Master in Science in Informatics (MSc-Informatics) and a Master in Public Health (MPH) that are integrated by their core specialization in *information systems* and the relationship with the HISP. Master education in general has become increasingly internationalized (Carnoy, 1999) and integrated with digital technologies. Master and doctoral programs in informatics (as in design) are highly internationalized. Whereas India and several Asian countries have advanced computer science and industry profiles, most universities of the South do not have the capacity needed for master's level education in information and communication technologies. Thus there is a great need for research qualification at doctoral and master levels: "Only these degrees will take the students to the research frontier where they get acquainted with the recent developments...and become familiar with the methods used to advance knowledge in the field" (Kaasbøll and Macome, 2002).

Analysis by the Swedish Agency for Research Cooperation with Developing Countries offers recommendations for sustainable high-quality international higher education programs: 1) they must be institutionalized in the university in the South, with joint South-North management; 2) links with leading scientific institutions must be retained, which are to become self-sustaining; 3) long duration and focus on capability building are required; 4) requirements must aim for master and PhD research qualification; 5) universities of the North must provide courses, supervision, and mentoring; and 6) the collaborating universities must have strong mutuality of research interests and realization of mutual benefits in sustained inter-institutional research relationships (Bhagavan, 1992 as cited by Kaasbøll and Macome, 2002). In the Master in Informatics, students work in international and interdisciplinary teams, alternating periods of studies and field research between Norway, Mozambique, and their own countries.

Collaboration 2: Research Qualification of Master and Doctoral Graduates. One of the distinctions of the HISP higher education program is its aim for Doctoral and Master research qualification in Informatics and Medicine. Research qualification is integral to non-dependency, sustainability, and reciprocity in both localization and internationalism. Principles of local construction of knowledge are especially important in information systems development that "is highly dependent on the culture, politics and resources" (Macome, 2002; Macueve, 2008). The faculty directors of the dual master programs associated with the HISP therefore recommend that information systems "should mainly be taught by teachers who know the local conditions." This perspective contrasts, for example, with the strategy of virtual universities such as the African Virtual University funded by the World Bank, which "does not take local context into consideration" (Kaasbøll and Macome, 2002).

Collaboration 3: Capability Building in Information Technology, Health and Higher Education Sectors. The health sector is an especially demanding domain for design because medicine and healthcare are integral to human and social development, community and national quality of life, and cross-sectoral economic development. The HISP takes the broad meaning of capability building and social development from Nobel Laureate Amartya Sen's writings on development, values, human freedom, and autonomy (Nussbaum and Sen, 1993; Sen, 1984, 1999, 2002). Sen observes that "[t]he field of health provides a rich ground" of convergence between doctors and philosophers who share common concerns regarding determinants of quality of life across countries and communities (Nussbaum and Sen, 1993, 3, 30–53) such as basic human rights to good health (Nussbaum and Sen, 1993, 242–269).

While pursuing their own research and learning, the doctoral and master students are also engaged in university-based teaching and in training and mentoring of health sector personnel. Table 12.3 shows: A) country participation in the International

Figure 12.3
Distribution of Health Information Systems Programme, health sector training, graduate education, and open source software development

Graduate Education & Training	Health Sector Training	Dual International Master Programmes MSc Informatics & MPH University of Oslo & University of Eduardo Mondlane	PhD Programmes, Informatics & Medical Faculties, University of Oslo	DHIS open source development global network	New National MSc Informatics Programmes established and/or in development (2005, 2008)
Students & Participants	More than 3,000 health sector staff in short & long term courses (2005 data)	55 international MSc Informatics alumnae & candidates (2006 data) 20 international Master in Public Health alumnae & candidates (2005 data)	45 doctoral alumnae & candidates (2008 data)	More than 100 Master & Doctoral students have contributed (2008 data)	
Countries	Ethiopia India Malawi Mozambique Nigeria Norway South Africa Tanzania-Zanzibar	Mozambique Norway	Norway	China Ethiopia Finland India Malawi Mozambique Nigeria Norway South Africa Tanzania-Zanzibar Vietnam	Mozambique National Master Programme (2005) Tanzania-Zanzibar (2006) Ethiopia (2008) Malawi (2008) Sri Lanka (2008)

Master Programmes in Informatics and Medicine; B) courses and training sessions for health sector personnel in the participating countries; and C) HISP Global Network nodes for open source software development in the HISP Global Network.

Collaboration 4: Health Information Systems Research and Implementation through Participatory Design. Participatory institutionalization of the HISP critically engages multiple levels of contextual research and iterative design, higher education for research leadership and collaborative project leadership, and training of district health personnel. The capability development of local health workers is critical to sustainable information systems implementation. Training sessions aim for each person's gaining an attachment with the collaborative process for gaining knowledge concepts and skilled practices needed to constitute a local culture of information for action. In many places, health information is still pen- and paper-based, so learning information and numeric concepts are preconditions for a future point of knowledgeable computer use. Clinic workers learn not only about use of the software but also gain understandings of health information and systems concepts. For ongoing learning "where you sit," tools associated with the DHIS need to be immediately usable and practical for users and, at the same time, designed as "vehicles for learning." For example, numeracy learning required to calculate health indicators is built into the suite of tools of the software application itself.

Collaboration 5: Open Source Software Development of District Health Information Software. The District Health Information Systems software is free open source software: "both gratis and with free distribution and redistribution of the source code" (Braa and Hedberg, 2002, 122). The DHIS design and development is based on a hybrid open source and Microsoft basis that has advantages of broad recognition of interface conventions, and institutionalization as a platform in wide circulation.

Since 2005, the HISP Global Network has been developing DHIS2 as an open source software from top to bottom. Given the extensive implementation of the current hybrid software and the emphasis on local appropriation and customization, the fully open source version adds complexity to the HISP collaboration. One of the leading Mozambican physicians and doctoral candidates asked, "What will happen to us computer geeks? We know how to make Microsoft tools work, but we don't know how to do open source programming." Going to the fully open source DHIS2 requires higher technical competencies of participating designers and developers, as well as the skills and reliable infrastructure required for collaborating virtually and across time and space. Challenges include instability of open source team compositions and higher technical literacy and conceptual knowledge of information systems at grassroots levels (Burasa, 2005; Lungo, 2008). These challenges come back recursively into the commitments to capability building through higher education and in continuous learning among health sector personnel at all levels.

Scandinavian Participatory Design and Adaptation in New Contexts

The HISP is a participatory design project that adapts Scandinavian participatory design to different contexts and conditions. DHIS development employs a strategy that the principal designer Calle Hedberg calls, "cyclical prototyping with guided user participation," adapting participative prototyping as the principal methodology for iterative design and modular development. Whereas "[p]articipative prototyping as described in the literature is usually quite formal and structured, with well-established user groups, channels of communication and conflict resolution," participatory systems development in the HISP is thought of as *cultivation* (Dahlbom and Janlert, 1996). Cultivation as a design strategy is conceived as:

> ...a slow incremental bottom-up process of...gradually transforming social structures where the resources are already available form the base. The precise outcome of the design process is not given, but is negotiated within a broader set of goals. The strategy is characterized... by *improvisations*...[and] by a strong emphasis on flexible negotiation keeping design options open. (Braa and Hedberg, 2002, 116)

Improvisation refers, for example, to the informality of communication between developers and users. Jørn Braa and Calle Hedberg (2002) explain that "any interested or innovative user...[has] full access to the development team."In guided user participation, "the development team normally has to guide users to a significant degree in understanding their own requests and how they can be implemented in practice" (Braa and Hedberg, 2002, 123).Hedberg, principal designer of the DHIS, estimates that he spends fifteen to twenty percent of his time on software development per se; "the remainder is devoted to extensive interactions with district health staff using the system and with the HISP staff involved in training, technical support, ongoing evaluation, and reporting" (Gregory, 2003, 70).[2] Guided user participation is highly valuable to the software designers but poses a dilemma as it is time-consuming and therefore only possible with a small subset of users among many systems users.

Adaptation of Scandinavian Participatory Design in New Contexts

Given critical shortages of national expert resources in Mozambique, a core multidisciplinary team was established comprised of senior researchers from the Ministry of Health, University of Eduardo Mondlane, and the Mozambican doctoral and master students in computer science and medicine, joined *ad hoc* by international master students. The augmented HISP research and development team highlights potential *mediating agencies* of collaborative design teams across disciplines, local and national governments, policies, and practices, and types of knowledge. In sustained designer-user relationships in participatory prototyping throughout the Mozambique, close interaction with field staff in local languages enabled inclusion of indigenous knowledge. New and locally informed data elements were created to register diseases specific to local food habits, for example, *konzo* ("tied legs"), an irreversible spastic paralysis in the lower legs caused by "cyanide poisoning from insufficiently processed bitter cassava" (Puri et al., 2004, 47). Furthermore, the knowledge needed to modify and update systems developed by proprietary expatriate-led projects was heretofore lost when foreign developers who owned the closed code departed the country.

Participation is essential; the context for participation must first be collaboratively constituted. Without participation, nothing will happen or last.

Adapting participatory design in new contexts means learning from other cultural traditions in participatory decision-making and other methodologies such as Participatory Rural Appraisal involving communities in development projects (Puri, 2003; Puri et al., 2004; Byrne, 2004; Byrne and Gregory, 2007; Byrne and Sahay, 2003). Reflecting on their experiences in adapting Scandinavian participatory design strategies in the HISP in India, South Africa, and Mozambique, Puri, Byrne, Nhampossa and Quraishi (2004) point to capability development as especially important in context-dependent participation strategies for information systems implementation.

> [T]he politics of design, the nature of participation, and the methods, tools and techniques for carrying out design projects are shaped with respect to the diversity of the socio-economic, cultural and political situations faced in each of these settings...[I]t is the importance of the contextual nature of participatory design that emerges most strongly (42).

To cultivate the capacity of local health care personnel to participate, "the unequal nature of social relationships and positions between different actors and also institutions was recognized from the outset" (Puri et al., 2004, 49). This speaks to "the how, rather than the why" of participation—"the *process* of participation" (Puri et al., 2004, 50). For example, beyond training in the functionality of the DHIS and training on use of data and information, intensive training was provided to women community health workers in India not only to enable them to be better "able to communicate on more equal terms" with the Primary Health Center hierarchy, but also for local health workers to be able to modify the information system on their own as needs and situations change.

Sustainable change requires significant investments of time and resources to realize the potentials of *design-in-use*, going from sites of technology design and production—and design intentions thereof—into situated use contexts, in which activities and interactions are accomplished by collectives of people, artifacts, technologies, and nature in actor-networks. By the nature of healthcare and health information, information systems need to be designed to be culturally and locally specific through reconfiguration and redesign while at the same time being designed in relation to national and regional health institutions and internationally circulating health and medical knowledge, including a multitude of standards of care, technical, and communication standards. The participatory approach engages the collective designer-user in joint definition of problems and adaptation to variable circumstances. Local adaptation and collaboration is always required rather than replication or "transfer of technology." The process involves establishing participatory committees place-by-place at district and health facility levels so that each local committee becomes its own sustainable collaboration with its networked communication between district, regional, and national hierarchies. The DHIS must take hold locally as the requisite basis for sustainable collaboration networked between grassroots to ministry levels.

Mutual learning and reciprocity among design collaboration partners and between designers, practitioners, and other users are key to success in intercultural, interdisciplinary, international, and inter-institutional contexts.

Mutual learning is a core tenet of participatory design in the Health Information Systems Programme and in Scandinavia. Regarding reciprocity in open source software design, HISP project leaders refer directly to *The Gift* by Mauss: "Already in 1925 Marcel Mauss showed how social interaction and rituals, as the interchanging of gifts, 'tied up,' confirmed and reproduced social institutions" (Mauss, 1954/1925 as cited in Braa and Hedberg, 2002, 119). The principles of mutual learning and reciprocity in transdisciplinary, transnational, and cross-cultural learning expand upon the classical base of action research. Action research offers a cyclical methodology "to build theory, knowledge, and practical action by engagement with the world in the context of practice itself" with the aim of "increasing the system's self-development capacity" (Elden and Chisholm as cited in Braa and Hedberg, 2002, 116).

Striving for participatory relations in design in new use and cultural contexts means that we engage in crossing boundaries that involve "encountering difference, entering onto territory in which one is a stranger and, to some significant extent therefore, unqualified"(Suchman, 2002, 142). A key principle is to recognize the knowledgeability of people in their practices and to pay close attention to *presence* and not only the *absence* of what we regard as familiar.

In a keynote address at the IFIP Working Group 9.4 Conference in 2000 in Cape Town, South Africa, Lucy Suchman related her experience in "the *hyperdeveloped* world of industrial research and development in the United States" to contexts of *design-in-use* and *technologies-in-use* that are distant—spatially, socio-culturally, infrastructurally— from sites of origin of technology design in the research centers of global companies (Suchman, 2002). Current work practices are often counter-posed as suspect in the face of visions of a technology-enabled future, whereas taking the ingenuity of social practices *in the present* as the starting point can open imaginatively onto alternative design practices. Rather than ascribing "resistance to change" or "traditional" and "stagnant" values to people and organizational culture in the situation-to-be-changed by technology design developed elsewhere, Suchman suggests that designers begin with "the premise that innovation and change [are already] indigenous aspects of technologies-in-use, work practice, and organizational life" (Suchman and Bishop 2000 as cited in Suchman, 2002, 143).

Respect for different knowledges as local and scientific, partial and multiple, opens further onto reciprocity of understanding across cultural contexts. In rural India, taking local knowledge of water and land reclamation seriously transformed possibilities for participatory collaboration between Indian community members with Geographic Information Systems scientific institutions from the longstanding mode of mandated participation for "inputs" to the scientists in charge (Puri, 2003). In the Child Survival Project in KwaZuluNatal, South Africa, local communities and regional health personnel needed to carefully work through the reinvention of international health indicators for local meanings of "risk,""safety," and "love in the home" for children two years old and younger for development of a Child Health Information System. Doing so meant accepting irreconcilable differences between medical knowledge and traditional beliefs and healing practices for certain childhood illnesses (Byrne and Gregory, 2007; Byrne and Sahay, 2003; Puri et al., 2004).

> *Participatory design is a culture of principled argument, in the most positive meaning that critique always offers a proposal in which conflict, mistakes, dilemmas, and contradictions become resources in design.*

The Scandinavian tradition of participatory design is marked by its regard for conflict and contradictions as resources in design explicitness regarding discussion of values in design and imagined futures. High value is put on autonomy of individual users and designers and open discussion for building consensus. Susanne Bødker writes, "Design is fundamentally a collective activity, in which the various practices of the participants meet in a process of mutual learning. This meeting creates conflicts that create new possibilities in design" (Bødker, 1991, 48). Conflict may, variously, refer to different perspectives, argument, heterogeneity, or contradictions (Gregory, 2003). Principled argument in participatory design may open onto a certain degree of high-spirited creative chaos on the way to arriving at consensual agreement, which may seem quite foreign in other design cultures and contexts.

Mistakes can also be valued as part of the process of mutual learning and reciprocity of understanding. Participatory prototyping can act as an important corrective to occasional design moves that override the realities of practice. "The longitudinal prototyping of software and standards...[aims] at confrontations between preconceptions of the research and the reality on the ground" (Braa and Hedberg, 2002, 117). In collaborative processes of design, sharing power—indeed, giving up control—is one of the hardest things to do, particularly for "principal designers." Yet this must be done in instances of participatory collaboration in which users, whose work will be affected by change, decide for a course of action in systems design even when principal designers or computer scientists believe the users' collective decision to be wrong (Damitrew and Gebreyesus, 2005). In the multi-layered collaboration of the HISP, these values translate into design for local autonomy to create adaptations at health district level and inform the theory and practice of *cultivation of cultures of information for action*.

> ***Respectful dialogue in which difference is valued is essential to intercultural sensitivity and collaboration; shared ground is co-created, not given.***

As Sharon Poggenpohl writes in this volume, collaboration entails valuing difference and preserving difference rather than seeking or imposing harmony from a singular central position. The highly diverse multi-country participants in the HISP value respectful dialogue in which everyone has the right in principle to speak his or her mind. The conditions for dialogue need to be jointly constituted to create the "in between space" for productive cross-cultural discussion. For example, to establish a community-based Child Health Information System in the Child Survival Project in KwaZuluNatal, South Africa meant working with communities' cultural heritage and acting in consonance with the cultural principle of *ubuntu* that refers to "collective personhood and collective morality" (Byrne and Gregory, 2007, 48). Yet, in many situations, unity and harmony are culturally valued in ways that inhibit open dialogue given long-standing social and political hierarchical relations in both community and professional settings. Constituting "shared ground" did not mean establishing "common ground." Reflecting on the project, Byrne and Gregory (2007) explain:

> We use the expression "shared ground" to point to the limits of achieving "common ground" given unresolved differences in meanings between community-based terms for child health problems and status in local languages and traditional belief systems and terms for health indicators

for child health monitoring and health practices that are based in the standardized terminologies of the national health system and the knowledge system of international public health. We also use "shared ground" to distinguish our discussion of striving for a "meeting ground"... from the concept of "common ground" proposed by Clark (1996) as more fully achievable through joint commitments in using language, than what we describe in the case study as co-construction of local meanings in which "common ground" remains only partially realized, as different—sometimes conflicting—meanings persist and co-exist in the language, beliefs, and practices of communities with distinct knowledge systems (Clark, 1996 as cited in Byrne and Gregory, 2007, 79 note2).

Formal scientific contributions and social commitments in which participatory relations in design are essential, expand designers' responsibilities, knowledge, and practice; these in turn "change the formal" through articulation of new theory and philosophy for design practice.

Theory building is vitally important in the HISP. Striving for both formal scientific and socially meaningful contributions is a foundational principle that comes from the early participatory design movement in Scandinavia. Commitments to societal values and participation expand the responsibilities of designers and result in transforming formal practices. In the 1980s, Kristen Nygaard and Pal Sørgaard argued that, "the capability of multiperspective reflection is essential for all computer professionals" (Nygaard and Sørgaard, 1987; Floyd, 2005; Nygaard, 1986). Their notion of *perspectivity* posited the intrinsically interdisciplinary nature of computing. Systems design through designer-user collaborations enables user participation in the development of methods and tools. During the same period, Peter Naur argued for his Theory Building View of programming: "[P]rogramming properly should be regarded as an activity by which programmers form or achieve a certain kind of insight, a theory, of the matters at hand" (Naur, 1985, 1992). Contemporary Scandinavian informatics continues to be characterized by its conceptualization as a multidisciplinary practice and by the influence of social theory in design.

The HISP is known for theory building regarding information infrastructure theory, standards-making that allows for local flexibility, strategies for horizontal and vertical "scaling," and "cultivation" that affords improvisation and autonomy of individuals and local teams. Information infrastructure theory is continuously developed to guide and reflexively elaborate informatics design practice as it is confronted by practical challenges (for richer details see Global Infrastructures at http://www.ifi.uio.no/research/groups/gi/hisp.html). An information infrastructure is characterized by its: 1) being shared by a large community of users and irreducibly interconnected, 2) having inherently open boundaries, and 3) enabling function for diverse rather than singular purposes and domains (Hanseth and Monteiro, 2004). The HISP cultivation approach to information infrastructure design entails "small incremental steps, sensitivity to the existing installed base, and flexibility to dealing with the rapidly changing political and institutional conditions" (Sahay and Walsham, 2006, 197). "Scaling" of information infrastructure encompasses political alignments, technical and practice standardization, and customization in context. In 2004, the HISP-India team was mandated by state government of Andhra Pradesh (population 75 million) to scale up from its nine pilot health districts to all twenty-three districts. This required moving rapidly from 49 to 1,500 primary health centers across the state's geographic territory of 15,000 square kilometers. Sahay and Walsham (2006, 196) describe what was being scaled as:

> ...a scaling up of complexity, best conceptualized or represented as a heterogeneous network [comprising] geography, numbers, technical systems, data and databases, user capacities, trainers, and socio-technical practices such as political negotiations that try to bring the network together.

Design For Negotiation of Disparate Logics

Designing for negotiation of disparate logics offers an alternative to translation of others' interests into one's own; doing so can support emergence of "spaces in between" and new "meeting grounds" for thinking and designing creatively with and across diverse cultures of disciplines, domains, cultures, institutions, and practices.

As designers, we need to take thoughtful responsibility for our design logics. My interest is in how we can understand the dynamics of logics that manifest in unfolding effects in the world that are reasonably, even if only partially, knowable with forethought and for which we can therefore take reflective responsibility.

In the design context, my use of the term "logic" does not refer to a mathematical logic that leads us to a determinate outcome; rather, I refer to logics that unfold in indeterminate ways that are yet shaped by dynamics that we can comprehend. Because the kinds of logics I have in mind cannot be subsumed under another logic, such logics may collide. Annemarie Mol suggests that logics are patterns related to the rationale of practices. "[T]he term 'logic'...invites the exploration of what is appropriate or local to do in some site or situation, and what is not...It may be implicit: embedded in practices, buildings, habits and machines" (Mol, 2008, 8). Logics co-exist and may interfere with each other in the "mixed events" of everyday life because they are embedded in practices (Bourdieu, 1990).

My sense of the necessity of designing for negotiation of disparate logics comes from my experience with how a "beautiful logic" was confronted by the logics of practice, as the *design logic* of an electronic health record prototype was confronted by the logics of patient care interactions, organizational regimes, the progressive unraveling of medical knowledge, and knowledge of a patient's health that is revealed as the logics of illnesses that unfold in particular bodies and patients' life contexts (Gregory, 2000). I found Helen Verran's proposal that we take responsibility for *working disparate knowledge traditions together* especially helpful (Watson-Verran, n.d.; Watson-Verran and Turnbull, 1995). Verran's analysis of disparate imaginaries opens onto the emergence of "third spaces" and "meeting grounds" between contrasting culturally-historically constituted social practices and ontic and epistemic commitments held by different communities (Verran, 1998). Design practice and designers are already positioned in between disciplines and collaborators from diverse domains in design projects. Verran's concern is with how we may get beyond the desire to "translate" difference into the familiar or dismiss difference as exotic "otherness.'"

Thinking about design for negotiation of disparate logics offers an alternative epistemological stance for comprehending multiple possible worlds within the world rather than counterpose a "real world" and "a world apart." Verran uses *disconcertment* to express the kind of subtle yet troubling interruptions to our usual ways of thinking when we are confronted with different forms of knowledge; these are valuable windows for cross-cultural understanding. For example, Verran's study of Yoruba plurality in counting, in contrast to the unity of numbers in English counting, revealed differences in how arithmetic is conceived, taught, and practiced. Approached as an argument about right and wrong ways of *thinking*, a different African logic in mathematics clashes with the Western scientific canon, allowing only for a relativist bridge between different logics. Approached as two generalizing logics grounded in different cultural *practices* of mathematics, "cross-overs and other combinations become possible" (Mol, 2008, 115n17).

A case example from a primary health center in rural India takes us into deeply sensitive cultural values in relation to maternal and infant mortality and the challenges posed in the HISP (Raghavendra, 2007). As a story of negotiation of logics, this brief moment of the DHIS becoming a system-in-use offers a window onto diverse logics of forms and rationales for health data collection between the computer-based software and household-based family health ledgers in which community health workers document vital information about health status once a year. It underscores cultural sensitivity and difference by undoing "the obvious" (Jordan 1978; Raghavendra, 2007).

What was first thought to be confusion about establishing denominators for maternal and child mortality and for ante-natal care and births in clinic or at home, in going from one data collection system to another for these key maternal and child health indicators—how to establish the base number reliably in learning how to calculate maternal and infant mortality—opened onto deeply cultural differences. In cultural context, if the "birth" didn't result in a live birth, then many people locally would rather not describe it as a "birth" or as a "death;" rather, there was a transitional soul temporarily here but quickly gone. It became clear that the confounding aspect went much deeper culturally: What does it mean to calculate maternal mortality and infant mortality in a setting where people do not refer to "death" of stillborn babies? How should "birth in hospital" and "ante-natal care" be calculated in settings where midwives play a key role in childbirth? Measures assumed as logically straightforward and universal—maternal and infant mortality—were suddenly confounded at the local level. Considerable discussion and careful listening were required of everyone to reach consensus and to reinvent the indicator as meaningful in the local contexts. The same issues arose in three DHIS training sessions that I attended in South Africa and India.

Challenges, Dilemmas, and Contradictions

Never an empty vessel. One's own unmarked ethnocentricity in expressing culturally specific positions as universal claims poses a challenge for all designers and design researchers in international collaborations. Lucy Suchman and Brigette Jordan (1989) critique *the fallacy of the empty vessel* in their comparative analysis of women's knowledge in mid-wifery and office work in relation to technology design and authoritative knowledge (Jordan, 1997). The metaphor of the empty vessel emanates from "the belief by those who design new technologies that there is nothing there in advance of their arrival" (Suchman and Jordan, 1989, 155). An alternative stance begins by acknowledging the partiality of one's knowledge and respecting the multiplicity of perspectival positions.

In the early years of the HISP in South Africa, a core refrain of the project discourse invoked that there was *no information culture* to characterize the local organizational cultures into which the DHIS system and participatory methodology would enter and heroically transform the "non" into the "new." The expression echoed influential writings from 1978 up to the early 1990s that continued to be widely cited as late as 2005 (Østmo, 2007). By its frequent citation and repetition, the phrase *no information culture* persisted after local cultures of action began to be institutionalized, and in the face of local health personnel's struggles to get information systems into place with scarce resources to do so. The HISP leaders and researchers thus expressed a variation of the fallacy of the empty vessel in collision with the professed design strategy of cultivation in which the resources already available form the base.

In a Master research study in Linguistics and Information Systems in Cape Town, South Africa, Lise Østmo (2007) employed discourse analysis methodology to analyze the HISP project writings and interviews with health facility managers and observational materials in their respective clinics, to understand the emergence of change—or *status quo*—in the clinics towards local cultures of information for action (Gouws and Gregory, 2005). She found that the health managers did not feel informed or included in participatory processes, and they lack resources to implement health information systems. Mozambican and Tanzanian doctoral and master students challenged the characterization of *no information culture* as it did not match their perceptions from field research. The Tanzanian students met local health workers working with some concepts of information, keen to advance their knowledge (Igira, 2008a; Igira, 2008b; Mukama, 2003; Sheikh (Shehe), 2005; Shidende, 2005). To craft a more culturally-sensitive HISP strategy in Mozambique, Emilio Mosse (2005) proposed a concept of *counter networks* (Castells, 1996) to underscore the need for system designers to appreciate the multiple situated social identities, relationships, roles, and status that health personnel already have in their communities.

All or nothing and winner take all. In health information systems, the "all or nothing" dilemma of technical systems is heightened because they are "practically useless for the health department unless the coverage of the whole state is obtained. For example, to be able to compute the immunization coverage of the state, data are required from all the reporting facilities collected in similar formats, using the same business logic for the calculation of the indicator" (Sahay and Walsham, 2006,198). A second dilemma—"winner take all"—further complicates achievement of coherence in information infrastructure, as there are limits to collaboration across systems posed by lack of technical interoperability, especially between proprietary (closed code) systems and open source systems.

Enduring inequalities. Most importantly, enduring power structures and obdurate hierarchies of inequality and dependency add sociopolitical constraints to equitable quality of life and human social development.

In Conclusion

What does this large-scale contextually located yet diverse model represent for design collaboration at large? The HISP experience offers a complex multi-level model for possibilities that we can reach for and potentially engage in directly regarding international and intercultural collaboration. Thinking deliberately of mutual learning as reciprocal understanding across contexts can further open onto reciprocity of design imagination, modification and transformation of design, and use. The HISP can be conceived as a model for multi-country graduate design education that highlights doctoral research qualification for leadership to advance design practice. As a globally distributed open source design and development network based on principles of reciprocity, the HISP experience is an invitation to think about the need for viable interactive interfaces with general license agreements that can encourage and support co-creation of design and knowledge of relevance both locally and transnationally. As designers, we are already in multidisciplinary and in between spaces, and we can also deliberately constitute design spaces for new kinds of participation and reciprocity. We can do so by adjusting how we practice collaboration in design, how we design interfaces, systems, and tools for collaboration, and through our choices about what we design and how we constitute inclusive partnerships and relations in design.

When we are able to combine formal scientific and social commitments in intercultural, international, and interdisciplinary collaborations, we open onto designers' reflections on our implicit theory and taken-for-granted underlying philosophical stance, as design practices, research methods, and knowledge relations are always intertwined. For example, mutual learning and reciprocity is not about "extracting knowledge," but more usefully thought of as "circulating knowledge" that is co-constructed through transdisciplinary design collaboration. We can embrace the underlying principles of participatory design in modes of open collaboration including open source and transdisciplinary design as meeting grounds for mutual learning and reciprocity in relations in design and reflective practice for iterative co-construction of knowledge.

Before closing, I wish to be clear that it is not my view that we can only realize social responsibility at the scale of the complex international collaboration I have described. We do not need to travel elsewhere; designers can create and act in so many ways at home—in our own places and regions. Nor is it my position that everyone should work at the urgent edge of social problems. Wherever we choose to work, we should always seek to understand the constraints we face and the power we have individually and collectively. It is my view that we can realize our power and responsibility most fully through open collaboration, in our full embrace of the special role that design and designers can play in interdisciplinarity of knowledge and participatory, reflective practice. We surely face unprecedented constraints. We also have unprecedented power through open and transdisciplinary collaboration and the new interactive means and media in our hands that can cross time and space to take up the opportunities that stand in front of us. If we recognize how we might combine our resources and actions in person and virtually, nationally and internationally, we can deepen and quicken our design knowledge and reciprocal learning in and through design collaboration.

Endnotes

1. For the Artful Integration Award to the Health Information Systems Programme by the Participatory Design Conference 2006, see http://www.pdc2006.org/.

2. This discussion of Scandinavian participatory design in the HISP is also informed by the author's personal communication with Calle Hedberg (March and April 2001, April 2002), an interview with Hedberg by the author (April 2002), and an interview with Hedberg by Erich Schienke for the Center for Ethics in Complex Systems, Rensselaer Polytechnic Institute, Troy, New York (March 2001).

References

Bourdieu, Pierre. 1990. *The Logic of Practice*. Stanford, CA: Stanford University Press.

Braa, Jørn and Calle Hedberg. 2002. The Struggle for District-Based Health Information Systems in South Africa. *The Information Society*, 18.2, 113–128.

Burasa, Patrick R. 2005. Challenges of Collaboration in Health Information Systems Development and Implementation in Developing Countries: The Global and Local Perspectives. Master of Science thesis. Oslo, Norway: Department of Informatics, University of Oslo.

Byrne, Elaine. 2004. A participatory approach to the design of a child-health community-based information system for the care of vulnerable children. Doctoral dissertation. Cape Town, South Africa: School of Public Health, University of the Western Cape.

Byrne, Elaine and Judith Gregory. 2007. Co-constructing local meanings for child health indicators in community-based information systems: the UThukela District Child Survival Project in KwaZuluNatal. *International Journal of Medical Informatics*, 76.S1, 78–88.

Byrne, Elaine and Sundeep Sahay. 2003. Health Information Systems for Primary Health Care: Thinking about Participation. In Korpela, M., R. Montealegre and A. Poulmenakou (eds.), *Proceedings of the IFIP TC8 & TCP/WG 8.2 & WG 9.4 Working Conference on Organizational Information Systems in the Context of Globalization*. Athens, Greece, June 15–17, International Federation for Information Processing, 237–249.

Bødker, Susanne. 1991. *Through the Interface: A Human Activity Approach to User Interface Design*. Hillsdale, NJ: Lawrence Erlbaum Associates.

Carnoy, Martin. 1999. *Globalization and educational reform: what planners need to know*. Paris, France: UNESCO.

Castells, Manuel. 1996. *The Rise of the Network Society*. Cambridge, MA: Blackwell Publishers.

Chilundo, Baltazar. 2004. Integrating information systems of disease-specific health programmes in low income countries: the case study of Mozambique. Doctoral dissertation. Oslo, Norway: Faculty of Medicine, University of Oslo.

Clark, H.C. 1996. *Using Language*. Cambridge, UK: Cambridge University Press.

Dahlbom, Bo and Lars-Erik Janlert. 1996. *Computer future*. Manuscript. Gothenberg, Sweden: Department of Informatics, University of Gothenberg.

Damitrew, Hirut Gebrekidan and Netsanet Haile Gebreyesus. 2005. Sustainability and Optimal Use of Health Information Systems: An Action Research Study on Implementation of an Integrated District-Based Health Information System in Ethiopia. Master thesis. Oslo, Norway: Department of Informatics. University of Oslo.

Dunin-Woyseth, Halina and Liv Merete Nielsen (eds.). 2004. Discussing transdisciplinarity: Making professions and the new mode of knowledge professions. *The Nordic Reader 2004*, 6. Oslo, Norway: AHO The Oslo School of Architecture and Design.

Epstein, Helen. 2001. Time of Indifference. *New York Review of Books*, April 12, 33–38.

Farmer, Paul. 2005. *Pathologies of power: health, human rights, and the new war on the poor.* Berkeley, CA: University of California Press.

Floyd, Christiane. 2005. Being Critical in, on or around Computing? Keynote address. In Bertelsen, O.W., N.O. Bouvin, P.G. Krogh and M. Kyng, (eds.), *Proceedings of the Fourth Decennial Aarhus Conference: Critical Computing - Between Sense and Sensibility.* Aarhus, Denmark, August 20–24. Aarhus, Denmark: Aarhus University, 207–211.

Garrett, Laurie. 2000. *Betrayal of trust: the collapse of global public health.* New York, NY: Hyperion.

Gibbons, Michael, C. Limoges, H. Nowotny, S. Schwartzmann, P. Scott, and M. Trow. 1994. *The New Production of Knowledge: The Dynamics of Science and Research in Contemporary Societies.* London, United Kingdom: Sage.

Gouws, Marius and Judith Gregory. 2005. Push-Pull Factors in Routine Health Management Information Systems: Towards a Conceptual Framework to Evaluate, Plan and Improve the Capacity and Influence of RHMIS Actors in Developing Countries. In Bada, A. and A. Okunoye (eds.), *Proceedings of the Eighth International Working Conference of IFIP WG 9.4.* Abuja, Nigeria, May 26–28. Abuja, Nigeria: International Federation for Information Processing, 320–331.

Gregory, Judith. 2000. Sorcerer's Apprentice: Creating the Electronic Health Record, Re-inventing Medical Records and Patient Care. Doctoral dissertation. San Diego, CA: Department of Communication, University of California at San Diego.

Gregory, Judith. 2003. Scandinavian Approaches to Participatory Design. *International Journal of Engineering Education* (Special Issue: Social Dimensions of Engineering Design), 19.1, 62–74.

Hanseth, Ole and Eric Monteiro. 2004. Understanding information infrastructure. http://heim.ifi.uio.no/~oleha/Publications/bok.html (accessed June 1, 2004).

Igira, Faraja Teddy. 2008a. The situatedness of work practices and organizational culture: implications for information systems innovation uptake. *Journal of Information Technology*, 23.2, 79–88.

Igira, Faraja Teddy. 2008b. *The interplay between transformation in everyday work practices and IS design and implementation processes: Empirical experiences from the health information system in Tanzania.* Doctoral dissertation. Oslo, Norway: Department of Informatics, University of Oslo.

Jordan, Brigitte. 1997. Authoritative knowledge and its construction. In Davis-Floyd, R. and C. Sargent (eds.), *Childbirth and authoritative knowledge: Cross-cultural perspectives.* New York, NY: Routledge, 55–79.

Jordan, Brigitte. 1978. Birth in Four Cultures: A Cross-cultural Investigation of Childbirth in Yucatan, Holland, Sweden and the United States. Montreal: Eden Press Women's Publications, Inc.

Kaasbøll, Jens and Esselina Macome. 2002. Developing sustainable research education in Sub-Saharan Africa. *Proceedings of the IFIP Working Group 3.2 Working Conference: Information Curricula, Teaching Methods and Best Practice.* Florianopolis, Brazil, July 10–12.

Kuutti, Kari. 2007. Design Research, Disciplines, and New Production of Knowledge. *Proceedings of IASDR 2007: Emerging Trends, Hong Kong Polytechnic University.* Hong Kong, November 12–15.

Lungo, Juma Hemed. 2008. Design-reality gaps in Open Source information systems development: An action research study of education and healthcare systems in Tanzania. Doctoral dissertation. Oslo, Norway: Department of Informatics, University of Oslo.

Macome, Esselina. 2002. The Dynamics of the Adoption and Use of ICT-based Initiatives for Development: Results of a Field Study in Mozambique. Doctoral dissertation. Pretoria, South Africa: University of Pretoria.

Macueve, Gertrudes Adolfo. 2008. Analyzing challenges and opportunities of the implementation of e-government initiatives for development through the lens of the capability approach: case studies from Mozambique. Doctoral dissertation. Oslo, Norway: Department of Informatics, University of Oslo.

Mendes, Lídia Soares. 2004. *Seguimento e atenção prestados aos doentes com tuberculose e infecção por HIV/SIDA após a alta do Hospital Geral da Machava*. Master in Public Health thesis. Maputo, Mozambique: Faculty of Medicine, University of Eduardo Mondlane.

Mol, Annemarie. 2008. *The Logic of Care: Health and the Problem of Patient Choice*. New York, NY: Routledge.

Mosse, Emilio Luis. 2005. Understanding the introduction of computer-based health information systems in developing countries: counter networks, communication practices and social identity: A case study from Mozambique. Doctoral dissertation. Oslo, Norway: Department of Informatics, University of Oslo.

Mosse, Emilio and Sundeep Sahay. 2005. The Role of communication practices in the strengthening of counter networks: Case experiences from the health sector of Mozambique. In Mosse, Emilio Luis, Understanding the introduction of computer-based health information systems in developing countries: counter networks, communication practices and social identity: A case study from Mozambique. Doctoral dissertation. Oslo, Norway: Department of Informatics, University of Oslo.

Mukama, Faraja. 2003. A study of health information systems at local levels in Tanzania and Mozambique. Master thesis. Oslo, Norway: Department of Informatics, University of Oslo.

Naur, Peter. 1985. Programming as Theory Building In Naur, P., *Computing: A Human Activity*, 1992. http://alistair.cockburn.us/crystal/books/asd/extracts (accessed February 23, 2006).

Nhampossa, Jose Leopoldo. 2005. Re-thinking Technology Transfer as Technology Translation: A Case Study of Health Information Systems in Mozambique. Doctoral dissertation. Oslo, Norway: Department of Informatics, Faculty of Mathematics and Natural Sciences, University of Oslo.

Nowotny, Helga. 2004. The Potential of Transdisciplinarity. In Dunin-Woyseth, Halina and Liv Merete Nielsen (eds.), Discussing transdisciplinarity: Making professions and the new mode of knowledge professions. *The Nordic Reader 2004*, 6. Oslo, Norway: AHO The Oslo School of Architecture and Design, 10–18.

Nowotny, H., P. Scott and M. Gibbons. 2001. *Re-Thinking Science, Knowledge and the Public in the Age of Uncertainty*. Oxford, United Kingdom: Blackwell.

Nussbaum, Martha C. and Amartya Sen (eds.). 1993. *Quality of Life*. Oxford, United Kingdom: Clarendon/Oxford University Press.

Nygaard, K. 1986. Program Development as social activity. In Kugler, H.G. (ed.), *Information Processing 86: Proceedings of the IFIP 10th World Computer Congress*. Amsterdam, Netherlands: North-Holland, 189–198.

Nygaard, K. and P. Sørgaard. 1987. The Perspective Concept in Informatics. In Bjerknes, G. et al. (eds.), *Computers and Democracy: A Scandinavian Challenge*. Brookfield, UT: Avebury.

Puri, Satish K. 2003. The Challenges of Participation and Knowledge in GIS Implementation for Land Management: Case Studies from India. Doctoral dissertation. Oslo, Norway: Department of Informatics, University of Oslo.

Puri, Satish K., Elaine Byrne, Jose Leopoldo Nhampossa, and Zubeeda B. Quraishi. 2004. Contextuality of Participation in IS Design: A Developing Country Perspective. In Clement, Andrew, Fiorella de Cindio, Anne-Marie Oostveen, Douglas Schuler and Peter van den Besselaar (eds.), *Proceedings of Participatory Design Conference 2004*. Toronto, ON, Canada. Toronto, ON, Canada: ACM, 42–52.

Raghavendra, Ranjini Canchi. 2007. Implementing Public Health Information Infrastructures in India: An Ethnographic Approach. Doctoral dissertation. Bailrigg, Lancaster, United Kingdom: Institute for Women's Studies, Lancaster University.

Sahay, Sundeep and Geoff Walsham. 2006. Scaling of Health Information Systems in India: Challenges and Approaches. *Information Technology for Development*, 12.3, 185–200.

Schuler, Douglas and Namioka, A. (eds.). 1993. *Participatory Design: Principles and Practices*. Hillsdale, NJ: Lawrence Erlbaum.

Sen, Amartya. 1984. *Resources, Values and Development*. Cambridge, MA: Harvard University Press.

Sen, Amartya K. 1999. *Development as Freedom*. New York, NY: Knopf.

Sen, Amartya. 2002. *Rationality and Freedom*. Cambridge, MA: Harvard University Press, The Belknap Press.

Sen, Gita, Asha George, and Piroska Östlin (eds.). 2002. *Engendering international health: the challenge of equity*. Cambridge, MA: Bradford/The MIT Press.

Sheikh (Shehe), Yahya Hamad. 2005. Improving routine health information management at health districts in Zanzibar: an action research study. Master thesis. Oslo, Norway: Department of Informatics, University of Oslo.

Shidende, Nima. 2005. Assessing the Quality of Routine Primary Health Care Data at Facility Level and in the Regional Database in Tanzania. Master thesis. Oslo, Norway: Department of Informatics, University of Oslo.

Strauss, Anselm L. 1993. Continual permutations of action. Hawthorne, NY: Aldine de Gruyter.

Suchman, Lucy A. 1994. Working relations of technology production and use. Computer Supported Cooperative Work, 21–39.

Suchman, Lucy A. 2002. Practice-Based Design of Information Systems: Notes from the Hyperdeveloped World. *The Information Society*, 18.2, 139–144.

Suchman, Lucy A. and Brigitte Jordan.1989. Computerization and Women's Knowledge. In Tijdens, Kea, Mary Jennings, Ina Wagner and Margaret Weggelaar (eds.), *Women, Work and Computerization: Forming New Alliances*. Amsterdam, Netherlands and New York, NY: North-Holland, Elsevier Science Publishers, 153–160.

Verran, H. 1998. Re-imagining land ownership in Australia. *Postcolonial Studies*, 1.2, 237–254.

Verran, Helen. 2001. *Science and an African Logic*. Chicago, IL: The University of Chicago Press.

Watson-Verran, Helen. n.d. Working Disparate Knowledge Traditions Together: Partially Connecting Ontic/Epistemic Imaginaries. Melbourne, VIC, Australia: Department of History and Philosophy of Science, University of Melbourne.

Watson-Verran, Helen and David Turnbull. 1995. Science and Other Indigenous Knowledge Systems. In Jasonoff, Sheila, Gerald E. Markle, James C. Petersen and Trevor Pinch (eds.), *Handbook of Science and Technology Studies*. Thousand Oaks, CA: Sage Publications, Inc.

Werner, David. 1980. *Where there is no doctor: a village health care handbook*. London, United Kingdom: MacMillan Education Ltd.

Østmo, Inger Lise. 2007. Health Information Management in Context: Discourse Analysis of HISP & District Health IS and Field Studies in Clinics and Hospitals in Cape Town, South Africa. Master of Arts in Linguistics & Informatics thesis. Oslo, Norway, Department of Linguistics, University of Oslo.

Acknowledgements

I wish to acknowledge all of the Health Information Systems Programme doctoral and master graduates and current students, all of my faculty colleagues and colleagues at large, and the many committed educators, supporters, leaders, and grassroots workers in public health that I had the honor and privilege to meet and work with along the way. This chapter is dedicated in memory of Marius Gouws and Satish Kumar Puri.

CONCLUSION

13

DESIGN INTELLIGENCE

Kees Dorst

Introduction

These days, some designers are successfully working on very complex problems that only a couple of years ago seemed far outside of their range and beyond their capabilities. They have discovered a hidden strength in design that makes it especially suited for the networked, dynamic problems our societies face today. But what is the special "design intelligence" that these designers bring to bear upon those issues? And how would design in general have to change to really live up to these new challenges?

This chapter will provide a bird's eye view of the established knowledge on design expertise and design intelligence. The backbone of this exploration will be a description of design ability (the knowledge and skills that make someone a designer), and a recently developed model on the nature and development of design expertise (how one becomes a designer). This provides us with a framework to look at the impact that the growing importance of research and of truly collaborative design should have on design research and design education.

The Need for Design Intelligence

In society, design is moving into a new role. Designers are asked to participate in the creation of solutions to problems that are far beyond what would normally be called "the design sector." This new application of "design intelligence" seems to be accompanying the increasing complexity of the world we live in. We are living through a communication revolution (mobile phones, the internet) and find ourselves newly connected in many ways to innumerable other people. This enriches our lives enormously. But by networking our society we have inadvertently networked our problems, too. Thus the blessed state of hyper-connectedness is also the source of a fundamentally new kind of very complex, networked problem.

We have now come to the point where many of the most important issues we face in today's society have become so complicated that they seem impervious to solution. This forces us to reconsider the old ways of problem-solving. Most of our traditional problem-solving strategies worked reasonably well in a well-ordered universe: when problems appeared, we could isolate them in a relatively separate problem arena, abstract from the details of the concrete problem situation, decompose the problem, analyze the sub-problems, solve them, and build together the sub-solutions—thus reaching an overall conclusion in due course. If all else failed, we could use authority or power to simplify the problem area by overruling some parties and by pushing through an envisaged solution.

But this strategy will not work at all for today's problems; our societies, economies, and cultures have lost these enclosed "mini-worlds" to a tangle of relationships within complex and overlapping networks, where power doesn't rest in one place anymore, and what truth there is to be found seems to become a matter of the perspective you take. The word "network" might actually be an understatement here, in that it still conjures up the image of a semblance of structure; in today's reality, everything is related in a giant tangled *knot*. Problems are so intimately related to each other (and there are so many dependencies between these interrelationships) that no matter how hard you try to pull just the one single string out of the knot, you will end up with the whole thing on your lap. You can see this happen all the time. Governments in particular are very much used to a hierarchical and purely analysis-based method of problem-solving (which they have organized in well-defined and reasonable government institutions), and they seem powerless to deal with today's complex issues, resulting in an endless parade of news items about botched government decision-making. And this doesn't only apply to governments: companies and institutions all around the world have been caught out by the sudden complexity of their problems. They are desperately searching for a new way of tackling these complex, networked problems.

More and more companies, governments, and institutions are turning towards the field of design for help. Designers have naturally been dealing with these kinds of complex, networked problems that involve multiple stakeholders for many years. And designers have been trained to come up with creative solutions that satisfy many of the relevant parties with their design solutions. Their "design thinking" involves the creative exploration of problems and the creation of solutions that somehow overcome the paradoxes in the problem area that would be insurmountable using traditional problem-solving (Dorst, 2003).

It is interesting to see that, through this realization, "design thinking" is being exported to areas that have traditionally not been considered part of the design field. This is happening all around us, in many different ways:

1. There is a clear trend in many professions to see their work as "designing." For instance, managers now "design" company policies and operational processes, and in education, teachers "design" a curriculum; medical doctors "design" therapies, etc. Many professions are now keenly interested in taking a design approach (van Heffen et al., 1999).

2. Design-type problem-solving is being incorporated into general education. Design is now taught in many high schools the world over. Knowing how to solve problems in a design-like manner is considered to be a natural and essential part of the mental makeup of the next generation (see www.spacesoup.nl).

3. More and more designers are being asked to participate in think-tanks and in all kinds of future-oriented workshops and projects. This is because they are used to looking at problems from different viewpoints, searching for novel solutions, and analyzing a problem quickly and creatively by proposing various solutions (see Suyling et al., 2005).

4. Many people with design training find their work outside of the design domain, but still report on applying their design thinking in their daily work (de Wilde, 1997).

We will now explore what is known about this newly valued "design intelligence," and we will address the challenge to develop it much further in the years to come. In the next sections, we will first deal with the nature of the design ability, and then we will discuss a model of the way in which design expertise develops.

The Nature of the Design Ability

What abilities and skills do you need to be a designer? Nigel Cross (1990) has summarized the early work in this area in his seminal paper "The nature and nurture of the design ability." In this paper, eight key design knowledge attributes and skills are defined that together define the design ability. He concludes that designers must have the ability to: 1) produce novel, unexpected solutions by 2) applying imagination and constructive forethought to practical problems, 3) using drawings and other modeling media as means of problem-solving. In doing this, they need to 4) deal with uncertainty and decision-making on the basis of limited information 5) in resolving ill-defined, "wicked" problems. They do this by 6) adopting solution-focusing strategies, 7) employing productive/creative thinking, and 8) using modeling media.

This list of abilities, impressive though it is, does not answer the question whether design is a special ability, or a distinct form of intelligence. It is very complex and diverse, and there doesn't seem to be an underlying coherence, a core "essential design ability" or guiding principle behind it all. And some of these abilities are not that special: they are quite widespread among the professions, or can be learned or taught in a fairly straightforward way (there are drawing courses to work on your graphic expressions and skills, and there is an extensive collection of clever tricks to stimulate creative thinking). On the other hand, not all of these basic design abilities can be learned easily. Some design abilities are very complicated (e.g., "resolving wicked problems"—it is even hard to imagine how one could develop such a skill at all). Some of the design abilities are deeply connected to the personality of a designer (such as "dealing with uncertainty"), and thus are virtually impervious to direct training.

For a better understanding, it could be useful to place this description of design ability within the framework of the six intelligences that the psychologist Howard Gardner (1983) has proposed. Gardner holds that there are several relatively autonomous human intellectual faculties. He discerns the following seven forms of intelligence: *linguistic, logical/mathematical, visual/spatial, musical, bodily/kinesthetic and personal (which includes interpersonal and intrapersonal)*. Design does not seem to fit easily in any of these distinct intelligences, or to be especially related to any of them. What then, could be the core of design? Or could it be an "intelligence" in itself?

To pursue this line of investigation, it is worth looking at the set of criteria that Gardner uses to define an intelligence, and use this as a filter against which claims for a distinct form of intelligence can be judged. Cross (2007, 41) mentions these criteria, and with him we will attempt to match "design intelligence" against them.

1) *Potential isolation by brain damage*. If forms of intelligence are to be places in discrete brain-centers, as Gardner seems to suggest, then they can be harmed through brain damage. Research from neuroscience agrees that part of the design ability, namely geometric reasoning and visual-spatial thinking, have specific locations in the brain.

2) *The existence of prodigies and other exceptional individuals*. Cross holds that there are examples of people that do display an exceptional ability in design, while not being exceptional in other abilities. Yet design does require an intense understanding of others, and an ability to empathize with the fellow human beings that designs are

created for. This precludes the occurrence of the classic, more or less autistic "idiot savant" in design.

3) *An identifiable core operation or set of operations.* Are there some basic mental information-processing operations that are special or unique to design? Cross believes that advances in computer simulation of design reasoning do point in this direction.

4) *A distinctive developmental history, and a definable set of expert, end-state performances.* This means recognizable levels of development or expertise of this intelligence in the individual. We will discuss a model of the development of design expertise in the next section.

5) *An evolutionary history.* Gardner argues that the forms of intelligence must have arisen through evolutionary antecedents, and this could be the case in design. Our closest relatives in the animal kingdom do make and use tools in a considered manner; this could well be a stepping-stone towards design.

6) *Susceptibility to encoding in a symbol system.* In design, the use of a specific vernacular ("designspeak") and the original and extensive use of modeling media does seem to bear this out.

7) *Support from experimental psychological tasks.* This is where the state of design research does not allow us to express any firm statement. We simply do not know yet. But this clearly is one of the directions for design research in the coming years—I will expand on this later.

In all, we have to agree with Cross that the verdict is inconclusive: we can't judge whether design could be classified as a separate intelligence. It could be that looking for this distinction is not the most productive way to go, anyway. Designers and design researchers alike tend to want to identify what distinguishes design from other disciplines. Some have done this by claiming that design is a special way of reasoning—design methodologists have discussed whether design should be considered a logical reasoning pattern in its own right, in addition to deduction, induction, and abduction (Roozenburg and Eekels, 1995, 72). In the end, thorough logical analysis of design does not seem to bear this out, and the idea has quietly been dropped. The motivation behind wanting to define design as special in this way is of course an emancipatory one: if design is a special case of reasoning or a special kind of intelligence, then through its distinctive features the design profession can be defended much more easily. Design agencies, design departments within companies, and schools of design within the framework of a university could benefit from such a special and separate status.

On the other hand, claiming a special status as a separate intelligence could easily lead to a further isolation of the design discipline within these contexts. If we critically consider the core design abilities discussed above, they actually seem to require all seven forms of intelligence that Gardner identified. This could mean that design generally is a broad, all-encompassing human activity that possibly does not absolutely require extreme intelligence in any of the seven varieties, but rather a special combination of these intelligences. This in itself could be a key feature if we compare design with many other professions that seem to lean more on one dominant kind of intelligence. The very broadness of its intelligence base could be the reason that people often feel there is something obscure about the design ability—it is a complex brew of traits.

This could also help to explain the many species of designers that we see in practice. Designers are an extremely diverse bunch of people; there are those who could be characterized as "entrepreneur," or "artist," or "rationalist," or "pragmatist," etc. Designers tend to take on these various roles in design teams—the combination of different strands of design intelligence could be a key reason to prefer designing in teams. In general, one could state that you need all kinds of design abilities and possibly all of Gardner's intelligences to achieve design quality. There have been experiments at several design schools to maximize the personality differences when assembling a design team, some using a Meyers-Briggs type indicator to test the students, others preferring the Kirton adaptor-innovator test (Kirton, 1989). These experiments have also been taken up in some design practices (Hirshberg, 1998; Sutton and Hargardon, 1996). When each of the team members is innovative or extreme in one or more of the seven forms of intelligence, and if they nonetheless share a broad understanding based on their education or common background (Valkenburg, 2000), rather special things can happen. The case studies do suggest that teams that are put together to form this kind of "collective design intelligence" are very successful indeed.

On Design Expertise

This first, descriptive approach has given us an idea of the scope of the design ability and the general makeup of what we could call design intelligence. But this model doesn't address the question of how this design ability is attained. To begin to answer this question, we turn to models of expertise development as they are used in many professions and see if we can apply them to the development of a designer. More specifically, we now turn to lectures and papers by Hubert Dreyfus (2002, 2003a, 2003b) in which he points out that the nature of the problem that is considered in a problem-solving situation depends very much on the level of expertise of the problem solver. Dreyfus classifies seven distinct levels of expertise, corresponding with seven ways of perceiving, interpreting, structuring, and solving problems.

1. A *novice* will consider the objective features of a situation, as they are given by experts, and will follow "the rules of the game" to address the problem.

2. For an *advanced beginner*, situational aspects become important, and there is sensitivity to exceptions to the hard rules followed by the novice. Maxims are used for guidance through the problem situation.

3. A *competent* problem solver works in a radically different way. He selects the elements in a situation that are relevant and chooses a plan to achieve the goals. Problem-solving at this level involves seeking opportunities and building up expectations. There is an emotional attachment, a feeling of responsibility accompanied by a sense of hope, risk, threat, etc., and a clear need for reflection.

4. A problem solver that then moves on to be *proficient* immediately sees the most important issues and appropriate plan, and then reasons out what to do.

5. The real *expert* responds to a specific situation intuitively and performs the appropriate action straightaway. There is no problem-solving and reasoning that can be distinguished at this level of working. This is actually a very comfortable level of professional achievement, and many professionals do not progress beyond this point.

6. With the next level, the *master*, a new uneasiness creeps in. The master sees the standard ways of working used by experienced professionals not as natural, but as contingent. A master displays a deeper involvement with the professional field as a whole. This attitude requires an acute sense of context and openness to subtle cues. In his/her own work, the master will perform more nuanced appropriate actions than the expert.

7. The world discloser or *visionary* consciously strives to extend the domain in which he/she works. The world discloser develops new ways things could be, defines the issues, opens new worlds, and creates new domains. A world discloser tends to operate on the margins of a domain, paying attention to anomalies and marginal practices that hold promise for a new vision.

Most of these levels are intuitively recognizable to anyone involved in design education or design practice. That in itself is a good sign, but of course this doesn't validate the model at all. To further develop this model, we must adapt it to the special character of the design profession and "anchor" the model by linking it more clearly to the existing knowledge in design research.

A first step in this direction has been taken (Lawson and Dorst, 2005, 2009), and we will briefly reiterate some of the points made in their work as a basis for further discussion. We will do this level-by-level.

0) *Naïve*

> This is an extra level that has been added, preceding the "novice" level of Dreyfus. This state is required in a model of design expertise since design-like tasks are not only performed by professionals, but also by ordinary people in their everyday life. This naïve state of designing is adequate for everyday use in conventional situations; it is based on personal, unsystematically gathered experience. Many students that enter design schools will display this naïve design behavior. They have a relatively superficial set of design solutions that they know and that they wish to emulate ("I want to make something like that"), leading to a very direct form of visual quotation. Students at this stage have no idea that design is a process, and they find it difficult to express what they know and what they want—they have not yet learned the language of design.

1) *Novice*

> Students starting out will have little knowledge of what the design activity entails. The main objective of education at this stage is the search for generic principles that link and classify precedents, replacing the isolated instances of the naïve designer. In this novice stage, the students encounter design as a formal process for the first time. To tackle the complexities of design, they also need to learn a whole series of techniques and methods of representation.

2) *Advanced Beginner*

> This might be the level normally attained during design education. The learning of a language for discussing and criticizing design distinguishes this state of expertise from the previous ones. Students acquire schemata or "design prototypes" (Gero, 1990). A further characteristic of this level is the recognition that design problems are highly individual and situated. Design problems at this level are considered to be less amenable to the use of standard solutions than they were at the naïve level of designing.

3) Competent

The advanced beginner begins to understand the enormous richness and variability of design situations and is becoming adept at dealing with a wide range of them. The competent designer is one who can actually handle and understand the normal kinds of situations that occur within the design domain. In process terms, a competent designer is likely to be able to become the creator of the design situation through strategic thinking. This means that by now such designers must be able to develop a brief with clients and understand the needs of their users.

We would expect most designers to generally progress from a broadly Naïve way of designing, through Novice and Advanced Beginner to Competent. However, at this point, the model should branch. There are at least three ways to go from the Competent state, and this progression depends very much on the mentality, personality, level of ambition, and insight of individual designers themselves. The states of Proficient, Expert/ Master, and Visionary should be seen in this light.

4) Proficient

A proficient designer may be thought of as one who is "good enough for the client." Graduates with some small degree of professional experience would be proficient designers. Professional bodies (e.g., RIBA in the UK for architecture) usually have a period of post-graduate practical experience as a requirement before admitting a student to professional membership. Working at this level means that the designer is good and probably successful in his/her chosen profession.

5) Expert/Master

The expert designer has a rather more developed set of guiding principles than the proficient designer. He or she is known for a certain approach or set of values. In the general literature about expertise of this kind, this is characterized by a more or less automatic recognition of situations. This can be used not only to recognize key features of the situation but also to suggest a range of appropriate actions that can be taken. The master designer has taken his/her set of guiding principles to a level of innovation such that their work is seen as representing new knowledge in the field. These designers are producing design ideas that are innovative responses to situations that may have been previously considered well understood. Such work is published and becomes the new precedent for other designers to study. This could be deemed "practice-based research."

6) *Visionary*

The visionary designer may be one who has become so interested in developing new ideas that the normally expected level of professional competence becomes less important. This may be a feature of expertise peculiar to the design world. The work of such designers may often not be realized, but it is deemed important as visionaries are explicitly redefining the design field that they are working in. The design world deliberately creates an opportunity for this with design idea competitions, exhibitions, and the publication of professional journals.

This model is described as a set ordering of discrete states, although it is far from clear that individuals would necessarily progress one level at a time. But the levels are distinct in that what is required developmentally to move up a level in each case is different and that each level comprises its own kind of problem-solving and reflection. Going through these stages is not a smooth linear progression towards expert-hood at all—it seems common for students to flatten out at some levels, almost repeating a successful formula, and then suddenly go through a period of confusion before emerging on a new plateau. What then triggers such a fundamental change of state? First, it is necessary to acquire sufficient knowledge on the lower level before one progresses. Second, it is necessary to undergo some mental realization that the newly acquired knowledge and skills can be used in a different way. This is an important point on which students and junior designers need to be coached: the jump from one level of expertise to the next does not come lightly.

The definitions of the levels are still sketchy, and not all the steps may be described unequivocally (this is very much a work in progress). Design reality is infinitely more complicated. For instance, we should be aware that these fundamentally different ways of looking at problematic situations can actually co-exist in a design project. Nobody is an expert on all aspects of design. On some issues we might be novices, on others we might be competent. Thus our ways of working as a designer will be mixed, too, changing between the kinds of problem-solving and reflection that are associated with the levels of expertise within a split-second.

The Future of Design Intelligence

Toward a New Design Practice

We started this chapter by stating that the design way of approaching problem situations, and its way of creating solutions through design thinking, is becoming a value in many areas of today's complex networked society. This is an inspiring and fascinating development, but it does not leave design untouched. It poses completely new challenges to designers. For one, designers have to become much more explicit about what exactly this "design intelligence" is that they can bring to a problem situation. Only then will they be able to position themselves in the right way and get recognition for their abilities and expertise. Design intelligence has to be defined in a new, clear, and open way. The challenge is not to isolate design by explaining how special it is, but to open up the field by defining the potential connections between professional design and the design-like reasoning in many other professions.

The new classes of problems that designers are beginning to deal with are posing new challenges for designers, potentially changing the very nature of the design profession. Designers now get involved in projects where their intuitive approach has to be augmented by a clear understanding of the complex problem areas for which they are designing. This does not happen easily: it includes studying the scientific research that has been done in complex socio-cultural problem areas, as well as the challenge to do research into these issues themselves. And the new designers have to listen to the "users" of their designs in a different way: the success of a solution to these socio-cultural problems depends on the participation of the stakeholders, not just in the role of experts that need to be consulted, but also as active contributors in the design process. Thus the future of design seems to point in the direction of closer and closer cooperation with many other disciplines. If we really want to live up to the challenge of tackling complex problems, we cannot do so alone. We need to move from design as a reasonably stand-alone activity to collaborative design.

This movement has recently been taken a fundamental step further at Stanford University in the development of a master course called "d.school" (see www.stanford.edu/group/dschool). In this school, young professionals from different fields (e.g., medicine, chemical engineering, information technology) get a crash course in design thinking and are then set to work on complicated design tasks under the guidance of a design specialist. Thus, "the designer" in the classical sense of the word seems to more or less have dropped out of the equation altogether. This could be a harbinger of a new, very significant turn in the development of the design profession. If this is trend of the future, the designer as an independent profession could even all but disappear, becoming absorbed into a co-design process. On reflection, this could be in line with the history of the design profession. If we take product design as an example, the traditional design profession came to the fore in the late 1800s as a separate profession because the industrial revolution made this specialization necessary. The creative process of creating a product design became so complicated that the natural link between design and production that had previously existed in the crafts was broken. Simultaneously, the need to bring cultural knowledge to bear upon otherwise "cultureless" objects of mass-production led to the creation of the autonomous artist-designer. The continuing growth of the complexity of the design field later led to the creation of the "integrating designer" after World War II. This type of designer really came to the fore from the 1960s onwards—a single designer who would span the areas of form-giving, ergonomics, technology, business, and marketing, integrating these aspects into a product. The complexities of these design challenges were partly addressed by adopting explicit methodologies from a more systematized profession like engineering. In the last decades, however, the complexities in the product design field finally proved too great for a single integrative designer, leading to the rise of "design teams" of different kinds of designers. Since then we have moved on to "participatory design" and recently, to "collaborative design." In real collaborative design, the position of "the designer" disappears into a team effort of many different parties: prospective users, stakeholders, and other specialists. If this development continues, it could spell the end of the industrial design profession as we know it (defined by its domination of the creative step in the creation of new artifacts), after only about one hundred-fifty years of existence. We could find ourselves in the interesting and paradoxical situation that while design is successfully spreading throughout society, the design profession is simultaneously disappearing.

A Designer-Centered View on Design Research

For some reason, the design research community has always had something of a blind spot for the study of design intelligence—indeed, it has had a blind spot for anything connected to the designer. There has always been an overwhelming focus on modeling and supporting the *process* of designing. But any study of design, and any method for aiding design activities, necessarily contains statements or assumptions about all four "dimensions of design activities" (Roozenburg and Cross, 1991): the dynamics of a design process, the designer, the design task, and the context in which the design activity takes place.

By focusing almost exclusively on design processes, design researchers have abstracted away from the designer, design task and context. This "bracketing" has led to the development of process-focused design models, theories, methods, techniques, and tools that are often implicitly supposed to be valid for *any* design task, and can be used by *every* designer, in any design context.

Anybody involved in design teaching and design practice will know that this is precisely the weakness of these "strong" process-focused models and methods: they are hard to apply to a concrete design task in a design situation, and they are hard to relate to the specific qualities of the actor, whether a design student, professional designer, a design team, or a designing organization. The art of being a designer is to determine *what to do when* in a complex design situation. This decision, what to do in a specific design situation, has to be based not only on the knowledge a designer has of the *design process*, but also on the diversity of *design tasks*, the *design problem situation*, and his/her own *capacities and ambitions*. Attaining this largely implicit knowledge of how to create designs within the context of all four elements of a design situation requires a lot of practice, acquired by years of design studio work on a broad array of different design problems. Through design exercises, students of design develop their own personality as a designer and their own approach to design problems and design situations.

But the fact that design research has been looking the other way, and until recently has defined itself quite narrowly as design methodology (thus focusing on the design process as the sole object of study), does not mean that designers, design tasks, and design contexts are beyond study or that they are beyond the realms of explicit knowledge. The models of the design ability and design expertise presented here could provide a first backbone for the development of a new, designer-focused branch of design studies. The classic remark at the end of every scientific paper is that "more research is needed." That is putting it very mildly in this case: we have hardly begun.

Clarity and Precision in Design Education

The models of the design ability and design expertise open up a whole field of study on design intelligence, concentrating on the properties of the designers and their development in design training and practice. Both the model of the design ability and the model of design expertise should be checked against developments in design practice, and they need to be made more internally consistent, rigorous, and complete.

Part of this urgency results from the recent shift in educational theory and practice towards competency-based learning. Different design schools have developed their own lists of design abilities that define the scope of their take on design. For instance, the Department of Industrial Design at the University of Technology Eindhoven in the Netherlands has formulated a competency framework that spans six core competencies: 1) ideas and concepts, 2) integrating technologies, 3) user focus and perspectives, 4) social and cultural awareness, 5) business and market orientation, and

6) form and senses. In addition to these six competencies that define the substantive domain of that industrial design department, there are four meta-competencies: a) design and research processes, b) multidisciplinary teamwork, c) self-directed and continuous learning, and d) analyzing complexity (see Overbeeke et al., 2004). Thus some of the general competencies, close to the Cross list of design abilities, are mixed with competencies that can be linked more specifically to the character of the design problems and design solutions that are part of the substantive design area (in this case, the design of intelligent products and environments). Through the rise of the competency-based view on professional and academic education, these explicit inventories of design abilities are becoming increasingly important. They are used to set and evaluate design education curricula, and by implication define the kind of designer that is being developed in a design school.

Another phenomenon that is a motivating factor for the study of design intelligence is that all over the world, design schools are moving towards academia. This results in a fresh need to define what "design at an academic level" is, more than just a kind of design that has been burdened with extra "research" to make it *look* more academic. A much extended and improved version of the expertise model could play a pivotal role in defining the academic power of design. The slow entry of design into the universities results in pressure on design schools to become much more explicit about their teaching methods, too. An extended version of the expertise model that has been described above could also be used to describe the development of design students (Dorst and Reymen, 2004), and it could lead to the development of testing methods that would enable us to more precisely target the position and learning possibilities for every student, at every point in their studies. Design exercises could be made much more specific, opening up the possibility for a much more efficient learning process (current teaching and learning practices become ineffective when executed under the staff-student ratio that is standard for other academic disciplines). Design methods and design tools could be provided to the design student at exactly the right time to foster the next step in their development. The further development of a model of design intelligence could thus lead to the development of new, more specific methods and tools for design practice and design education.

The Design Research Agenda

In order to live up to these expectations, there are several directions in which the design expertise model has to be developed. We can distinguish four main questions, corresponding with four directions for design research:

1. We should explore the different kinds of reflection and problem-solving that take place on every level of expertise. For instance, the kind of problem that

is perceived by the designer at the novice level (How can I use my methods?) is quite different from that on the advanced beginner's level (When should I use this particular method/rule of thumb?). The reflection that takes place on the novice-level deals with the rules themselves, while the reflection for the advanced beginner centers on the applicability of a rule in a specific design situation.

2. This can then help us define and study the transitions that link the different levels of expertise. What does a designer need to learn to get from one level to the next? How can he/she do that? What problems stand in the way of learning the next set of skills? It has been observed before that the acquisition of design skills is not a gradual process, but that it goes in leaps and bounds. But what are the conditions under which such leaps occur?

3. A third stream of research should be focused on enriching this model with aspects of design learning that might not be captured so easily in this skill-oriented learning model: the development of the declarative and process knowledge of the designer, and the acquisition and use of "design prototypes."

4. Finally, the models of design ability and design expertise should then be combined in one coherent model of design intelligence.

There are several means we can use to attack these issues. An extensive literature survey is in order, spanning several disciplines. There is much more theoretical work on expertise development to be found in educational research and in the field of educational psychology. On the empirical front, a detailed longitudinal study needs to be set up. We need to actively follow students in their education, minutely tracing their development. Designers in practice should be interviewed and other research techniques could be used to trace their development in the higher steps of the expertise development model. In addition to this longitudinal study, cross-sectional research could support more in-depth analysis of a specific level of expertise or a specific transition within the model.

Concluding Remarks

The development of design research away from its exclusive focus on design processes and toward the more inclusive study of design tasks, design contexts and, above all, the properties of the designer (design ability, design expertise, and design intelligence), is going to be a huge challenge in the coming years. The emergence of such a new, broad type of design research requires a true paradigmatic shift. To create clarity, understanding and insight in the wonderful but complex design arena, not just on the separate subjects of design process, design task, design context, and design intelligence but on their interaction, the repertoire of research methods will have to diversify.

Design researchers will have to move away from purely observational research methods towards action-research and experimentation (in a way, this is the same movement towards a more design-like approach, in the face of the complexity that I discussed in the context of social problems at the beginning of this chapter). To do this, design researchers will have to descend from their ivory towers and work with designers, engage with the issues they are struggling with, and involve designers as equals into their discussions. This call for renewed contact will fall on fertile ground within the design professions: designers in the field realize that the challenges they are now facing (the growing complexity of design problems, globalization, sustainability, the opportunities opening up in the socio-cultural arena) require a fundamental rethinking of the design professions. Design practitioners are looking for ways to articulate their knowledge and abilities afresh, and for ways to really incorporate research and collaboration into their practice—not as an afterthought, but as an integral part of the value proposition that a design professional brings to the world.

This is the moment when design research and design practice, which have grown so far apart over the last forty years, are to finally meet again. The future belongs to those that can create a new synthesis of design research and design practice: from that integration, the new design profession will emerge.

References

Cross, N.G. 2007. *Designerly Ways of Knowing*. Basel, Switzerland: Birkhauser.

Cross, N.G. 1990. The nature and nurture of the design ability. *Design Studies,* 11. 3, 127-140.

de Wilde, J. 1997. *Passie voor produktontwikkeling*. Utrecht, Netherlands: Lemma.

Dorst, K. and I.M.M.J. Reymen. 2004. Levels of expertise in design education. In Lloyd, P. et al. *The changing face of design education, Proceedings of the 2nd International Engineering and Product Design Education Conference, Faculty of Industrial Design Engineering*. Delft, Netherlands, 2-3 September.

Dorst, K. 2003. The problem of design problems. In Cross, N.G. and E. Edmonds (eds.). *Expertise in Design: design thinking research symposium 6*. Sydney, Australia: Creativity and Cognition Studios Press, 135–147.

Dreyfus, H.L. 2002. Intelligence without representation – Merleau-Ponty's critique of mental representation. *Phenomenology and the Cognitive Sciences*, 1. 4. 367–383.

Dreyfus, H.L. 2003a. From Socrates to Artificial Intelligence: The Limits of Rule-Based Rationality. Unpublished lecture notes of the first 2003 Spinoza Lecture at the University of Amsterdam.

Dreyfus, H.L. 2003b. Can there be a better source of meaning than everyday practices? Unpublished lecture notes of the second 2003 Spinoza Lecture at the University of Amsterdam.

Gardner, H. 1983. *Frames of Mind: the Theory of Multiple Intelligences*. London, United Kingdom: Heinemann.

Gero, J.S. 1990. Design prototypes: A knowledge representation schema for design. *AI Magazine*, 11.4, 26–36.

Hirshberg, J. 1998. *The Creative Priority*. New York, NY: Harper Business.

Kirton, M. (ed.). 1989. *Adaptors and Innovators: styles of creativity and problem solving*. New York, NY: Routledge.

Lawson, B.L. and K. Dorst. 2005. Acquiring Design Expertise: a first attempt at a model. Keynote lecture for Hi 05. Computational and Cognitive Models of Creative Design: Sixth International Roundtable Conference Hron Island Australia ,10-14 December,

Lawson, B.L. and K. Dorst. 2009. *Design Expertise*. Oxford, United Kingdom: Architectural Press.

Overbeeke K., R. Appleby, I. Janssen Reinen, and D. Vinke. 2004. Nine Competencies, six units: Industrial Design Education at TU Eindhoven. In Lloyd, P., N.F.M. Roozenburg, C. McMahon and L. Brodhurst L. (eds.), 2004. *The Changing Face of Design Education*. Delft, Netherlands: Delft University of Technology.

Roozenburg, N.F.M. and J. Eekels. 1995. *Product Design: Fundamentals and Methods*. Chichester, United Kingdom: Wiley.

Roozenburg, N.F.M. and N.G. Cross. 1991. Models of the design process: integrating across the disciplines. In Hubka, V. *Proceedings of ICED 91*. Zürich, Switzerland: Heurista.

Suyling, P., D. Krabbendam, and K. Dorst (eds.). 2005. *More than 8 design ideas for the integrated living of mentally handicapped people in society*. The Hague, Netherlands: Dutch Ministry of Health Wellbeing and Sports.

Sutton, R.I. and A. Hargardon. 1996. Brainstorming Groups in Context: Effectiveness in a product design firm. *Administrative Science Quarterly*, 41, 685–718.

Valkenburg, A.C. 2000. The reflective practice in product design teams. PhD thesis. Delft, Netherlands: TU Delft.

van Heffen, O., P. Maassen, and A. Rip (eds.). 1999. *Sociale wetenschappen van ontwerppraktijk naar ontwerppraktijk*. Enschede, Netherlands: Twente University Press.

Index

Name Index

Author Notes

Toby Bottorf is the Director of Design at WGBH Interactive in Boston, where he oversees a staff of more than a dozen designers producing award-winning websites for a number of PBS television series, including *NOVA*, *American Experience*, *Masterpiece Theatre*, *ZOOM*, *Arthur*, and *Between the Lions*. From 1995 to 2004, Toby was the founder and principal of Firehaus Design, a studio that specialized in applying user-centered design methods to projects in informal learning. A frequent speaker at conferences, he has taught graduate-level interaction design at the Institute of Design, Illinois Institute of Technology and the Massachusetts College of Art.

Kees Dorst, Ph.D., is Associate Dean of Research and Professor of Design on the faculty of Design, Architecture and Building at the University of Technology, Sydney, and a Senior Researcher in Design at Eindhoven University of Technology. He has published numerous articles and four books, most recently, *Understanding Design—175 reflections on being a design*er (2006) and *Design Experience* (2009) with Bryan Lawson. Trained as an Industrial Design Engineer at Delft University of Technology, he also studied some philosophy at the Erasmus University Rotterdam. He has worked as a product designer and a researcher, and he has studied the ways in which designers work.

Judith Gregory, Ph.D., is a member of the Design Research faculty of the Institute of Design, Illinois Institute of Technology, where she is Co-Coordinator of the Doctor of Philosophy in Design Program and faculty lead for the Rethinking Health initiative. Also appointed as Adjunct Professor in the Human-centered Informatics Research Group, Department of Communication, Aalborg University, she previously was an Associate Professor in Informatics, University of Oslo, and Professor II, Oslo School of Architecture and Design. A founding member of the Nordic Design Research Society (2005) and co-editor of the *CoDesign* special issue on Design Participation(s) (2008), Judith is active in doctoral design education, international design research, participatory design, health informatics, and cultural historical activity theory conferences.

Birgit Helene Jevnaker, Ph.D., is Associate Professor at BI Norwegian School of Management's Innovation Department, Oslo, where she conducts research on design/innovation, service design, and collaboration between designers and business. She has explored new practices of product innovation, entrepreneurship, knowledge and learning in a variety of organizations and settings. Jevnaker's many articles are published internationally, and she co-edited *Management of Design Alliances*, pioneering studies of design and business strategy. She created new courses on managing design and creative projects in both business and design schools, and she organizes executive leadership programs. She is a member of the international committee of European Academy of Design and the research advisory board of Design Management Institute, Boston.

Kari Kuutti, Ph.D., is a Professor in Human-computer Interaction in the University of Oulu, Finland, and he also holds teaching positions at University of Helsinki and Helsinki University of Technology. His research interest is in theories of human-computer interaction and design and in computer support for collaborative design processes. He has been working in design since the mid-1990s, first in the context of mobile phones and smart products together with industrial designers, and later in the context of intelligent and ubiquitous environments and urban spaces together with architects and urban designers.

Tom MacTavish, Associate Professor at the Institute of Design, Illinois Institute of Technology, teaches courses related to Interaction Design history, theory, and practice. Previously, he directed the Motorola Lab Center for Human Interaction Research and NCR Corporation's Human Interface Technology, where he participated in the full range of product conceptualization and development including strategy formulation, user and technology research, concept development, and product implementation. These activities resulted in products that used recognition technologies (handwriting, speech, and image) and interaction technologies (synthetic speech, multimodal interaction, and context-aware systems), which benefited from formal methods for experience design and prototyping (design research, user-centered design, usability evaluations, and rapid prototyping).

Aaron Marcus is President of Aaron Marcus and Associates, Inc. in Berkeley, California, where he researches and designs user interfaces, information visualization, and cross-cultural communication. He is the Editor-in-Chief of *User Experience*, a member of the ICOGRADA Design Hall of Fame (2000), a Fellow of AIGA (2007), and a member of CHI Academy (2009). He has written or co-written five books and 250 articles. Aaron is the world's first graphic designer to work with computer graphics (1967 at AT+T Bell Labs); he founded one of the first computer-based graphic design firms (1982). He has taught at Princeton, Yale, University of California Berkeley, and Hebrew University Jerusalem.

Sharon Helmer Poggenpohl edits and publishes the international scholarly journal *Visible Language*. Formerly a professor at the School of Design, Hong Kong Polytechnic University and Institute of Design, Illinois Institute of Technology in Chicago, she coordinated post-graduate programs in Design at the former, and co-coordinated the Doctor of Philosophy in Design at the later. In 2007, with colleagues, she designed a new Master of Design offering in Hong Kong, Interaction Design, one of only three in Asia. Graduate education in design has been her focus for over twenty years; she recently completed a research study for Cumulus on research and graduate education. A recipient of three teaching awards, she is concerned with learning strategies in design as they support practical action and formalization of design knowledge through publication.

R. Roger Remington is the Massimo and Lella Vignelli Distinguished Professor of Design at the Rochester Institute of Technology. For the past twenty years, he has developed a unique scholarly resource there, the Graphic Design Archive, a project that preserves and interprets the original source materials of thirty Modernist design pioneers. He has written three books on design history, the latest of which is *Design and Science—The Life and Work of Will Burtin* (2007). Two prominent schools in Germany, the Dessau Department of Design, Anhalt University of Applied Sciences in Dessau and the Hochschule für Gestaltung in Schwäbisch Gmünd, welcome him as a guest professor.

Keiichi Sato is Professor and Co-Coordinator of the Doctor of Philosophy in Design Program at the Institute of Design, Illinois Institute of Technology. His research and teaching focus on design theories and methodologies, interactive systems, and human-centered system integration. Recent projects include robotic system integration for health/elderly care and scenario-based design information management. A Fellow of the Design Research Society and recipient of best paper awards at ASME DTM, IEEE Robot-Human Interactive Communications, and ACM-IEEE Design Automation conferences, he has been developing collaborative research with institutions abroad as well as interdisciplinary initiatives within the university. He taught at Kyoto Institute of Technology and Osaka Institute of Technology, and he was visiting professor at Musashino Art University and Darmstadt University of Technology.

Nicole Schadewitz, Ph.D., is a Lecturer in Design at the Open University in the United Kingdom. She is involved in the production of the new distance-learning course in Design Thinking. Before joining the Open University, Nicole completed her Ph.D. at the Hong Kong Polytechnic University's School of Design. Her dissertation identified recurring, successful solutions to facilitate international collaboration in remote design education. Her current research looks at how social networking sites support peer learning and collaboration in distance design courses at the Open

University. She also maintains a wiki on cross-cultural collaboration. Her interests include cross-cultural design learning, collaboration in design, design patterns, and design in and for emerging markets.

Tetsuo Tomiyama, Ph.D., is Professor in the Faculty of Mechanical, Maritime and Materials Engineering of Delft University of Technology. Prior to this appointment, he was Professor at Research into Artifacts, Center for Engineering (RACE) of the University of Tokyo. He is interested in a variety of subjects related to design, including design theory, design methodology, function modeling, knowledge-intensive engineering, distributed autonomous intelligence, manufacturing paradigms, lifecycle engineering, and service engineering. His current research topics are complex systems architecture, self-maintenance, service CAD, human-machine collaboration in manual tasks, and design education.